CRIMINAL PROCEDURE:

The Administration of Justice

CRIMINAL PROCEDURE:

The Administration of Justice

Charles F. Hemphill, Jr.
M.S., Doctor of Jurisprudence

GOODYEAR PUBLISHING CO., INC.
SANTA MONICA, CALIFORNIA 90401

Library of Congress Cataloging in Publication Data

Hemphill, Charles F.
    Criminal procedure.

    1. Criminal procedure—United States. 2. Criminal
justice, Administration of—United States. I. Title.
KF9619.H34   345'.73'05   77-21985
ISBN 0-87620-213-X

To my wife, Phyllis Davis Hemphill

Copyright ©1978 by GOODYEAR PUBLISHING COMPANY, INC.
Santa Monica, California

Y-213X-1
ISBN 0-87620-213-X

Current Printing (last number)

10 9 8 7 6 5 4 3 2 1

Printed in the United States of America

Production Editor: Pam Tully
Illustrator: Tanya Maiboroda
Designer: Linda M. Robertson
Cover: Tanya Maiboroda and Linda M. Robertson

CONTENTS

The administration of justice requires absolute equality, "not out of tenderness for the accused but because ... civilization ... by respecting the dignity even of the least worthy citizen, raises the stature of all of us and builds an atmosphere of trust and confidence in government."

Justice Frankfurter, United States
  Supreme Court, in *Stein* v. *New
  York,* 346 US 156, 73 S Ct 1077
                            (1953)

PREFACE

This book was written for individuals preparing for a career in law enforcement, corrections, or court administration; practitioners already in those fields; and readers who simply want to know how the courts function.

It is hardly necessary to restate the seriousness of crime in America, and its impact on almost every detail of our daily lives.

While the problem of crime is only one of the many responsibilities that require the time and attention of police officers, it continues to be perhaps the most serious in its overall challenge.

No attempt has been made to set out the laws and court decisions of a specific area of state. The broad, controlling principles are presented, along with some of the important exceptions. The student should gain familiarization with specific laws in the particular area, bearing in mind that these broad principles may be constantly altered by court decisions and statutory changes.

The administration of justice is concerned with the processes by which the government seeks to convict and correct an individual for a criminal violation. It is therefore concerned with the way the police determine whether a criminal violation has been committed; the way in which they collect evidence against the suspect; the way in which evidence is presented to and evaluated by the courts; and if guilt is found, the way in which punishment or correction is imposed.

It is important that the suspected violator is legally taken into custody, brought to trial, properly handled in the event of conviction, and given the facilities needed for a satisfactory return to society.

From a legal standpoint, then, this book deals with our system of criminal procedure, as distinguished from the subjects of substantive criminal law and the law of evidence. Terms used are defined in the glossary, if not otherwise clarified.

The book is purposely devoid of detailed attention to methods for preventing criminal violations. However, it should be understood that the preventive approach lies in the background of practically all our police activities, court systems, and correctional programs.

It should be pointed out that courts are often in disagreement, and that an isolated court decision may be found that is contrary to almost every settled rule of law. If the United States Supreme Court has passed on a specific issue, then that decision is controlling, regardless of what any prior court had decided. In some instances, the text in this book states that the courts are in general agreement on a legal point. This means that the United States Supreme Court has not handed down a decision on this dispute. There may be a few contrary decisions by state courts, but the great majority of the high state courts that have ruled on this issue are in agreement. To specifically list the states that have lined up on one side or the other would be beyond the space limitations of this book, in many instances. An expression of this general agreement of the courts is not an opinion of the author, but is the consensus from independent court decisions. Footnotes are included, where believed helpful.

The criminal law in this country undergoes constant change. To add to the problem, many court decisions are written in legal terminology that even judges and lawyers have trouble in interpreting.

This book will attempt to span the attitudes and practices that sometimes exist between those who work in the criminal justice field and our court systems.

I want to express appreciation to Mr. John F. Pritchard for his practical help and assistance. I also wish to thank Anita M. Hemphill for editing and Dianne Haines for typing. Tanya Maiboroda prepared the drawings.

Charles F. Hemphill, Jr.
Long Beach, California

CRIMINAL PROCEDURE:

The Administration of Justice

The methods we employ in the enforcement of our criminal law have aptly been called the measures by which the quality of our civilization may be judged.

Chief Justice Warren, United States Supreme Court, in *Coppedge* v. *United States,* 369 US 438 (1962)

chapter one

CONCEPTUALIZATION

At all times and everywhere, civilized people have maintained an organization of laws prohibiting those acts which menace society. At the same time, governments seek to provide individual rights to all persons. Consequently, it is necessary to strike a balance between absolute personal liberty and the necessary authority of government.

The purpose of this chapter is to describe the systems used in the United States to administer justice in criminal cases. The material in this chapter outlines the aims and requirements of our systems, and the interplay between the individual roles assumed by investigative and police officials, government agencies, and the courts.

THE RESTRICTIONS ON INDIVIDUALS

No man has a right to take over the lives of others. A free society cannot exist if individual members are allowed to disrupt its functions without restraints of any kind. Every civilization in history has adopted criminal laws to control those who harm others.

Each nation and government throughout the world has a responsibility to administer a system of justice for its subjects. By the methods used to carry out this responsibility, some governments stamp themselves as harsh, repressive, and unresponsive to the basic values of human decency. Some other governments, however, seek to uniformly follow laws and procedures that are at once firm but fair.

1

Conceptualization

We may describe criminal laws and procedures as the disciplines of freedom, conceding that this may seem to be a contradiction of terms. Every law takes away some measure of individual freedom, but the freedom taken away is often the kind that the community can ill afford to let its members have.

It may be argued, for example, that everyone is entitled to live without hindrances or restrictions of any kind. But most of us will agree that we should never have the freedom to chop off our neighbor's head whenever the impulse strikes us.

WHAT IS THE ADMINISTRATION OF JUSTICE?

The administration of justice is the machinery for enforcing the provisions of criminal law. The application of these legal restraints or criminal laws serves to control the excesses of individuals. The terms *administration of justice* and *criminal procedure* may be used interchangeably to mean *that which provides or regulates the steps by which law violators are brought to account.*

In this process, "justice is the constant and perpetual desire to render every man his due. It places all persons on an equal footing, requiring each to conform his acts and will to the requirements of the law."[1]

THE AIMS AND ACTIVITIES OF THE ADMINISTRATION OF JUSTICE

The basic concern of the administration of justice is the elimination of crime and misconduct. At the same time, the system should allow as much freedom as possible to every individual.

There are five basic activities that should be considered in the administration of justice:

1. The first area of concern should be to get at the root causes of crime. This should be followed with preventive programs or techniques that will steer away the potential offender before he becomes involved.

2. The second area of concern should be to discover criminal activity, as early as possible. This is because evidence may be

---

1. Henry Campbell Black, *Black's Law Dictionary,* Revised Fourth Edition by The Publisher's Editorial Staff (St. Paul: West Publishing Co.), 1968.

lost unless an investigator knows a crime was committed. The concern here is not only to develop and preserve evidence, but to also bring the responsible person to trial. Confirmed criminals sometimes state that prompt apprehension and conviction are effective factors to discourage the criminal repeater.

3.	The third area of concern is that of basic fairness in determining whether the accused is or is not responsible for the crime. This trial procedure should cause as little disruption to the personal life and business affairs of the accused as is necessary to assure that he will remain available to the court until the case is concluded.

4.	The fourth area of concern is to rehabilitate the offender so that he will not again disrupt the lives of others, or to remove him from society if he cannot be rehabilitated.

5.	The fifth area of interest is the concern of punishment. This does not mean punishment as a vindictive act, but isolation from society as society's way of retaliating for wrong. As we will observe, this is an area where there are differences of opinion as to what punitive measures should be used, and under what circumstances.

Part of this area of concern is to house the offender so that the public is safe from the convict's destructive acts, and so that the convict is safe from other offenders. At the same time, penal or jail detention quarters should make available rehabilitation facilities and opportunities.[2]

THE STEPS IN THE CRIMINAL PROCEDURE SYSTEM

Under the legal system in the United States, there is a definite series of steps that are taken in the handling of any person who is believed to have violated the law. This procedure has been set up by the courts and the legislatures of all the states, as well as by the federal courts and the United States Congress. In this process, a number of rights and safeguards are guaranteed to every accused person, in both the state and the federal courts.

The process is started by the commission of the crime. It proceeds through the investigation by the appropriate police

2. Judge Edmund J. Leach, Jr., "A Plan for Meaningful Justice," *Federal Probation,* May 1975, pp. 37–38.

agency, to a decision to prosecute, to an arrest, to detention in jail or freedom to await trial while out on bail, to the criminal trial, to the sentencing, to the serving of the sentence or release on probation, to a return to freedom on the street.

Individuals who commit only one crime during their lifetime are taken through this series of steps only one time. Individuals who are criminal repeaters (recidivists), may go through the cycle time after time.

THE NONFEDERAL APPROACH TO POLICE WORK IN THE UNITED STATES

Foreign countries, especially some of those in Europe, make use of a structured "police system." This is usually a well-arranged series of agencies and departments, beginning at the local level and organized with increasing responsibility. Local units report to progressively higher ranks of command, with a single head or board in charge of activities on a national level.

An individual studying police activities in the United States could assume that a system of this kind is followed in this country. This is because several agencies may be observed working together. Police work in the United States, however, utilizes a nonfederal or nonsystem approach. Local, state, and federal officers will usually cooperate closely, since all have the common objective of upholding the law, but they are separate entities.

These agencies function in differing roles and capacities. Each type of officer derives authority from an individual law. Each agency knows that there must be a generous amount of cooperative team-work to earn the respect and assistance of the other.[3]

THE RELATED AND DIFFERING ROLES OF THOSE INVOLVED IN THE SYSTEM

The overall aim of the administration of justice is the elimination of crime and delinquency.

Our plan for dispensing criminal justice is an example of law under stress—of interests that are in conflict. The system must

---

3. See John N. Ferdico, *Criminal Procedure for the Law Enforcement Officer* (St. Paul: West Publishing Co., 1975), for additional background on the criminal justice system.

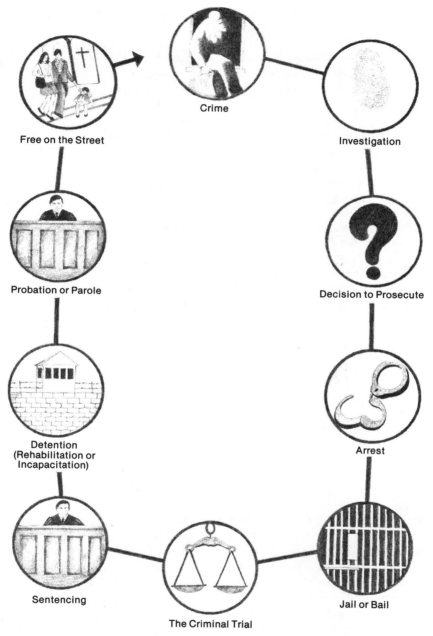

Figure 1–1.   The Cycle of the Administration of Criminal Justice

protect the law abiders, the people of the whole community. Yet, at the same time, the system must serve a smaller group of individuals, the law breakers.

Experience indicates that society can never be truly protected by any procedure that does not protect the rights of its members. Unquestionably, there has been increased emphasis on the rights of the individual in recent years. From the viewpoint sometimes expressed by the courts, the benefits derived by the general public rest on the fact that every member is given his individual rights. Even the most obvious indications of guilt or calloused criminality do not justify a court, public official, or police officer deciding that the accused has forfeited his expectation of legal safeguards.

Quite obviously, the rights of society and the rights of an individual offender are sometimes in conflict. In looking out for the rights of the accused it may be painfully apparent that the victim of a crime has done nothing wrong, while the perpetrator has gone far out of his way to do deliberate harm.

In general, the system works to dispense evenhanded justice. However, there are occasions when a detached observer may wonder who is the victim and who is the beneficiary of the system. For example, a woman may hesitate to report a forcible rape, especially when she considers the ordeal ahead of her. Even reporting the matter may be a trying experience. She may fear that newspaper publicity will turn her boyfriend against her. It is possible that an unscrupulous defense attorney will subject the most reputable woman to some real indignities in the cross-examination at the time of the trial.

There are also occasions when an elderly, perhaps senile person who has been victimized by a confidence man may receive neither sympathy nor the return of the loot.

It is apparent, then, that there are uneven spots in the operation of the system and in the performances of some of those who administer it.

For his part too, the criminal may not get the things that he needs from the system. In the thinking of the public, the arrest and trial of the suspect seem to be the most important aspects of criminal activity. The TV and news reporters focus on the fugitive apprehension and the chase, or the sensational aspects of the trial. After the sentence, the curtain falls, and the public interest is drawn away to new crimes and new court battles.

An obvious truth is that the convicted individual is one in serious need of help—something that will encourage him to live within the law. Unfortunately, this help is frequently not forthcoming.

6

It is a basic intention of the criminal justice system to provide this kind of help. One of the problems here is that the individuals who figure in the operation of the system may lose sight of this objective. The investigating police officer has a number of specific duties that he must perform. When a criminal violation is reported, he has the job of interviewing the victim and witnesses, and of determining the facts. He is expected to collect and preserve whatever evidence can be found, making searches and seizures that are within the standards set by the courts.

Then too, it is the officer's responsibility to present the available proof to the prosecuting attorney. A warrant may then be issued and an arrest made by the policeman, with the accused being afforded his rights, including an opportunity to make bail.

During this process, the officer must sift out the truth as to what happened, probing the versions of the victim, the accused, and the independent witnesses that can be located. Later, the officer may be called upon to participate in the trial, testifying impartially, but as a witness called for the prosecution.

Through all of this, the investigating officer may concentrate so intently on sending the guilty individual to prison that he loses sight of the fact that the conviction pinpoints a person in society who is in need of help. Solution of every case is important, and should never be de-emphasized. At the same time, it is desirable to ask, "What can I do to make the accused realize he will continue to be a loser so long as he's determined to buck the rules of society?"[4]

The federal or state prosecutor who handles the case may be concerned only with the record of conviction that he can compile.

The trial judge who hears the case may be concerned only with the maintenance of proper rules and standards of evidence in the courtroom, and in making certain that he is not reversed on appeal.

The appellate judge may be thinking within the very narrow limits of the technical rules of procedure and evidence that have been followed since the days of the common law. He may be so intent on the protection of individual rights that he is drawn away from the purpose of a criminal trial—the finding of truth as to guilt or innocence.

The probation or parole officer who is assigned the case may be so intent on the rehabilitation of the prisoner that he or she ignores the overriding interests of society in general.

All of these patterns add up to the fact that there may be times

---

4. For additional source material, see Ronald L. Carlson, *Criminal Justice Procedures for Police* (Cincinnati: W. H. Anderson Co., 1970).

when an official in the criminal justice system may become carried away with the particular role that he plays. On occasion, individuals may function independently within the criminal justice framework, rather than in relation to the basic objectives of the system.

On the whole, however, all of these participants play their assigned roles, at the same time relating their performance toward an improved system of criminal justice.[5]

The private citizen, too, has a role to play. He has a responsibility to immediately report every violation of the law, to willingly participate in jury duty, and to support peace officers and the courts in handling their obligations. As a taxpayer, the citizen must, for example, support projects that give promise for rehabilitation and that will induce a criminal to conform to the rules of society.

The individual citizen cannot pick and choose among good laws and bad laws, according to his individual tastes and conscience, without destroying the whole concept of the rule of law. The only real protection against crime is respect for the law. The habit of voluntary compliance is at the heart of the civilizing and liberalizing influence of the justice system. In this sense, law is the very fabric of a free society.

Public opinion as to what is right and necessary varies from generation to generation. Laws must be changed regularly if they are to keep up with public attitudes. Ideas as to proper conduct are always changing or evolving, and no law can be said to represent a final truth.

For example, in colonial America the pilgrims had a law that everyone who attended church must carry a gun, to defend against a surprise attack by unfriendly Indians. Somewhat later, around 1890, several states passed statutes that required the installation of hitching posts and a watering trough for horses to be maintained in front of every county courthouse. Laws of this kind are now completely out of keeping with the needs of society.

SUMMARY

No government can allow complete freedom for individual members of society. There must be restrictions on individual actions that work against the common good. A program or system for the administra-

5. For additional source material, see John C. Klotter and Jacqueline R. Kanovitz, *Constitutional Law for Police* (Cincinnati: The W. H. Anderson Co., 1968).

tion of justice must be concerned with stamping out the root causes of crime; with discovering and investigating criminal activity at the earliest possible moment; with treating the criminal fairly; with rehabilitation of the offender; with isolating the offender from society when necessary; and with incarcerating the offender in a way that is safe to the public and the offender as well.

There is a "nonsystem" approach to police work in the United States, with local, state, and federal investigative and police agencies operating independently. Almost always, however, these agencies do work in cooperation. The individuals who are involved in the operation of the criminal justice system have differing, but related roles. Each functions within an individual sphere, but ties into the whole. These interwoven responsibilities and functions will be examined in more detail in the following chapters.

QUESTIONS

1. Can a society have absolute freedom without surrendering some rights and privileges? Why?

2. What is a government's responsibility in setting up a criminal justice system?

3. What is the basic concern of the administration of justice?

4. Is it more important to get at the root causes of crime or to rehabilitate offenders so they do not repeat their criminal acts? What are reasons for your answer?

5. Should the police investigator, the prosecutor, the judge, and the parole officer all work together toward eliminating crime and delinquency? Or should their basic aims be more individualized?

6. Is it essential for a private citizen to accept responsibility for a government's criminal justice program? Why?

Further Readings in Criminal Justice

BASSIOUNI, M. CHERIF, *Criminal Law and Its Processes* (Springfield, Ill.: Charles C. Thomas Publishers, 1969).

BLANCHARD, ROBERT E. *Introduction to the Administration of Justice* (New York: John Wiley and Sons, 1975).

FERDICO, JOHN N. *Criminal Procedure for the Law Enforcement Officer* (St. Paul: West Publishing Co., 1975).

Conceptualization

GAMMAGE, ALLEN Z., AND CHARLES F. HEMPHILL, Jr.   *Basic Criminal Law* (New York: McGraw-Hill and Co., 1974).

INBAU, FRED EDWARD   *Criminal Law and Its Administration* (New York: The Foundation Press, 1974).

ISRAEL, JEROLD H., AND WAYNE R. LAFAVRE   *Criminal Procedure in a Nutshell* (St. Paul: West Publishing Co., 1976).

KLOTTER, JOHN C., AND JACQUELINE R. KANOVITZ   *Constitutional Law for Police* (Cincinnati: The W. H. Anderson Co., 1968).

LEONARD, V. A.   *The Police, The Judiciary, and The Criminal*, 2d ed. (Springfield, Ill.: Charles C. Thomas Publishers, 1975).

PERKINS, ROLLIN M.   *Criminal Law and Procedure*, 3d ed. (Brooklyn: The Foundation Press, 1966).

RUTTER, WILLIAM A.   *Criminal Procedure*, 5th ed. (Gardena, California: Gilbert Law Summaries, 1973).

WESTON, PAUL B., AND KENNETH M. WELLS   *The Administration of Justice*, 2d ed. (Englewood Cliffs: Prentice-Hall, Inc. 1973).

. . . there is in this country no superior, dominant, ruling class of citizens. There is no caste here. Our constitution . . . neither knows nor tolerates classes among citizens . . . The humblest is the peer of the most powerful. The law regards man as man, and takes no account of his surroundings . . .

**Justice John Marshall Harlan,
United States Supreme Court,
dissenting in *Plessy* v. *Ferguson*,
163 US 539 (1896)**

chapter two

LEGAL AUTHORIZATION FOR THE SYSTEM

The criminal justice system, while based on law, is run by people.

The purpose of this chapter is to set out the background and the historical basis for the development of the criminal justice system in this country. This material examines the legal origins of the system, and shows how the processes of criminal justice developed alongside the origins of the United States government.

DEVELOPMENT OF THE U.S. GOVERNMENT AS IT RELATES TO THE CRIMINAL JUSTICE SYSTEM

Stripped of the protection and services provided by organized government, most of us would be hard put to protect our lives or property for very long. But we do not like to turn over control of our personal freedoms and possessions to others, unless there is some way to hold these custodians responsible.

In organized society, power is universal, permanent, and necessary. Our job as citizens is not to seek to escape that power, but to control it. Whenever we allow someone else to govern, we must see to it that the power does not get out of hand.

We can better understand our criminal justice system by first examining the legal basis or authorization for our government and its powers.

Legal Authorization for the System

Unique at the time of its inception, the U.S. Constitution served as a blueprint for the first representative government of, by, and for the people. The founding fathers planned our government with a system of checks and balances controlling the executive, legislative, and judicial branches in a way they hoped would forever protect the United States from the dangers of dictatorship, tyranny and totalitarianism.[1]

The Revolutionary War—Shaper of the U.S. Constitution

The government of the United States, as we know it today, did not spring into being overnight. The revolutionary war began as a protest by thirteen divided, squabbling British colonies that resented being governed unfairly and from a great distance. Most of the colonial leaders were not in favor of actual revolt at the outset. Still regarding themselves as loyal Englishmen, they wanted control over their own internal affairs and wanted to be treated as well as other subjects of the crown.

The colonial leaders looked for solutions to their grievances by writing petitions to the king, staging protests, holding meetings with the royal governors, and making nonimportation agreements.

It is not easy to simplify the causes of the revolutionary war. One hundred fifty years had passed since the first settlement. From a few starving Massachusetts and Virginia settlers, the colonists had become prosperous merchants, ship owners, planters, and self-sufficient farmers. Most had come as free Englishmen and permanent settlers, regarding themselves as a class above the occupants of a conquered English colony. Perhaps most of the differences with the mother country stemmed from the opposing viewpoints as to the proper political relationship between the government of King George III and the colonies.

With the French and Indian wars, England ran up large debts. The king's ministers refused to acknowledge that great wealth came to England from the New World, and that colonial dependence brought considerable trade to the English merchants. The British government reasoned that taxes and trade restrictions on the colonists were needed to pay for colonial protection. One thing led to

---

1. For source material, see Edward Conrad Smith, ed., *The Constitution of the United States, With Case Summaries,* 9th ed. (New York: Barnes and Noble, 1972), and Edward S. Corwin and J. W. Peltason, *Understanding the Constitution,* 4th ed. (New York: Holt, Rinehart and Winston, 1967).

another, and the protests and demonstrations became more heated. Communications with England were very poor, and many of the governmental officials made no effort to explain the colonial viewpoint. When force was used to break up protest meetings, the settlers took up arms.

Even after the war broke out, the majority of the colonists were not seeking to form a unified nation. Most considered that they had joined together only long enough to fight the redcoats, and that the colonists would then return to their status as separate units. James Madison, who was later to become the third President of the United States, commented that the union was temporary and "will but little survive the present war."

The individual colonies had so many different interests that many of the people had no real desire to unify. The New England states were engaged in manufacturing and ship building and wanted no restrictions on trade. The southern, slave-owning colonies were determined to oppose efforts to stop the slave trade. The small colonies were suspicious of the larger ones. States with a "one crop" economy feared national taxation of their produce, while the seaboard areas wanted to tax exports. A number of the states had boundary disputes that they refused to have settled by a national government.

Then too, the dispute with the mother country arose from a dislike for a far away, overbearing government. The colonists had no intention of fighting a war, only to experience a similar problem in America.

In order to air their common grievances against the crown, all the colonies except Georgia sent delegates to the First Continental Congress in Philadelphia in 1774. This was intended as a peaceful meeting for the purpose of possible reconciliation, and a statement of grievances was sent to the king by representatives of this meeting.

On April 19, 1775, open fighting broke out at Concord, Massachusetts. A Second Continental Congress assembled on May 10, 1775, and resulted in the Declaration of Independence on July 4, 1776, as a powerful inducement to unification. The colonies then united for a time under the Articles of Confederation, and the union remained workable until the British general, Cornwallis, surrendered at Yorktown, in October, 1781. After the war it was soon apparent that the organization set up under the Articles of Confederation did not have the powers to cope with the governmental needs of the country.[2]

2. Eriksson, *American Constitutional History*, Chapter 7, 1933.

Legal Authorization for the System

The Congress that had been established under the Articles of Confederation met in February, 1787, calling for a convention to revise the government. In four months, beginning in May, 1787, delegates from all the states except Rhode Island worked out a proposed constitution that was submitted to conventions of the people in the individual states. Eventually adopted, this constitution provided for the establishment of a united national government when ratified by nine of the 13 states. This was submitted to the people on September 28, 1787.

Many Americans were still not enthusiastic about a centralized national government, and the new government did not obtain the required nine-state approval until April 30, 1789. North Carolina and Rhode Island continued to exist as separate governments until after the new nation imposed a tax on foreign imports, including items shipped from North Carolina and Rhode Island into the other states.

In effect, then, our Constitution was the result of a long, evolutionary process. The leaders of this country based the authority for the government and its criminal justice system on the Constitution, which in turn derives its authority from assemblies of the people. This was accomplished without additional fighting or the bloodshed that frequently follows a revolutionary movement.[3]

By any standard, our Constitution is a magnificent document. The writing style, alone, makes it noteworthy as literature. More importantly, it sets out the rights of individuals, and the guarantees that prevent these rights from being eroded away.

In addition, the writers of the Constitution recognized that it would be a mistake to rigidly impose their own ideas on people in the future. To some degree, every society falls heir to the passions, hates, and attitudes of prior generations. Realizing this, the framers of this document left the Constitution flexible, so that it can be altered to the human needs and understandings of each generation. In short, the limitations on the Constitution are the limitations of civilized man himself.

The Constitution as an Extension of Earlier Democratic Ideas

The establishment of democratic government in the United States was achieved largely through the leadership and sacrifices of

3. John C. Klotter and Jacqueline R. Kanovitz, *Constitutional Law for Police* (Cincinnati: The W. H. Anderson Co., 1968), pp. 3–5.

the colonists. But it represented the realization of the hopes and dreams of those who had worked toward individual freedom for thousands of years. For the first time in history, a representative government was set up which gave the citizens themselves the responsibility of looking out for the interests of the public at large.

It is true that earlier attempts at democratic government had been made long before in the ancient Greek city states. These systems had been set up on a very small scale, however, with direct, rather than representative government. These early systems did not approach the government of an entire people and, after a short time, the Greek democracies were not able to hold out against their enemies.

Democracy, as a government of the people, involves rule by laymen, rather than by those who are specially trained for the task. It can be argued that the interests of the nation would best be served in many cases if the most intellectual and competent citizens were given the reins of government. History indicates, however, that it is often only a matter of a short time before political leaders who are not responsible to the public turn into tyrants. There is an overriding moral value in self-government. In general, the democratic system effectively sets up and guarantees the rights of the individual members of society.

THE U.S. CONSTITUTION AS AUTHORIZATION FOR THE CRIMINAL JUSTICE SYSTEM

The U.S. Constitution is the fundamental or supreme law of the nation. Unlike the "unwritten constitutions" of some countries, it was recorded for everyone to read. It establishes representation—the way in which individuals are involved in and participate in the government. The Constitution sets out the beginnings of the criminal justice system by authorizing the establishment and operation of the United States Supreme Court. In the years since ratification of the Constitution, Congress has passed a number of laws which authorize more courts and spell out the organization and mechanics of the system. These enactments have been supplemented by regulations set forth in the United States Administrative Code and the codes of civil and criminal procedure. Congress has specified what kinds of behavior are criminal. The federal courts try those accused of criminal misbehavior and interpret how the laws are to be applied.

LEGAL AUTHORIZATION FROM STATE CONSTITUTIONS

Systems similar to the federal model have been used to set up the state criminal justice systems. As early as 1776, the colonial states began to adopt written state constitutions. In these documents, the people were declared to be the ultimate source of power and of governmental authority. The language used in two of these constitutions is as follows:

Massachusetts
The whole people covenants with each citizen, and each citizen with the whole people that all shall be governed by certain laws for the common good.

Georgia
We, therefore, the representatives of the people, from whom all power originates and for whose benefit all government is intended, by virtue of the power delegated to us, do ordain . . . that the following rules and regulations be adopted for the future government of this state.

Like the U.S. Constitution, the state constitutions include provisions for setting up state criminal justice systems. For example, the California Constitution provides:

Article VI, Section 1—The judicial power of this State is vested in the Supreme Court, courts of appeal, superior courts, municipal courts, and justice courts. All except justice courts are courts of record. [Courts whose acts and judicial proceedings are perpetually recorded through use of a court reporter or stenographer are considered courts of record.]

STATE PENAL CODES AND COURT INTERPRETATIONS

State penal codes also serve as the basis for the criminal justice system. In some instances, the state constitution provides the broad outlines, while court interpretations and penal codes give additional clarification and substance to the general plan spelled out by the constitutional provisions.

SUMMARY

The basic legal authorization for the federal system of criminal justice is obtained from the U.S. Constitution. This basic authority has been expanded by federal criminal laws passed by Congress, by interpretations of the Constitution, and by Congressional enactments in cases reaching the Supreme Court of the United States. While this authorization started with the U.S. Constitution, no one source of authority can be considered all-inclusive.

In a similar fashion, legal authority for the state criminal justice systems stems from individual state constitutions. These state constitutional provisions have become more detailed as a result of state legislative enactments (state penal codes) and court interpretations. Some of these court interpretations come from the Supreme Court when state constitutional provisions, state penal codes, or state court decisions are in conflict with the federal laws.

QUESTIONS

1. Describe why the American colonies were not politically united before the start of the revolutionary war. List reasons for opposition to colonial unification prior to the war against England.

2. Show briefly how the U.S. Constitution resulted from a drawn-out evolutionary process.

3. List some of the sources for the ideas incorporated into the United States Constitution.

4. Explain how the U.S. Constitution is the legal basis for the criminal justice system. In turn, from which group of persons does the United States Constitution derive authority?

5. How does authority for a state criminal justice system derive from the state constitution?

6. Describe how some additional authority for the criminal justice system may derive from state statutes.

7. How may court interpretations provide an additional basis for the criminal justice system? Give explanations.

Men are not to be exploited for the information necessary to condemn them, and a prisoner is not to be made the deluded instrument of his own conviction, and such an exploitation of interrogation, whatever its usefulness, is not a permissible substitute for judicial trial.

Justice Felix Frankfurter, United States Supreme Court, in *Culombe v. Connecticut,* 367 US 568 (1961)

chapter three

IMPLICATIONS OF CIVIL RIGHTS

The purpose of this chapter is to outline the specific legal rights that are available to everyone in this country—both criminals and law-abiding citizens alike. These rights will be examined individually and we will take a brief look at their origins. This chapter will also explain how the courts interpret and apply these specific rights, and the implications to be drawn from the courts' interpretations.

INDIVIDUAL RIGHTS PROVIDED IN THE U.S. CONSTITUTION

In one sense, it is somewhat ironic that the accused must be furnished every protection of the legal system that he is charged with violating. Nevertheless, this is a basic part of the criminal justice system in this country.

Certain inalienable rights are set out in the U.S. Constitution and these rights cannot be taken or bargained away. They work to the benefit of society as a whole, but they furnish specific protection to individuals.

Most of these safeguards were incorporated into the first ten amendments to the U.S. Constitution. They form the Bill of Rights, which was ratified on December 15, 1791. One other important safeguard, that of *habeas corpus,* was included in the Constitution proper. *Habeas corpus* protects American citizens from illegal detention or imprisonment.

The first ten amendments to the Constitution are as follows:

Amendment I
Congress shall make no law respecting an establishment of religion, or prohibiting the free exercise thereof; or abridging the freedom of speech, or of the press; or the right of the people peaceably to assemble, and to petition the Government for a redress of grievances.

Amendment II
A well regulated Militia, being necessary to the security of a free State, the right of the people to keep and bear Arms, shall not be infringed.

Amendment III
No soldier shall, in time of peace be quartered in any house, without the consent of the Owner, nor in time of war, but in a manner to be prescribed by law.

Amendment IV
The right of the people to be secure in their persons, houses, papers, and effects, against unreasonable searches and seizures, shall not be violated, and no Warrants shall issue, but upon probable cause, supported by Oath or affirmation, and particularly describing the place to be searched, and the persons or things to be seized.

Amendment V
No person shall be held to answer for a capital, or otherwise infamous crime, unless on a presentment or indictment of a Grand Jury, except in cases arising in the land or naval forces, or in the Militia, when in actual service in time of War or public danger; nor shall any person be subject for the same offense to be twice put in jeopardy of life or limb; nor shall be compelled in any criminal case to be a witness against himself, nor be deprived of life, liberty, or property, without due process of law; nor shall private property be taken for public use, without just compensation.

Amendment VI
In all criminal prosecutions, the accused shall enjoy the right to a speedy and public trial, by an impartial jury of the State and district wherein the crime shall have been committed, which district shall have been previously ascertained by law, and to be informed of the nature and cause of the accusation; to be confronted with the witnesses against him; to have compulsory process for obtaining witness in his favor, and to have the Assistance of Counsel for his defense.

Amendment VII
In Suits at common law, where the value in controversy shall exceed twenty dollars, the right of trial by jury shall be preserved, and no fact tried by a jury, shall be otherwise re-examined in any Court of the United States, than according to the rules of the common law.

Amendment VIII
Excessive bail shall not be required, nor excessive fines imposed, nor cruel and unusual punishments inflicted.

Amendment IX
The enumeration in the Constitution, of certain rights, shall not be construed to deny or disparage others retained by the people.

Amendment X
The powers not delegated to the United States by the Constitution, nor prohibited by it to the States, are reserved to the States respectively, or to the people.

Fifteen specific safeguards in the Bill of Rights regulate criminal procedures and trials. Those rights regarding illegal search and seizure of evidence, as well as the issuance of search warrants, are frequently explored in courses on Evidence and will not be considered here.

For our purposes, individual treatment is given to eight of these basic rights in other sections of this book. There are specific discussions on:

1. Grand jury indictment in federal cases;
2. Prosecution a second time for the same offense (double jeopardy);

3.   Requiring an individual to give testimony against himself;

4.   The right to a fair trial;

5.   The right to be advised specifically of the charge;

6.   The right to an attorney;

7.   The right to bail at a reasonable figure; and,

8.   The prohibition against cruel or unusual punishment.

The remaining rights of the accused, as specified in the Bill of Rights, are discussed in this chapter. In addition, another right was set out in the Constitution prior to the ratification of the Bill of Rights and the other amendments. This is the right of *habeas corpus* which appears in Article I, Section 9.

HABEAS CORPUS

Hundreds of years ago, the king of England could clap an individual into jail and hold that person indefinitely without trial. In 1215 A.D., in one of the celebrated moments in English history, fifteen of the English barons united in a confrontation against King John. A particularly harsh ruler, John had taxed the barons heavily to pay for wars in France that had been fought to keep some of John's holdings on the continent. In addition, John had taken away many of the civil and private rights that the barons and city dwellers had acquired by custom over hundreds of years. Although as individuals they were relatively powerless, the fifteen lords together controlled most of the armed men in the country. Meeting King John in a meadow at Runnymede, the barons forced the king to sign a list of demands that had been drawn up by the barons and church authorities.

King John reluctantly agreed to the lords' demands, thereby establishing the principle that even the English king was not above the law. The fifteen lords were motivated by personal interests; they demanded restoration of their "ancient and accustomed liberties." Happily for future generations, the barons served more than their own best interests. The rights they had secured for themselves were soon claimed by all the English people, and the document signed by King John came to be known as the Magna Charta (sometimes spelled Magna Carta), or Great Charter.

The following items in Chapter 39 of the Magna Charta were among the rights conceded by King John:

24

No free man shall be seized or imprisoned, or stripped of his rights or possessions, or outlawed or exiled, or deprived of his standing in any other way, nor will we proceed with force against him, or send others to do so, except by the lawful judgment of his equals or by the law of the land.

Habeas corpus is the Latin term for the rights conceded by John in Chapter 39 of the Magna Charta. Over the years, *habeas corpus* has come to mean that any authority or official holding someone under arrest may be forced to come into court with that individual to explain to the court whether there is legal justification for holding that person. If no legal basis is found, the court can order release from custody.

The writ of *habeas corpus* was considered so important to the cause of personal freedom that the American colonists included it in the U.S. Constitution. They believed that it was one of the most cherished rights of their English heritage. Article I, Section 9, of the U.S. Constitution reads:

2.   The Privilege of the Writ of Habeas Corpus shall not be suspended, unless when in Cases of Rebellion or Invasion the public safety may require it.

State courts may not inquire into the reasons why persons are held by federal authorities, but the federal courts do have jurisdiction to determine if persons are being improperly held by either state or federal authorities.

State courts uniformly grant the writ to cover situations of unauthorized state detention. The California Penal Code, Section 1475, provides:

Application for the writ is made by petition, signed either by the party for whose relief it is intended, or by some person in his behalf, and must specify:

1.   That the person in whose behalf the writ is applied for is imprisoned or restrained of his liberty, the officer or person by whom he is so confined or restrained, and the place where, naming all the parties, if they are known, or describing them, if they are not known;

2.   If the imprisonment is alleged to be illegal, the petition must also state in what the alleged illegality consists;

3.   The petition must be verified by the oath or affirmation of the party making the application.

Implications of Civil Rights

In typical cases involving the writ, a suspect is taken into custody but is not formally charged with a crime. This usually occurs when investigating officers feel they know who committed a crime but do not have enough evidence to convince the prosecutor to authorize a warrant.

A suspect is at a psychological disadvantage if he is held in an unfamiliar place and subjected to intense questioning. There is a greater likelihood that he may confess if held incommunicado and cut off from his friends and associates.

Whenever there is an illegal restraint, a writ of *habeas corpus* may be issued. The courts take the approach that exploratory inquisitions can get out of hand if allowed to continue for very long. Therefore, a police official cannot hold a suspect for any lengthy period of time on a mere hunch. A complaint must be filed or the suspect released.[1]

THE RIGHT TO A PUBLIC TRIAL

Free people have always had a distrust of secret governmental activities. If trials are not conducted in the open, there is always the possibility that the court can be used either as an instrument of persecution or to cover up criminality. When courtroom activities are under public scrutiny, there is a stronger likelihood that the proceedings will be fair, both to the accused and to the public interest.

The Sixth Amendment to the U.S. Constitution includes a provision that "in all criminal prosecutions the accused shall enjoy the right to a . . . public trial. . ." The constitutions of the majority of the states also include this guarantee.[2] Even if it is not spelled out in the state constitution, the federal courts have ruled that this is an essential right in either a state or federal prosecution.[3] The courts do not agree, however, as to whether this is a right solely for the benefit of the accused, or whether it is also a right of the general public.

So long as the trial court judge acts reasonably, the higher courts almost invariably allow him to run his own court. The judge must have a free hand to do his job in an orderly, businesslike way, keeping the trial free from outside influences. If there is good cause

1. Rollin M. Perkins, *Criminal Law and Procedure,* 3d ed. (Brooklyn: The Foundation Press, 1966), p. 834.
2. California State Constitution, Art. I, paragraph 13.
3. In re Oliver, 333 US 257 (1948).

to feel that a spectator is threatening or intimidating a witness, the judge may order the spectator thrown out of the courtroom. In addition, the judge may instruct the prosecuting attorney to look into the possibility of filing a criminal charge against the spectator.

The accused must be allowed to have his friends and relatives present but they are not allowed to act as a cheering section for him. These friends and relatives forfeit their right to remain in the courtroom if they make a public show of sympathy or blurt out comments.

As a part of the accused's right to a public trial, judges usually try to accommodate spectators. If available seating space is limited, however, the judge has only to make a reasonable allotment of space for the accused's relatives and friends.

THE RIGHT TO A JURY TRIAL

The U.S. Constitution, Article III, provides the right to a trial by jury for ". . . all crimes, except in cases of Impeachment, . . ." In addition, the Sixth Amendment to the U.S. Constitution specifies that this shall be "by an impartial jury of the State and district wherein the crime shall have been committed."

From a legal standpoint, the defendant in a federal prosecution has the right to a jury on any serious charge—that is, any violation that carries a possible penalty of more than six months imprisonment.[4]

The federal courts have also ruled that the accused is entitled to a jury in any state criminal prosecution where the penalty involves a possible sentence of more than six months imprisonment.[5] This result was reached by the courts on the basis that it is a requirement of fundamental fairness under the due process clause of the Fourteenth Amendment of the U.S. Constitution, which must be applied to all the states.

The federal courts, however, do give the states leeway as to how many people are required to make up a jury. The federal requirement for a jury is twelve persons and the verdict must be unanimous.[6]

4. Patton v. US, 281 US 276 (1930).
5. Duncan v. Louisiana, 391 US 145 (1968) and Dyke v. Taylor Implement Co., 391 US 216 (1968).
6. Apodaca v. Oregon, 404 US 404 (1972).

On appeal to the federal courts, it has been held that a state jury may consist of as few as six individuals, provided this is the state law.[7] The federal courts have also ruled that the verdict of a state court jury does not necessarily have to be unanimous, if this is allowed by state law.[8]

In the federal courts and most state courts the accused can waive his right to a jury trial, and be tried by the judge alone. This approach may be used if the defense attorney feels that the judge might be less disturbed by some aspects of the case than would a jury. The prosecutor, however, can insist that a jury trial be held, regardless of the accused's desire to waive the jury.[9]

The accused's right to ask for a waiver is usually studied closely by the courts, as they want to make certain that he does not surrender his rights without understanding them. Therefore, some states require the accused to have his attorney present when he asks the judge for a waiver, while some other states do not allow the accused to give up his right to a jury trial under any circumstances.[10]

THE RIGHT TO A SPEEDY TRIAL

The Sixth Amendment of the U.S. Constitution provides that "in all criminal prosecutions the accused shall enjoy the right to a speedy . . . trial." This provision, of course, takes care of the situation in the federal courts. The constitutions of most states have similar provisions, some using the identical language of the federal provision.

The right to a speedy trial is important to both the general public and the individual. Even if a man has committed a crime, it is not fair to "keep him on the hook" forever.[11] Without a speedy trial, the accused may suffer real hardship, whether or not he is kept in jail. His savings may be used up and his chances for future employment may be seriously harmed. Conviction, of course, always carries a stigma. But even if the accused is found innocent, he and the

7. Williams v. Florida, 399 US 78 (1970).
8. Johnson v. Louisiana, 496 US 356 (1972).
9. Singer v. US, 380 US 24 (1965).
10. See Rollin M. Perkins, *Criminal Law and Procedure,* 3d ed. (Brooklyn: The Foundation Press, 1966), pp. 909–911.
11. John C. Klotter and Jacqueline R. Kanovitz, *Constitutional Law for Police* (Cincinnati: The W. H. Anderson Co., 1968), pp. 273–278; and Rollin M. Perkins, *Criminal Law and Procedure,* 3d ed. (Brooklyn: The Foundation Press, 1966), p. 904.

members of his family may be held up to public scorn until after the trial.

What this provision means, then, is that the case will be thrown out completely if the prosecutor delays beyond a reasonable time. This is not the kind of legal situation where the accused can be granted a new trial, because that would not cure the problems caused by delay.

Although there are some states where there is no constitutional or statutory requirement for a speedy trial, the United States Supreme Court has said that this is such a basic requirement for fairness that it is essential. The due process requirement of the U.S. Constitution applies to all state prosecutions.[12]

In addition to the requirements laid down by the United States Supreme Court, statutes in a number of states require the accused to be brought to trial within a specific period after an indictment or information is filed. Obviously, a trial cannot begin if the accused is in flight and his whereabouts are unknown. The California Penal Code requires the initiation of a trial within sixty days.[13] Statutes in other states, however, frequently allow a longer period of time. When the state law does not specify a time period between the indictment and the trial, the court determines what it considers to be a reasonable length of time.

The machinery of the courts is geared for orderly, deliberate processes. While the accused has the right to a speedy trial, the prosecution is also entitled to have a reasonable time to prepare its case and to make ready for trial. The accused cannot insist that his trial be set at too early a date to allow the matter to be investigated, witnesses to be located, and physical evidence to be analyzed. Then too, the case must wait its place on the court calendar, provided this in itself is not an unreasonable time. The test is what is reasonable under all the circumstances.

Under England's early legal system, the prosecutor was allowed to bring the accused to trial as soon as charges were filed, unless he could show a strong cause for delay. Under the present system in the United States, the accused cannot be forced to trial until he has had reasonable time for preparation. Statutes in a number of states entitle the defendant to a specific period after his plea is entered (generally three to five days) as a matter of right.

In allowing the accused enough time to prepare, the courts will

12. Klopfer v. North Carolina, 386 US 610 (1967).
13. California Penal Code, Section 1382.

usually grant a continuance if they are shown reasonable cause, even after the time for trial has been set. Generally, the courts will allow a considerable time to pass before forcing a criminal trial for which the accused insists he is not ready. The decisions make it clear, however, that mere stalling for time will not be allowed by either side in the contest.

The right to a speedy trial does not come into play until charges have been filed. In some cases, the authorities may not get the kind of break that enables them to solve the case until long after the crime takes place. There is nothing in the law that requires the prosecution to bring charges in a speedy manner. The prosecution can hold off until the prosecuting attorney is satisfied that a solution has been reached, provided the charges are filed prior to the running of the statute of limitations.

If, however, the accused can show that the prosecutor has deliberately delayed the filing of charges to get some kind of tactical advantage, he can sustain a claim of substantial prejudice to a fair trial under the due process clauses of the Fifth and Fourteenth Amendments to the U.S. Constitution. Showing that there was a lapse of thirty-eight months between the commission of the crime and the filing of prosecutive action, with no other extenuating circumstances, would not be regarded as a delay chargeable to the prosecution.[14]

The constitutional prohibition against unreasonable delays is not limited to the trial alone. The convicted person must be sentenced within a reasonable time after being found guilty. Probation and revocation hearings must also be held within a reasonable time.

THE RIGHT TO CONFRONT WITNESSES

The Sixth Amendment to the U.S. Constitution gives an accused person the right ". . . to be confronted with the witnesses against him . . ."[15] The framers of the Constitution included this provision because there is less likelihood of a witness swearing to an untruth if he must face the accused.

14. U.S. v. Marion, 404 US 307 (1971).
15. This is apparently a right that has been recognized in the courtroom for a long time. The Biblical account of the Romans in Acts 25, Verse 16 (Revised Standard Version) states: ". . . it was not the custom of the Romans to give up any one before the accused met the accusers face to face, and had an opportunity to make his defense concerning the charge laid against him."

As stated by the Supreme Court in *Greene* v. *McElroy*:[16]

> ... it is ... important where the evidence consists of the testimony of individuals whose memory might be faulty or who, in fact, might be perjurers or persons motivated by malice, vindictiveness, intolerance, prejudice or jealousy.

Then too, the confrontation privilege allows for cross-examination of the witness. This permits the adversaries in the criminal trial to inquire into the witness' motives, and to look into the relationships that existed between the accused and the witness at the time of the alleged violation. This confrontation also helps the jury in sorting out conflicting testimony by evaluating the way in which the witness testifies. If he seems straightforward and confident, he may damage the defendant's case. If, however, the witness is unsure of himself, a reasonable doubt of guilt may be created.

This fundamental right to confront each witness applies to both state and federal prosecutions, according to the decision of the United States Supreme Court.[17] The accused has no right to confront witnesses before a grand jury or at a legislative inquiry. However, the right does apply to the preliminary hearing, since the accused is attempting to prove that the charges against him are without basis in fact, and this can be done by discrediting the prosecution's witnesses.

A juvenile has the same right to confront witnesses. This is true whether the juvenile is prosecuted in a regular criminal trial or by special juvenile hearings or proceedings that are held in lieu of a trial.[18]

The courts have interpreted the right of confrontation to require that the defendant be physically present whenever evidence or verbal testimony is offered for either side. If an argument is being made about a point of law, however, the judge may bar everyone from the courtroom except the attorneys and the judge.

There are times, however, when the courts say that the accused has forfeited his right to confront the witnesses against him. One of these situations is that in which the accused jumps out the window and makes his escape. Here, the courts say that the accused's right still existed and he simply did not stay around to take advantage of

16. Greene v. McElroy, 360 US 474, 79 S Ct 1400 (1959).
17. Pointer v. Texas, 380 US 400 (1965).
18. In re Gault, 387 US 1 (1967).

it. The trial would go on, whether or not the accused was recaptured and returned to the courtroom.

In some situations the accused may insist on attempting to disrupt the trial. Proper procedure calls for the judge to warn the accused, and to take action if he persists in disruptive tactics. The Supreme Court has indicated in prior cases that the judge may have the accused held in a nearby room until he agrees to conduct himself properly, or may have him bound and gagged while the trial proceeds. In all instances, however, the trial judge must give the accused a reasonable opportunity to control his behavior, prior to taking action against him.

THE RIGHT TO OBTAIN WITNESSES

The Sixth Amendment to the U.S. Constitution guarantees the right to subpoena witnesses who may furnish evidence for the accused. This is the same right that the prosecutor has to call witnesses for the government. The Supreme Court has decided that this right also applies to defendants in state criminal trials.[19]

The trial judge is allowed reasonable discretion regarding this right. Before he will authorize the spending of money to bring witnesses, he must have some assurance that the potential witness actually has some information and that it will have a bearing on the case. Experience shows that if a confirmed criminal is allowed to call any person he wishes, he may request subpoenaes for some of his old prison associates who would like a trip out of the penal institution where they are confined.

SUMMARY

A number of specific civil rights are guaranteed to everyone in this country. These rights can neither be taken nor bargained away. Most of these civil rights were incorporated into the first ten amendments to the U.S. Constitution, which is known as the Bill of Rights. There are some additional guarantees in the U.S. Constitution, however.

These rights include freedom of speech, freedom of the press, the right to assemble peaceably, freedom to petition the government to correct wrongs, the right to bear arms, and immunity from being

19. Washington v. Texas, 388 US 214 (1967).

required to quarter soldiers in private homes. Other rights include guarantees against unreasonable searches and seizures, the right to an indictment before trial in major federal crimes, the right to be put in jeopardy only once for one crime, and the right to refuse to testify against oneself. In addition, the accused in a criminal trial has the right to a speedy trial, a public trial, and a trial in the district and state where the crime is supposed to have been committed. The accused also has the right to call witnesses, to be informed of the nature of the charge, and to have an attorney in cases with a serious penalty. In addition, bail may not be set in an excessive amount, and any punishment inflicted may not be cruel or unusual. In addition, the person under detention has the right of *habeas corpus*—a legitimate complaint must be filed or the person who is restrained must be immediately released.

QUESTIONS

1. What is the Bill of Rights?
2. Explain what is meant by *habeas corpus*.
3. Does the accused always have the right to a public trial?
4. Is the accused guaranteed the right to a jury trial? If so, under what circumstances?
5. Does the accused have the same constitutional rights, whether the prosecution is for a felony or for a misdemeanor? Explain your answer.
6. What period of time must elapse before the courts will say that the accused was not given a speedy trial?
7. Why is the right to confront witnesses considered an important constitutional right?
8. What action may the judge take if the accused tries to pick a fight with a government witness?

It is not the function of the police to arrest, as it were, at large and use an interrogation process at police headquarters in order to determine whom they should charge before a committing magistrate . . .

Justice Felix Frankfurter, United States Supreme Court, in *Mallory* v. *United States*, 354 US 449 (1957)

chapter four

THE POLICE PROCESS

The purpose of this chapter is to describe the functions of the police force, especially as these functions relate to the power of arrest. This material will first consider what an arrest consists of. Information as to the sources of the power of arrest will then be covered, as will the right to make an arrest with a warrant.

It is also the purpose of this chapter to include some cautions as to the responsibilities of the officer making an arrest. The individual being detained has clearly defined rights, and these should be observed, both to avoid a personal lawsuit and to make sure evidence obtained in connection with the apprehension is legally admissible in court.[1]

THE PURPOSE OF AN ARREST

A criminal arrest has two basic purposes:

1. To make certain that the accused does not flee to some distant place or go into hiding. This insures the accused's availability when the case comes to trial.

2. To give protection to the community, since the offender may commit other crimes.

---

1. See William A. Rutter, *Criminal Procedure,* (Gardena, California, Gilbert Law Summaries, Publisher, 5th Edition, 1973), pp. 11–13.

ARREST DEFINED

According to the understanding of the courts, an arrest takes place when any person is held or detained against his will. In the words of a case that the courts use as a guide, arrest "is a restraint, however slight, on another's liberty to come and go."[2] In the transcript of *State* v. *Shaw,* arrest is described as "coercion exercised upon a person to prevent the free exercise of his powers of locomotion."[3]

Another case used as a guide by legal authorities and judges states that to arrest is "to deprive a person his liberty, . . . taking him under real or assumed authority, for the purpose of holding or detaining him to answer a criminal charge."[4]

Mere Restriction May Not Be an Arrest

As to the detention aspect of an arrest, the test is whether the person under restraint is free to move about. When an individual has been wrongfully locked out of a club in which that person holds membership, or is ejected from a bar without cause, no arrest has been made, although a recovery of money damages may be made in a lawsuit in civil court. As long as the individual is still free to go into other clubs of his choice, there has been no arrest. In this situation, the wronged person has not been confined to one location.

The mere fact that a person has been restrained does not, in itself, constitute an arrest. To be considered an actual arrest, the detention must be for the specific purpose of bringing an individual before a court or legal authority in connection with a prosecution, or for the administration of some other aspect of justice. If the detention is for other reasons, the facts may constitute a kidnapping, false imprisonment, or unlawful detention. Merely holding a person against his will for personal motives is not the kind of intent necessary for the act to be classified as an arrest.

Physical Force Is Not Necessary to an Arrest

It is not essential that the individual being placed under arrest be subdued, handcuffed, or held down. The restraint aspect of an arrest is just as valid when the arrestee peaceably submits to authority, whether it is real or assumed.

2. Turney v. Rhodes, 155 SE 112.
3. State v. Shaw, 50 A 863, 73 Vt 149.
4. Ex parte Sherwood, 15 SW 812.

In general, an arrest is made in one of two ways: (1) by submission to the custody of the arresting authority or (2) by being overpowered by the officer's force.[5] As stated by a Massachusetts court, either "Physical seizure by the arresting officer or submission to the officer's authority and control is necessary to constitute an arrest."[6]

There are, however, some exceptions to the two types of arrest just described. If the arrestee is so drunk that he cannot give his consent, or if he is unconscious, the consent requirement is skipped by the courts. When the officer intends to arrest and the arrestee has been reduced to a state of control, then the courts say that an arrest actually has taken place.[7]

The California Penal Code, Sections 834 and 835, defines arrest in the following manner:

An arrest is taking a person into custody, in a case and in the manner authorized by law. An arrest may be made by a peace officer or by a private person.

An arrest is made by an actual restraint of the person, or by submission to the custody of an officer. The person arrested may be subjected to such restraint as is reasonable for his arrest and detention.

The courts occasionally have difficulty determining whether or not an arrest has occurred. In the majority of these cases, the intent of the arresting officer to take a person into custody is the distinguishing element that makes an arrest different from mere questioning, detention, or street interrogation.

Mere Words Don't Constitute an Arrest

An arrest involves more than mere words spoken by an officer. When a person accompanies a policeman at the officer's request, an arrest has not necessarily been made. In fact, when the suspect goes along voluntarily and words of arrest are never spoken, he has not been taken into custody, and therefore has not been arrested. The would-be arrestee is still free to go his own way if he agrees to first

5. California State Penal Code, Section 835. And see Rollin M. Perkins, *Criminal Law and Procedure,* 3d ed. (Brooklyn: The Foundation Press, 1966), p. 806.
6. Thomas v. Boston Pub. Co., 189 NE 210, 285 Mass 344.
7. R. Gene Wright and John A. Marlo, *The Police Officer and Criminal Justice* (New York: McGraw-Hill Book Co., 1970), pp. 182–86.

go along with the police officer "for the purpose of clearing himself."[8]

Even though no force has been used, the courts say that a suspected shoplifter has been arrested if he or she submits to a command from the store manager to remain in the manager's office until the police arrive. If, in fact, the person is not a shoplifter at all, the courts take the position that a "false arrest" has been made by the store manager. The falsely accused individual may bring a damage suit against the store and the store manager in a civil court.

Citizen Arrests

Although arrests are usually made by peace officers, the law has established no legal requirement of this kind; arrests may also be made by private persons. Whether arrests are made by private persons or peace officers, they may be placed in two categories: (1) those made without a warrant, and (2) those made on the basis of a warrant issued by a court or other authorized body.

Sources of the Power to Arrest

In some states, the courts continue to look to the common law for the authority to arrest and for restrictions on this authority. Changing social conditions, however, have caused practically all jurisdictions to change or delete some of the technical aspects of the common law.

There is no uniformity among the states as to legal sources of the power to arrest. In California, the powers of arrest are spelled out by statute.[9] Some such statutes can be found in practically all jurisdictions.

Why Is It Important for an Arrest to Be Lawfully Made?

Many police training programs and the written instructions directed toward new officers emphasize that all arrests must be made in a lawful way. In many departments, however, the beginning policeman never becomes fully aware of the importance of this. At least three basic reasons must be considered:

First, if the arrest is not lawful, the courts say that none of the

8. Williams v. United States, 189 Fed 2d 693.
9. California Penal Code, Sections 836, 837, 847.

evidence obtained at the time of arrest may be used by the government to prove the case in court against the accused. Experienced investigators know that a criminal may be taken by surprise at the time of arrest. In many instances, the criminal may still be in possession of identifiable loot, weapons, or objects that could prove the case against him. In the case of an unlawful arrest, these items can't be introduced as evidence, and the prosecutor's case may be seriously damaged or lost. This is simply one of the variations of the so-called exclusionary rule applied by the Supreme Court to all arrests, either state or federal. In essence, this rule excludes the prosecution from presenting any physical or tangible evidence received during an unlawful search or arrest.

One of the arguments given by the U.S. Supreme Court in support of the exclusionary rule is that the government (federal or state) should not be allowed to profit by its own mistakes or wrongful acts. A second, and important argument, is that when evidence resulting from an unlawful arrest is not allowed, the police learn from their mistakes and know not to make improper arrests in the future.

Still a third argument given by the Supreme Court is that a policy of this kind is necessary to maintain the integrity of the courts. On the other hand, many practical police officials have long believed that the exclusionary rule only serves to make a game of the judicial process. Frequently, the police officer on the scene must make a judgment in a matter of seconds as to whether to arrest or to ignore facts that point to the probability that a crime was committed. To free the criminal in a situation of this kind seems to be a disservice to the public at large. The English courts have always admitted illegally obtained evidence without any appreciable loss of respect for the court system.

Also, some of the decisions of the state courts have pointed to the fact that the federal exclusionary rule seems to overlook one of the basic objectives of the criminal courts—that of making certain that the accused is convicted only on *trustworthy* evidence. Normally, evidence obtained during an illegal arrest is just as reliable and trustworthy as evidence legally obtained.[10] The argument can therefore be made that the criminal's recourse should be a private, or civil, lawsuit against the officer who illegally arrested that offender.

In a well-known New York state case, the celebrated judge, Benjamin F. Cardozo, of the New York Court of Appeals, pointed

10. People v. Cahan, 282 P 2d 905.

39

out the most basic objection to the exclusionary rule: "The criminal is to go free because the constable has blundered."[11]

It is also important to note that the exclusionary rule may not be very effective as a means for the courts to "discipline" police officers for failure to make proper arrests. In the usual situation, several years may pass before a conviction is appealed to the Supreme Court and, thereafter, sent back for a new trial. In the meantime, policemen involved in the original arrest may have transferred, retired, or left the force. Rather than grant release because of an improper arrest, a number of authorities on constitutional law feel it would be preferable to admonish the arresting policeman, or to allow the accused person to sue for false arrest. Why frustrate justice because of police mistakes?

Nevertheless, the exclusionary rule is the law. It is required by the Supreme Court and police officers should, therefore, strive to make a lawful arrest in every case.

In addition to problems relating to the exclusionary rule, an unlawful arrest may result in a costly lawsuit against the arresting officer and his department by the person who was wrongfully detained. While the officer can usually present a good defense in this type of case, a lawsuit of this nature is expensive and time-consuming at best. Also, all illegal arrest situations work against good public relations.

In the eyes of the average citizen, one of the principal functions of the police is to safeguard the democratic process. If we can't expect the police to abide by the laws, then how can we successfully hold private citizens accountable for criminal violations? As phrased by Justice Louis D. Brandeis of the Supreme Court: "If the government becomes a lawbreaker, it breeds contempt for the law; it invites every man to become a law unto himself; it invites anarchy."[12]

Arrests Must Be Made Without Any Show of Malice or Bias

Not only should every arrest be made in a lawful manner, but the apprehension must also be accomplished without any show of malice or bias. It is the duty of the peace officer to restrain the accused and bring him to trial, not to stand in judgment of the criminal. Experienced trial attorneys usually agree that any display of bias or malice will work to the advantage of the lawbreaker. A dis-

11. People v. Defore, 150 NE 585.
12. Olmstead v. United States, 277 US 438.

play of this kind may be used by the defense attorney to convince the jury that those in authority are actually persecuting his or her client.

Officers are often called upon to arrest individuals who have committed acts that are so repulsive that the accused seems to have forfeited all claim on human decency and respectability. Nevertheless, the arresting officer must remain completely objective—"he has a job to do and must perform it to the best of his ability." The officer should never indicate, by word or deed, any disapproval of the accused or the accused's activities. It is the policeman's duty to protect the rights of all individuals of all classes, whether or not they seem to deserve consideration.

As stated in the somewhat stilted, but powerful, language of an 1889 Kentucky case:

> . . . those who administer the law should be especially alert, and stand like a wall between the passion of the hour and the object of it, insuring him, however humble, an impartial trial. Without this barrier no citizen is safe. Remove it and the liberty, or what is more, the life of every individual is in danger.[13]

ARREST WITH A WARRANT

Experience shows that most individuals do not willingly come in to court to answer criminal charges that have been brought against them. For this reason, the early English courts established a procedure whereby a document was issued and signed at the time charges were filed, ordering the arrest of the *body* of the accused. This early court document has come down to us in modern times as a *warrant of arrest,* an *arrest warrant,* or simply as a *warrant.*[14]

There are some differences from state to state as to just what information must be included in a warrant of arrest but basically the document must be a written court order instructing a law enforcement officer or some other specially named individual to take custody of the accused's person.[15]

---

13. Dilger v. Commonwealth, 11SW 651, 88 Ky 550.

14. See Rollin M. Perkins, *Criminal Law and Procedure,* 3d ed. (Brooklyn: The Foundation Press, 1966), p. 791, for the background of the arrest warrant.

15. The Restatement of Torts, Section 113, states that a warrant is a written order directing the arrest of a person or persons issued by a court, body, or official having authority to order an arrest. In re Riddle, 131 Tex Crim 563, 101 SW 2d 268, the court noted that a warrant of arrest is the legal authority by virtue of which the officer takes the person accused of an offense into custody and retains that individual.

Purpose and Importance of Arrest Warrants

A warrant is simply a document which provides the legal right to make an arrest. A warrant gives the policeman the protection which is not otherwise available to him. If time permits, therefore, the officer should obtain a warrant in advance of arrest. This was clearly not the practice of policemen a generation or two ago, but decisions of modern courts have made this reversal of attitudes most important in present day law enforcement.[16]

Most of the early settlers in this country came from Europe to enjoy the freedom that the new land promised. Because of this heritage, today's American citizen is often quick to oppose anything that he regards as a restriction on his freedom. This may explain why an otherwise law-abiding person may strenuously protest a traffic ticket, even though he admits that traffic laws are essential to the safety and well-being of the public.

Moreover, the courts of this country, following the opinions of the Supreme Court, have consistently said that no person shall be deprived of freedom unless legal safeguards have been carefully observed. An arrest warrant is generally regarded as one of the most important of these safeguards.

Today, it is the duty of the court, magistrate, or judge issuing an arrest warrant to make an unbiased evaluation of the facts which indicate that a particular individual has violated a criminal law. In issuing the warrant, the court commits itself. We must, therefore, expect that the court system supports its own procedures when attacked from the outside, unless the facts definitely show that the magistrate acted out of malice or bias.

Arrest by warrant is the only type of arrest expressly approved by the U.S. Constitution, and by the constitutions of many of the states. As we will see, an arrest without a warrant is clearly an exception to the rule. If the facts do not satisfy one of several well-defined exceptions, the courts consistently hold that an arrest without a warrant is unlawful.[17]

For many years, the federal courts did not apply the standards and requirements of the federal law to arrests made by state officers. However, in *Ker* v. *California* (1963) the Supreme Court ruled that state and local peace officers would thereafter be held to the same constitutional requirements as federal officers.[18]

16. See V. A. Leonard, *The Police, the Judiciary, and The Criminal,* 2d ed. (Springfield, Ill: Charles C. Thomas Publishers, 1975), pp. 20–27.
17. State v. Mobley, 83 SE 2d 100, 240 NC 476.
18. Ker v. California, 374 US 23, 83 S Ct 1623.

Limitations on the Right to Arrest in the U.S. Constitution

The Fourth Amendment to the U.S. Constitution places some definite limitations on the right to arrest, as well as the right to search:

> The right of the people to be secure in their persons, houses, papers, and effects, against unreasonable searches and seizures, shall not be violated, and no Warrants shall issue, but upon probable cause, supported by Oath or affirmation, and particularly describing the place to be searched, and the persons or things to be seized.

This does not mean, however, that all arrests without warrants or searches and seizures without warrants are forbidden. What this does say, in effect, is that a warrant of arrest can't be issued unless someone comes before the committing magistrate or court official and swears under oath, or affirms, that probable cause exists to indicate that a crime has been committed by the accused. This constitutional restriction on the issuance of warrants keeps the process from becoming an automatic or capricious thing. In other words, it reduces the possibility that accusations may be brought without reasonable basis or that the complaining witness may be carried away by suspicions alone. Similar restrictions have been included in a number of state constitutions.

It is important to note that an official public body, such as a grand jury, may issue a valid warrant of arrest without swearing to the facts. This is because members of the grand jury are sworn in at the time they assume their duties, so the courts regard all deliberations of this body as being under a continuum of the oath.

A Warrant May Be Used for Only One Arrest

A warrant of arrest may be used only once. When it is necessary to arrest the accused a second time, a new warrant must be obtained. We find only one exception to this requirement. When a person under arrest manages to escape the officer who had custody may immediately follow and rearrest without a warrant, anyplace in the same state.[19]

---

19. See the statutes of Alabama, Arizona, California, Iowa, New York, and a number of other states which permit this practice.

Where May a Warrant Be Used?

As a general rule, an arrest warrant is valid only in the state in which it is issued.[20] One state can't empower its police officers to act in another jurisdiction. This idea is basic to our recognition of the separate powers of the states under our federal system.

If a warrant has legal effect outside the state where it is issued, this must come about because of statutes passed in the latter state. This does not mean, however, that a warrant from another state does not have any effect whatever. It is true that the arrest power created by the warrant is limited by the boundary lines of the state. However, the warrant may still be used in the second state as the basis for issuance of a fugitive warrant. In a situation of this kind, the original warrant is used as the basis for extradition.

The Uniform Close Pursuit Act

It is inaccurate to state that a peace officer of one state can never make an arrest outside his own jurisdiction. A number of states have adopted a statute commonly called the *Uniform Close Pursuit Act*. As enacted in New York, this statute reads:

1.   As used in this section, the word "state" shall include the District of Columbia.

2.   Any peace officer of another state of the United States, who enters this state in close pursuit of a person in order to arrest him, shall have the same authority to arrest and hold in custody such person on the ground that he has committed a crime in another state which is a crime under the laws of the state of New York, as police officers of this state have to arrest and hold in custody a person on the ground that he has committed a crime in this state.

3.   If an arrest is made in this state by an officer of another state in accordance with the provisions of subdivision two, he shall without unnecessary delay take the person arrested before a local criminal court which shall conduct a hearing for the sole purpose of determining if the arrest was in accordance with the provisions of subdivision two, and not of determining the guilt or innocence of the arrested person. If such court determines

20. U.S. v. Trunko, 189 Fed Supp 559.

44

that the arrest was in accordance with such subdivision, it shall commit the person arrested to the custody of the officer making the arrest, who shall without unnecessary delay take him to the state from which he fled. If such court determines that the arrest was unlawful, it shall discharge the person arrested.

4.   This section shall not be construed so as to make unlawful any arrest in this state which would otherwise be lawful.

5.   Upon the taking effect of this section it shall be the duty of the secretary of state to certify a copy of this section to the executive department of each of the states of the United States.

6.   This section shall apply only to peace officers of a state which by its laws has made similar provisions for the arrest and custody of persons closely pursued within the territory thereof.

7.   If any part of this section is for any reason declared void, it is declared to be the intent of this section that such invalidity shall not affect the validity of the remaining portions of this section.

8.   This section may be cited as the uniform act on close pursuit.[21]

Under the terms of the Uniform Close Pursuit Act, the courts have uniformly held that the officer who gives chase must actually be in "hot pursuit" at all times and must make an immediate arrest. The officer cannot make a legal arrest when any break has occurred in the continuity of the chase. Also, the courts have indicated that they will carefully examine the facts surrounding any arrest of this kind, to make certain that officers have not overstepped their authority.

The Uniform Fresh Pursuit Act

While some states have adopted the Uniform Close Pursuit Act, others have adopted a similar "Uniform Fresh Pursuit Act." The Iowa Code (Section 756–1), which includes the latter act, limits the pursuit to felony cases only. Illinois, however, allows pursuit for both misdemeanors and felonies. Because of differences in state laws, police officers should be familiar not only with their own state statutes, but with those of adjoining states as well.

21. McKinney's *Consolidated Laws of New York*, Section 140.55.

Who May Serve a Warrant of Arrest?

Under our modern legal system, a warrant of arrest is usually directed to officers of the law. Centuries ago in England, however, private persons were frequently told to serve the warrant under the common law.

In those days, only a handful of peace officers enforced the law in all of England. By tradition, individual citizens had the responsibility to make an arrest. These old ideas of arrest were brought to this country by the colonists and they continue to be a part of our legal tradition. There are still a few jurisdictions where a warrant of arrest may yet be directed to a private citizen, although this has been changed by statutes in some areas.[22]

Under federal criminal procedures, warrants must be directed to a federal officer, but they are usually routed to the U.S. Marshal, sometimes referred to as the USM. If the location of the accused is known, the warrant is usually served by the U.S. Marshal. When the whereabouts of the accused is unknown, he is considered a fugitive. It is then the responsibility of the FBI, Secret Service, Postal Inspectors, or other federal officers who possess arrest powers to conduct the investigation, locate, and arrest the wanted person.

Before the American Revolution, colonial agents of the king of England had adopted the practice of obtaining "blank" arrest warrants. These warrants did not contain the name of the arrestee. Blank warrants were used by the king's agents for "fishing expeditions," where they arrested people on whim or suspicion. Denounced by James Otis and other revolutionay patriots, the use of a blank warrant has long been forbidden by the U.S. Supreme Court.[23]

When May A Warrant Be Issued?

Generally, an arrest warrant may be issued at any time of the day or night, on holidays or on weekends. The courts insist that arrests be made on a warrant whenever possible. As a result, the courts must make sure that magistrates or other officials are always available to issue warrants. This practice had its origins under early English law when business contracts were invalid if made on Sunday but warrants of arrest were obtainable on any day.[24]

22. Randolph v. Commonwealth, 134 SE 544, 145 Va 883.
23. Henry v. U.S., 361 US 98, 80 S Ct 168.
24. Parish v. State, 30 SO 474, 130 Ala 92.

When May a Warrant Be Served?

Although a warrant may be obtained at any time, this does not mean that it may be served at any time of the day or night. Statutory restrictions generally say when a warrant may not be served. Usually, no time restrictions are placed on serving a felony warrant.[25]

If a warrant is issued for a violation less serious than a felony, for instance, a misdemeanor or lesser grade of offense, then the statutes in a number of states require that it shall be served during daylight hours. The general rule is that servants of the law should not engage in activities which may result in disturbances or cause terror in private homes at night. Since most people will not flee the country to avoid a misdemeanor warrant, the arrest may just as well be made during daylight hours.

As set out in Section 840 of the California Penal Code:

> If the offense charged is a felony, the arrest may be made on any day, and at any time of the day or night. If it is a misdemeanor, the arrest cannot be made at night, unless upon the direction of the magistrate, endorsed upon the warrant, except when the offense is committed within the presence of the arresting officer.

What Must a Warrant of Arrest Contain?

The required contents of a warrant of arrest depends on provisions of the constitution, procedural rules, and statutes in each particular state. A few statutes and court cases have gone so far as to say that the warrant must set out each element of the charged crime, but most courts have never insisted on this.[26]

In the absence of other specific requirements, five usual requirements for a valid arrest warrant are:

1. The accused must be named or sufficiently identified, so that the police officer knows who to arrest.

2. The nature of the charge must be specifically set out. In other words, the kind of crime must be named: arson, robbery, rape, etc.

25. Miles v. Wright, 194 P 88, 22 Ariz 73.
26. Ellis v. Glascow, 168 SW 2d 946.

3.   The warrant must be issued in the name of the state or Federal Government.

4.   It must be directed to an individual or class of individuals legally designated to serve it. Most modern-day warrants are directed to any peace officer in the state, as a class, so that it may be served by any one of them.

5.   The magistrate or issuing official must sign the warrant.

An additional, or sixth requirement, is imposed in some states: the warrant must be dated, and the place of issue must be named. This may include either the city or the county where the warrant was issued.

The Accused Must be Named or Identified in the Warrant

A warrant for the arrest of any person must specify his name or describe him so clearly that the officer does not arrest the wrong man. This was true under common law and has been continued through Supreme Court decisions.[27]

When the name of the person is unknown, a warrant is sometimes issued in the name of "John Doe." This "John Doe" warrant is worthless, however, unless it contains enough additional information that the person intended for arrest is definitely identifiable on the basis of descriptive information. This may include the accused's street address, peculiarities of appearance, or other distinctive information. Under these requirements, a warrant is sufficiently specific if it calls for the arrest of "the redheaded truck driver named 'Bud,' employed by the United Refrigeration Company, who lives at 825 South Ivy Street, Arlington, Virginia."

In the past, the courts have not been overly technical concerning the requirement for naming the accused, so long as it was clear who was to be arrested. The full and complete name need not be placed on the warrant. The investigating police officer must be careful, however, when supplying information for the preparation of a warrant if the arrestee is a father or son who uses the same name, followed by Sr. or Jr.

As indicated earlier, a "general warrant," signed by the magistrate in blank and filled in by a police officer at the time of arrest, is a nullity.[28] This type of warrant does not allow the magistrate's

---

27. Bean v. Best, 93 NW 2d 403, 77 SD 433; West v. Cabell, 153 US 78, 14 S Ct 752.
28. Rafferty v. People, 69 Ill 111; West v. Cabell, 153 US 78, 14 S Ct 752.

independent evaluation of the evidence against the accused prior to the time of arrest.

The Police Officer's Responsibility in Serving a Warrant of Arrest

Execution of a warrant of arrest is a very formal process. An officer's failure to execute the warrant amounts to disregard for a lawful court order. He is then subject to punishment for contempt of court.

As was previously pointed out, one of the functions of an arrest warrant is to give legal protection and authority to the apprehending officer. If the officer does not abuse this authority and the warrant appears to be proper or "fair" on its face, the officer has no obligation or duty to look into the events that resulted in the issuance of the warrant. A policeman is legally wrong if he delays an arrest for even a few minutes in order to satisfy himself that the warrant is based on reliable information. The true facts will be sifted out when the accused comes into court. Belief that the accused may not be guilty is beside the point during the arrest procedure.

In other words, the validity of an arrest warrant does not depend on whether a crime was actually committed. In some cases, the accused may not be guilty at all, but the evidence available to the investigating officer and the magistrate, at the time of the investigation, may be sufficient to convince a reasonable, prudent magistrate that arrest is justified. When the magistrate issues a warrant based on reasonable appearance, and a policeman arrests on this warrant, the accused can't bring a legal action against either the magistrate or the arresting officer. This holds true, even if the accused is later found not guilty.

Continuing in somewhat the same vein, when the arrest warrant appears to be proper on its face, the officer must serve it. In turn, he is protected in the event of a civil lawsuit for false arrest, regardless of what an investigation may prove later.

The Police Officer Must Serve an Arrest Warrant, Even if it Brings Financial Loss to the Accused

When an accused person is arrested at his place of business, the result may be that the arrestee will lose a considerable amount of money. However, the courts have said:

When a warrant, valid in form and issued by a court of competent jurisdiction, is placed in the hands of an officer for execution, it is his duty to carry out its demands without delay, and he incurs no liability for its proper execution, however disastrous may be the effect on the person against whom it is issued.[29]

A situation in point here might be that of a farmer who is engaged in harvesting a highly perishable crop. Unfortunately, the warrant must be served at a time which is critical to his livelihood. Clearly, though, this difficulty has been created by the actions of the accused, not by the arresting officer. In a situation of this kind, the arresting officer can't reasonably delay an actual apprehension while the accused hurries to save his perishable produce.

Then too, from a practical standpoint, experienced peace officers point out that any delay or "favor" granted to the arrestee may greatly increase the risk that the accused may attempt to escape. This is particularly true when the accused's plight seems desperate.

Common sense must, of course, be followed in making any arrest. When the person named in the warrant is operating a small business alone, it is obvious that some provisions must be made to lock the building or to have an officer remain at the scene until a responsible person can protect the assets involved. Similarly, when a parent or guardian of a small child is arrested, a juvenile or other officer must take charge of the child, at least until a responsible family member can be located.

Practically all law enforcement agencies provide regulations that cover these and other unusual arrest situations. In case of doubt, however, it may be advisable to obtain instructions from the legal officer or prosecuting official assigned to the jurisdiction.

Altering a Warrant

The courts have generally held that any substantial, or *material*, alteration of a warrant of arrest made after it has left the hands of the issuing magistrate, causes it to be illegal. An arrest can't be made legally when based on such a warrant. As one court said, "A warrant altered without the magistrate's authority is no longer his warrant."[30]

---

29. O'Neil v. Keeling, 288 NW 887, 227 Iowa 754; Malone v. Carey, 62 P 2d 166, 17 Cal App 2d 505.
30. Haskins v. Young, 19 NC 527.

The courts have, however, allowed the amendment of a warrant when the basic facts of the document have not been altered. For example, a correction on the return date has been permitted.[31]

How Long is a Warrant Good?

A criminal warrant of arrest is generally regarded as indefinitely "good." It does not die of old age. However, statutes of limitations in most jurisdictions prevent prosecutions of all but the most serious crimes after a specified period, which is commonly three years.

The Constitution of the United States, as well as a number of state constitutions, grant the accused the right to a speedy trial. When he has made no attempt to flee or go into hiding, law enforcement officers must attempt to serve the warrant within a reasonable time after the filing of the criminal charge or the issuance of the warrant. This allows time for the accused to receive notice of the complaint while witnesses in his behalf are still available. The accused also has the right to expect execution of the warrant within a reasonable time so that memories will be fresh as to the alleged events in the case. On the other hand, the courts have not been definite as to just what is regarded as a reasonable time to execute the warrant. In one California case, an unexplained delay of 140 days in attempting to serve the warrant was held to be unreasonable.[32]

Must the Warrant be in the Arresting Officer's Possession?

In states where the English common law is still followed, the arrest warrant must be in the possession of the arresting officer at the time of apprehension. Fortunately, this requirement has been changed by statute in most jurisdictions because improvements in communication and transportation have made the old common law requirement impractical. It is not unusual, however, for an accused to say, "I can't be arrested unless the warrant is in the officer's pocket." After some reflection on the matter one realizes that this demand is not entirely unreasonable. The accused needs to know

31. Kelly v. Gilman, 29 NH 385.
32. Rost v. Municipal Court of Southern Judicial District, 184 Cal App 2d 507; 7 Cal Rptr 869; 85 ALR 2d 507.

why an arrest is being made and should be told the nature of the charge for which the warrant was issued.

As to requiring the arresting officer to carry the warrant, a number of states have taken the approach set out in the California Penal Code:

> An arrest by a peace officer acting under a warrant is lawful even though the officer does not have the warrant in his possession at the time of the arrest, but if the person arrested so requests it, the warrant shall be shown to him as soon as practicable.[33]

The Officer's Right to Deputize Another to Make the Arrest

Many years ago in England, the sheriff was given authority by the king to summon any able-bodied male over the age of fifteen to assist in making arrests. When a group of these men was called upon, they formed what was known as a "posse comitatus," or, more simply, a posse.

In time, the courts recognized that any duly constituted officer could call on private citizens in time of need, requiring their help in preventing a crime or in making an arrest. This right is recognized today by the courts and a person who refuses to help, without proper justification, is, under modern statutes in most states, guilty of a misdemeanor.

A citizen who is deputized by an officer in an emergency generally cannot be sued for false arrest when he acts in good faith in following the officer's commands. However, when a private individual who is attempting to make a citizen's arrest calls on another for aid, the latter may be sued when the arrest is unlawful.

The Officer Must Make Known His Intention to Arrest

It has long been settled law in most jurisdictions that an individual may use force in his own self-defense when he thinks that he is being threatened with serious injury, death, or loss of his personal liberty. When an attempt is made to arrest this individual by an

---

33. California Penal Code, Section 842.

officer who doesn't make his identity known, then self-defense may legally be claimed.

Under common law rules, a person who was to be arrested had the right to prior notification as to the identity of the officer and the reasons for the apprehension. This notice, as practiced today, may work in either of two directions. It may prevent the arrestee from thinking that he is being assaulted, thus assuring that he will not draw a weapon in self-defense; or, it may remove the element of surprise, giving the dangerous criminal notice of an impending arrest and providing him an opportunity to shoot at the approaching officer.

In some states, therefore, proof that the police officer was wearing a uniform or a badge may be considered sufficient notice of the impending arrest and of the identity of the officer. Specific statements are included in the codes of a number of states as to just what must be said by the arresting police officer. This statement is sometimes called a "notice of arrest."

However, modern statutes generally allow the arresting officer to dispense with his notice of arrest when he can reasonably show that alerting the person to be arrested might result in harm to a bystander or to himself. Likewise, the notice of arrest may be ignored when the officer can establish that the arrest would have been jeopardized or that the giving of the notice would have been useless.

The Use of Force in Making an Arrest

When any arrest is made, potential for serious danger to the police officer exists. Thus, the right to arrest carries with it the right to use "reasonable force" in accomplishing the apprehension. This force may be used without the slightest hesitation when it is needed. The policeman acts unlawfully, however, when he uses more than reasonable force in making the arrest.

A certain number of people may be expected to resist arrest and subsequently to claim, without justification, that they were "beaten up" by the police. Some criticism has been leveled at the courts in recent years because of the needless attention given to such unjustified claims. Nevertheless, one of the problems of modern police administration is to consistently refute allegations of brutality.

In most states, a person who is aware that he is being arrested by a police officer has no legal right to resist. As stated by one court:

A citizen subjected to attempted arrest by one known to be a police officer must submit quietly and settle his rights at the station and in the courts, not on the street corner.[34]

In addition to what the courts have said, we should note that forceful resistance to arrest is generally a crime by statute. Nor does the accused have the right to insist that the officer justify the criminal charges against him before he will submit. A policeman who makes an arrest need not retreat or desist before the accused is in custody.[35]

An experienced officer sometimes keeps physical resistance to a minimum in this type of situation by explaining that the problem is beyond his authority. He explains that he will take the accused to the station house or to the committing magistrate where the matter can be explored in detail. In making decisions regarding the use of force in arrests, "the courts should not lay down rules which make it so dangerous for officers to perform their duties that they will shrink and hesitate from action which the proper protection of society demands."[36]

Using Handcuffs On the Prisoner

Our courts have always said that the arresting officer has the right to take reasonable action to prevent the escape of his prisoner once he has been arrested and to insure his own and the prisoner's safety. Therefore, he may use handcuffs to restrain an individual arrested for a felony. The courts have upheld this action, even in cases where the arrested person made no attempt to flee or offer physical resistance.[37]

Police officers must be particularly careful about using force when arresting a female suspect. Officers are sometimes criticized or accused of using undue force when they handcuff a woman of good reputation for a minor offense. On the other hand, when they have a reasonable basis for believing that she might offer physical resistance, draw a concealed knife, or throw herself from the police car, handcuffs are legally justified. Of course, the arresting officer should request the services of a female police officer or matron. As a practical matter, though, a policeman can't always plan arrests in advance.

34. People v. Baca, 55 Cal Rptr 681.
35. Commonwealth v. Duerr, 45 A 2d 235, 158 Pa Super 484.
36. Stinett v. Virginia, 55 F 2d 644.
37. Firestone v. Rice, 38 NW 885, 71 Mich 377.

Breaking Into a Dwelling or Other Building To Make an Arrest

Under the common law in England, a man's home was, without doubt, his castle. He could lawfully defend it against all intruders. This privilege was not allowed, however, against law enforcement representatives. In the colorful language of a case decided in 1604, the court said the "liberty or privilege of a house doth not hold against the King."[38]

At that time in England, when an officer had proper authority to make an arrest, the common law allowed him to break into a building to accomplish the apprehension. The common law made a distinction, however, between a dwelling house and other types of buildings. Only the windows or doors of a dwelling could be broken, whereas the walls, floors, roof, or any part of another building could be breached.

The common law rules on breaking and entering still apply in some states. In other jurisdictions these have been somewhat modified by statutes. Differences mainly relate to arrests for misdemeanors. Statutes in some states limit breaking and entering to felony arrests under a warrant only; some also allow the right of the officer to break and enter for a misdemeanor but only after the issuance of a warrant.

On the other hand, practically all courts insist upon a clear notice of authority to the occupants, as well as a statement of purpose. The courts also require that the occupants be given an opportunity to open the door. After police authorities have taken these preliminary steps, officers may break and enter when the occupants refuse to cooperate or fail to reply to the requests.[39] Here again, requirements are usually governed by statutes in the individual states and differences do exist.

The Right to Search as a Part of the Arrest Process

Conversely, the courts are in agreement that the arresting officers have a right to search any person who is taken into custody after a lawful arrest. The immediate purpose of this search is to deprive the prisoner of any weapons that might be used to attack the offi-

38. Semayne's Case, 77 Eng Rep 194.
39. R. Gene Wright and John A. Marlo, *The Police Officer and Criminal Justice* (New York: McGraw-Hill Book Co., 1970), pp. 182–84.

cers, to effect the prisoner's escape, or to enable the prisoner to commit suicide. Additionally, the arresting officers have the right to search for fruits of the crime, such as stolen goods. They may also search for instrumentalities used to commit the crime, such as a gun, fraudulent check passing equipment, etc. They may also retain as evidence other items taken from the person arrested that tend to prove his guilt.[40]

Any evidentiary weapons or materials taken from the prisoner should be immediately identified by location, date, and initials, so that the officers may use this identification to recall the circumstances of the arrest when the matter comes to trial. As soon as the evidence is identified, it should be turned over to an evidence custodian. Departmental rules for the handling of evidence should be followed closely since procedures of this kind are set up to conform to the legal experience and advice of attorneys hired for that purpose.

At times, the arresting officers may know in advance that the person taken into custody could not have had access to weapons or evidence. When this is the case, and a search is made merely to harass the arrestee, the prisoner's rights have been violated.

Women prisoners often present unusual arrest and search problems. Defense attorneys often try to obscure the real issues in the case by claiming that the apprehending officer took unwarranted liberties with a female prisoner. Sometimes police officers fail to realize how extensively a case may be jeopardized when doubt is planted in the jurors' minds. This accounts for the fact that a female police officer or matron should be present when the officers have any advance notice that a woman or girl is to be taken into custody. When a police woman is available, she may be used to make any search that is justified by the facts.

Most law enforcement agencies also have definite rules concerning the treatment of all female prisoners. From a legal standpoint, the apprehending officer should strive to deprive the female prisoner of the opportunity to harm anyone. At the same time, he should be in a position to refute any claim that he took undue liberties with the female arrestee. If the officer on the scene has serious doubts as to his safety or that of anyone else, however, he should instantly resolve doubt in favor of protecting all officers and members of the public who are present.

---

40. Paul B. Weston and Kenneth M. Wells, *The Administration of Justice*, 2d ed. (Englewood Cliffs: Prentice-Hall, Inc., 1973), pp. 42 and 61.

Holding in Jail or Detaining, Without Filing a Criminal Charge

At one time, police officials often legally placed suspects in jail, without actually filing charges against them. In a number of jurisdictions the courts required the release of the prisoner unless a criminal complaint was filed within seventy-two hours or some other specified period of time. In the meantime, the suspect remained in custody.

In sensational crimes when considerable pressure was received from the public or the press, the law enforcement agency might utilize a "dragnet" to round up known criminals or persons who had used a similar *modus operandi,* or criminal operating technique. Frequently, these subjects were held while they established an alibi or were eliminated through investigation.

Decisions of the Supreme Court that bear on this problem have abolished detentions of this kind. All suspects must be advised of their rights, provided attorneys, charged, and arraigned before a committing magistrate without undue delay. In fact, because of these Supreme Court cases, some judges believe that any detention of any mere suspect is unlawful, even when the person is held for only a very short time. Yet, a legal position that absolutely forbids any detention of a suspect is completely unrealistic from a law-and-order standpoint. Good law enforcement demands that all police officers be alert, probing investigators, constantly aware of circumstances which may indicate that a crime is being committed or has been committed. Often, the officer is able to observe an individual fleeing from the scene of a crime. Under such circumstances, the officer may feel that an immediate investigation should be made and that the suspect should be held. He sometimes observes flight of this nature even before a crime has been reported or the victim is aware of it. On other occasions, the victim may be lying dead or so seriously injured that he is unable to cry out.

Even under the above circumstances some judges and students of the criminal law think that any detention or restraint on the part of the policeman, even to question briefly, is improper from a constitutional standpoint. Other state courts clearly disagree, and an opinion of a California court illustrates this:

> There is, of course, nothing unreasonable in an officer's questioning persons outdoors at night . . . and it is possible that in some circumstances even a refusal to answer would, in the light of other evidence, justify an arrest . . .[41]

41. People v. Simon, 290 P 2d 531, 45 Cal 2d 645.

On the other hand, the Supreme Court has failed to spell out clear guidelines for police officers in most of these situations. Some legal authorities think that the Supreme Court Case, *Rios* v. *United States,* should be interpreted as giving police authorities reasonable right to detain and question when the policeman has "reasonable grounds for inquiry" prior to the time that the suspect is stopped.[42] Just what is meant by "reasonable grounds for inquiry" has not been clarified.

Other courts have used somewhat similar language. State decisions have said that, when "reasonable suspicion" is aroused, a peace officer may detain and make investigative inquiries less than either an arrest or a search.[43] Here again, the courts leave doubt as to just what is meant by "reasonable suspicion," but it seems to be more than a mere "hunch" and less proof than that required to provide "reasonable cause."

Fortunately, in recent years several states have passed statutes giving the police officer limited right to stop a suspect but appeals to the Supreme Court have not yet been made. Therefore, we do not know whether detentions of this kind are legally proper. Accordingly, we have no settled guidelines in situations that have arisen from the application of these laws but "reasonableness" seems to be the test.[44]

The New York law that covers these detention situations is known as the "Stop and Frisk" statute. It reads as follows:

Temporary Questioning of Persons in Public Places; Search for Weapons

1. In addition to the authority provided by this article for making an arrest without a warrant, a police officer may stop a person in a public place located within the geographical area of such officer's employment when he reasonably suspects that such person is committing, has committed or is about to commit either (a) a felony or (b) a class A misdemeanor defined in

42. Rios v. United States, 364 US 253, 80 S Ct 1430.

43. People v. Salerno, 235 NYS 879.

44. "The reasonable belief required may result from the policeman's own observations . . . police are privileged to reach inside a suspect's clothing and pat-down outer clothing, if he believes the person may be armed and dangerous." William A. Rutter, *Criminal Procedure,* 5th ed. (Gardena: Gilbert Publishing Co., 1973), p. 19.

the penal law, and may demand of him his name, address and explanation of his conduct.

2.   When upon stopping a person under circumstances pre-scribed in subdivision one a police officer reasonably suspects that he is in danger of physical injury, he may search such person for a deadly weapon or any instrument, article or substance readily capable of causing serious physical injury and of a sort not ordinarily carried in public places by law-abiding persons. If he finds such a weapon or instrument, or any other property possession of which he reasonably believes may constitute the commission of a crime, he may take it and keep it until the completion of the questioning, at which time he shall either return it, if lawfully possessed, or arrest such person. L1970,c.996,s 1,eff.Sept.1,1971.[45]

Stopping an Automobile

Nearly all courts agree that a peace officer who has authority to regulate or investigate traffic problems may stop a motorist to verify the legality of his driver's license, whether he is physically fit to drive, and other matters related to traffic safety and control. When the driver is detained to determine whether he has committed a criminal violation unrelated to traffic, however, we find dispute among the courts as to whether the arrest is illegal. This is not true when the reasonable cause test for an arrest without a warrant has previously been met.

In *Brinegar* v. *United States,* Supreme Court Justice Jackson ex-pressed the attitude that rights of an officer to detain may vary with the seriousness of the situation. In that opinion he stated:

If . . . a child is kidnapped and the officers throw a roadblock about the neighborhood and search every outgoing car, it would be drastic and undiscriminating use of the search. The officers might be unable to show probable cause for searching any particular car. However . . . it might be reasonable to sub-ject travelers to that indignity if it was the only way to save a threatened life and detect a vicious crime. But I would not strain to sustain such a roadblock and universal search to sal-vage a few bottles of bourbon and catch a bootlegger.[46]

45. McKinney's *Consolidated Laws of New York,* Section 140.50.
46. Brinegar v. U.S., 338 US 160, 69 S Ct 1302.

Apparently then, court decisions have not furnished absolute guidelines to the police officer as to when he may detain and question any and all suspicious individuals. In those jurisdictions where state statutes have been passed, officers must rely upon these statutes until the rulings are limited or struck down by the courts. In other jurisdictions, the officer runs the risk of making an improper detention, unless the known facts appear to warrant immediate action. From a practical standpoint, any police officer should strive immediately to develop facts that will bring suspicious activities under the requirements of a "probable cause" arrest.

Bringing the Accused into Court by Use of Citations, Summons, or Appearance Tickets

Law enforcement protection in any community suffers unless the working police officer is able to stay on the job. Yet, the necessary mechanics of law enforcement consume a great amount of the peace officer's time. When an arrest is made, the prisoner must be taken to the police station or county jail, a complaint must be filed against the prisoner, and booking and searching processes must be completed. The accused must have an opportunity to call his lawyer, to make bail, and to be arraigned before a committing magistrate. All of these activities take time.

On the other hand, when the arrest does not involve a serious crime, there is little likelihood that the accused will flee. In addition, the type of person who becomes involved in minor violations may not be a criminal in the accepted sense of the word. To subject this violator to an arrest may cause him embarrassment in front of his neighbors. Undoubtedly, he would prefer to come into court on his own volition. In addition, the public image of law enforcement is improved when officers are able to devote the bulk of their time to serious crime and preventive programs.

By custom, then, and subsequently by statutory authority, a number of jurisdictions have worked out procedures whereby certain types of violators are not forcibly compelled to go to jail. This is accomplished by using a written notice to appear, backed by the issuance of a warrant if the violator does not go into court on his own initiative. These notices to appear are called *citations, summonses,* or *appearance tickets,* depending on the term used in the particular jurisdiction. Statutes in some states limit the kinds of violations for which these notices may be used. We should, however, note that the issuance of one of these documents does not constitute an arrest; it serves as a substitute for an arrest.

An appearance ticket, as described in the *New York Code of Criminal Procedures,* is as follows:

> An appearance ticket is written notice issued and subscribed by a police officer or other public servant authorized by law to issue the same, directing a designated person to appear in a designated local criminal court at a designated future time in connection with his alleged commission of a designated offense. A notice conforming to such definition constitutes an appearance ticket regardless of whether it is referred to in some other provision of law as a summons or by any other name or title.[47]

SUMMARY

An arrest takes place whenever an officer or citizen assumes to act in an official capacity and detains an individual against that person's will. Arrests are made to insure that the accused will remain available for trial and to give protection to the community, since the accused may continue in crime.

It is essential that an arrest be lawfully made, since evidence found at the time of the arrest cannot be used in the courts unless the arrest was proper. If an arrest is made on the basis of a warrant already obtained, this problem does not arise. The reasoning here is that the court, magistrate, or judge who issued the warrant did so after an unbiased evaluation of the facts to make certain there was probable cause for believing the accused committed a crime.

A warrant is valid for only one arrest and may be served only in the state where issued. The warrant must be served by the person or class of officer to whom directed. There are usually no limitations as to when a felony warrant may be served but in many states a misdemeanor warrant must be served during daylight hours. The warrant must: (1) name or clearly identify the accused, (2) state the specific charge, (3) be issued in the name of a state or Federal Government, (4) be directed to the class of officer or person who will serve it, and (5) must be signed by the issuing official.

The officer must serve the warrant, regardless of financial loss that may result to the person arrested. An arrest warrant may be

47. McKinney's *Consolidated Laws of New York,* Section 150.10.

invalid if altered on its face. A warrant is good indefinitely. Usually, it need not be carried by the arresting officer, but must be exhibited to the accused when it can be obtained. Ordinarily, an officer has a right to deputize any adult to assist in making an arrest. Reasonable force may be used in making an arrest but excessive force makes the officer himself guilty of a criminal assault. Officers are governed by state statutes as to when they may break into buildings to make an arrest. This can usually be done only after giving notice of identity and of the intent to arrest. The right to search is a part of the arrest process. The officer may look for weapons or instrumentalities of the crime, as well as proceeds or fruits of the crime.

An officer's right to detain and search on suspicion—the right to "stop and frisk"—has not been completely settled by the courts. Usually, when his suspicions have been aroused, an officer may detain a suspect briefly and make a "pat-down" search, even though he does not have reasonable cause to believe the suspect has actually committed a crime.

To avoid actual arrests, persons accused of minor offenses and misdemeanors may be ordered to appear in court at a later date. To accomplish this, the arresting officer issues a citation, a summons, or an appearance ticket to the accused. This allows minor violators to remain free until time of trial.

QUESTIONS

1. List two basic purposes in making an arrest.
2. List the basic elements or requirements that must be met before an individual is considered to have been arrested.
3. Explain whether physical force is necessary to effect an arrest. Give reasons for your answer.
4. Explain why it is important for an arrest to be lawfully made.
5. What is the basic legal use or purpose for a warrant?
6. Explain what limitations the U.S. Constitution imposes as to the kinds of searches and seizures that may be made in connection with an arrest.
7. If a person is arrested and escapes from jail, may the original warrant be used to rearrest?
8. Where may an arrest warrant be served?
9. Describe basic features of the Uniform Close Pursuit Act and the Uniform Fresh Pursuit Act. What are basic differences in the two acts?

10. When may a warrant of arrest be served? Who may serve it?

11. List the basic requirements of a valid warrant of arrest.

12. Describe how the accused must be identified or named in a warrant.

13. Should the police officer arrest the individual named in the arrest warrant, even though so doing may bring financial loss to the person apprehended? Does the police officer have any responsibility to the person being arrested in a situation of this kind? Explain.

14. What is the effect of altering the face of an arrest warrant?

15. For how long is a warrant good?

16. Must the arresting officer have the warrant in his possession at the time of apprehension? Explain the rights of the person arrested in this regard.

17. Explain how an officer may deputize someone, and under what circumstances.

18. When may force be used in an arrest? If force is used, how much is permissible? When may handcuffs be applied?

19. When, if ever, is an officer allowed to break into a dwelling to make an arrest?

20. What right is there to search a prisoner in connection with an arrest? Elaborate.

21. May a person be held in custody without a warrant being filed? Explain.

22. What are an officer's rights in a "stop and frisk" situation? Explain.

23. When an officer stops an auto, does this mean that an arrest is made? How far can the officer go in searching the car without a warrant? May evidence obtained in a search of this kind be used in court? Explain.

24. Describe the process whereby an accused is brought into court by means of a citation, summons, or appearance ticket.

. . . [I]t is the command of the Fourth Amendment that no warrants either for searches or arrests shall issue except upon probable cause . . .

Justice William O. Douglas, United States Supreme Court, in *Henry* v. *United States,* 361 US 98 (1959)

chapter five

ARREST WITHOUT A WARRANT; BAIL

The purpose of this chapter is to explain those circumstances under which an arrest may be made without a warrant. Whenever possible, a police officer should obtain a warrant prior to making an apprehension. There are times, however, when it is apparent to the officer that the criminal will escape before a warrant can be obtained. This kind of problem will be considered in this chapter.

Bail will also be discussed in this chapter. The right to bail, how bail is handled, and alternatives to bail will be explained.

THE POWER OF A MAGISTRATE TO ARREST WITHOUT A WARRANT

For almost as long as legal records have been in existence, magistrates of the English courts have had the power to arrest without a warrant. This includes the power to verbally order an arrest after the magistrate has witnessed a breach of the peace or the commission of a felony. Although this authority is seldom used by modern day magistrates in America, it has been commonly included in state arrest statutes. In a number of jurisdictions the power has been extended to permit an oral order of arrest by the magistrate for any felony, misdemeanor, or public offense committed in his presence.[1]

1. Rollin M. Perkins, *Criminal Law and Procedure*, 3d ed., (Brooklyn: The Foundation Press, 1966), p. 789.

COMMON LAW—PEACE OFFICER ARRESTS WITHOUT WARRANT

The English common law courts also recognized the legality of some other arrests made without a warrant. The usual justification given was that time simply did not permit the obtaining of a warrant. Four kinds of situations were recognized:

1. An arrest could be made by an officer without a warrant for a felony or a breach of the peace attempted or committed in the officer's presence.

2. An arrest could be made by the officer if facts were brought to his attention that gave him reasonable grounds (probable cause) to believe that a felony had been committed by the accused.

3. An arrest could be made by an officer when a private citizen came to the officer and made the charge that the accused had committed a felony.

4. An arrest was legally proper when, upon later proof, the accused had actually committed a felony. (This type of arrest is no longer proper, according to U.S. Supreme Court decisions that subsequently will be summarized.)

WARRANTLESS ARREST FOR A FELONY COMMITTED IN THE PRESENCE OF AN OFFICER OR CITIZEN

Statutes now in effect in most states have continued the police officer's common law right to arrest without a warrant for any felony committed in his presence. The great majority of states have not limited this authority of arrest to felonies. Most have extended the policeman's right to any type of violation—whether it be a felony, misdemeanor, or public offense—so long as it is committed in his presence.[2]

A good number of states also have passed statutes granting a citizen the right to arrest without a warrant. Some of these statutes limit this right to felony violations; others include misde-

---

2. ". . . the Supreme Court [of the United States] has expressed strong preference for arrest warrants, . . ." Jerold H. Israel and Wayne R. LaFavre, *Criminal Procedure in a Nutshell,* (St. Paul: West Publishing Co., 1976), p. 98.

meanors; some also specify public offenses as well as felonies and misdemeanors. All of these statutes require that the offense shall have been committed in the presence of the person making the arrest.

The courts clearly have had problems in interpreting "within the presence" of the officer or citizen making the arrest. Generally, they have indicated that a crime is committed within the presence of the arresting officer when he is made aware of the crime through his physical senses.

In one case, two police officers were attracted to the scene of a beating when they heard the victim's outcries. As soon as they arrived at the location of the assault the attack ceased, so the crime was not actually seen. The total facts, however, indicated that the accused undoubtedly had committed the criminal assault. The accused then turned on the two policemen, killing both to escape arrest. The defense maintained that the policemen had made an illegal arrest, since the original beating was not "within their presence." The court upheld the conviction of the accused, pointing out the original crime, the beating, was within the hearing of the police officers. The court also noted that "this was in their presence, as contemplated by the law."[3]

When state statutes authorize a policeman to arrest for any public offense committed in his presence, the courts have held that this authority applies to all violations including traffic misdemeanors. It is not limited to those violations that constitute a breach of the peace.[4]

When criminal action has actually ceased by the time the police arrive on the scene, then a warrantless arrest cannot be made; the crime is not within the presence of a police officer. If, however, some of the action continues after the patrol car arrives and the assailant tries to break down a door to get at the victim a second time, the crime is considered to be committed in the presence of the policemen responding to the call.[5]

When an officer is alerted to the perpetration of a crime through his sense of smell, the act is also committed within his presence. This also justifies an arrest without a warrant.[6]

3. Dilger v. Commonwealth, 11 SW 651, 88 Ky 550.
4. Smith v. Hubbard, 91 NW 2d 756, 253 Minn 215; Oleson v. Peacock, 251 P 23, 68 Utah 507.
5. People v. Foster, 176 NE 2d 397.
6. Massa v. State, 19 SW 2d 248, 159 Tenn 428.

Arrest Without a Warrant on Probable Cause

The courts have clearly established the fact that an arrest without a warrant must be based on something more than a policeman's "hunch" or unsupported suspicion. Common law cases and modern statutes in practically all jurisdictions also allow a policeman to make a warrantless arrest on "reasonable grounds to believe that a felony was committed" or on "probable cause." These two terms are synonymous, since they are used interchangeably by the courts.[7]

Reasonable Cause to Believe

To know when he can make an arrest of this type, the police officer must understand what the courts mean when they use the terms "probable cause" or "reasonable grounds to believe." This is often difficult to do since court opinions vary from case to case. Generally speaking, though, probable cause is made up of a quantity of proof that rests somewhere between mere suspicion and the kind and quantity of evidence that it takes to convince a highly skeptical person.

The California statutes covering arrest with a warrant are set out in the California Penal Code, Sections 835 and 836:

> A peace officer may make an arrest in obedience to a warrant, or may, pursuant to the authority granted to him by the provisions of Chapter 4.5 (commencing with Section 830) of Title 3 of Part 2, without a warning, arrest a person:
>
> 1. Whenever he has reasonable cause to believe that the person to be arrested has committed a public offense in his presence.
>
> 2. When a person arrested has committed a felony, although not in his presence.
>
> 3. Whenever he has reasonable cause to believe that the person to be arrested has committed a felony, whether or not a felony has in fact been committed.

The person making the arrest must inform the person to be arrested of the intention to arrest him, of the cause of the arrest, and the authority to make it, except when the person making the arrest

7. See Wong Sun v. U. S., 371 US 471 (1962) and Beck v. Ohio, 379 US 89 (1964).

has reasonable cause to believe that the person to be arrested is actually engaged in the commission of or an attempt to commit an offense, or the person to be arrested is pursued immediately after its commission, or after an escape.

The person making the arrest must, on request of the person he is arresting, inform the latter of the offense for which he is being arrested.

Police Determination of Probable Cause

To determine whether probable cause exists, the court somehow must place itself in the officer's shoes, making an analysis of the facts known to him at the time of the arrest. In this total picture, the tribunal must consider what the investigating officer actually saw, what eyewitnesses told him, and what he learned from informers. In this process, the apparent sincerity and conviction of the witnesses must be considered and eyewitness identifications evaluated. The tribunal must ascertain whether any physical evidence was available and to what extent this material pointed to the suspect. The court has to determine whether the physical description of the suspect matched that of the person involved in the crime, and the availability of automobiles, weapons, or tools of the type that might have been used in the crime must be considered. In addition, the policeman may be allowed to use his knowledge of criminals to ascertain whether or not the criminal was in the area at the time; whether the suspect spent an unusual amount of money that could represent proceeds from the crime; whether the suspect was known to carry a gun; as well as a long list of other possibilities.

The policeman who makes the decision to arrest must summarize all of these bits of information and balance them against any indications that the suspect was not involved. If the total picture is "sufficient . . . to warrant a man of reasonable caution in the belief that a crime has been committed by the accused, then probable cause exists."[8]

In making his evaluation, the police officer uses a great number of fragmentary indicators. When taken together, these point to a conclusion of probable guilt. On the other hand, probable cause may be based upon only one or two pieces of evidence. For example, when a man is known to have passed large numbers of bills with serial numbers identifiable as loot from a bank robbery, while the

8. Draper v. U.S., 358 US 307, 79 S Ct 329.

license number of his car has been recorded as that of the get-away vehicle, then the element of probable cause likely has been satisfied.

The fact that a suspect previously served time in the state prison, with no other evidence to implicate him, is not enough for probable cause.[9] However, a reliable report that the suspect has recently engaged in a crime similar to that under investigation may be relied upon as part of the inference of probable cause.[10]

> When the police act without a warrant, they initially make the probable cause decision themselves, although it will be subject to after-the-fact review by a judicial officer. . . . If the arrest is on a warrant . . . the question is whether the magistrate acted properly, not whether the police officer did.[11]

Arrest on the Oral Accusation of Another

Under the common law, a peace officer had the right to arrest without a warrant when a third person came to him and charged the accused with a felony. The early English courts took the view that the responsibility rested with the person who had made the accusation, not with the officer who made an improper arrest. In 1817, this idea was reversed by a decision of the English courts.

Since then, variations of the former view have been incorporated into the statutes of some of our states. In the words of several of these laws, the peace officer must have "satisfactory proof" or "reasonable grounds to believe" that a felony was committed. Unfortunately, court interpretations of these statutes are somewhat lacking. They usually say, however, that "reasonable grounds to believe" means the same thing as "probable cause." Therefore, when an officer makes a legal arrest without a warrant under these circumstances, he must have probable cause. The fact that a third party reported to the officer and charged the accused with a felony is merely a circumstance to be considered by the officer in deciding whether he has probable cause to arrest. This information alone may be controlling, but not necessarily sufficient to convince a man of reasonable caution that an offense has been committed.

9. Beck v. Ohio, 379 US 89, 85 S Ct 223.
10. Brinegar v. U.S., 338 US 160, 69 S Ct 1302.
11. Jerold H. Israel and Wayne R. LaFavre, *Criminal Procedure in a Nutshell,* (St. Paul: West Publishing Co., 1976), pp. 97–99.

Felony Arrest Must Be Lawful at the Time it is Made

As noted earlier, under the common law requirements, a felony arrest without a warrant was lawful when subsequent evidence proved that the accused had actually committed a felony. This was true even if the arresting officer did not have probable cause at the time of arrest and the crime was not committed in his presence.

Several cases decided by the United States Supreme Court have clearly struck down this "save the officer" common law provision. The Supreme Court has held, in effect, that *each arrest must stand on its own merits at the time it is made.*

In *Henry* v. *United States,* the Court stated that "[a]n arrest is not justified by what the subsequent search discloses."[12] *Rios* v. *United States* declared that when an arrest without a warrant is unlawful at the time it is made, nothing that happens thereafter can cause it to be lawful.[13] Again, in *United States* v. *Como,* a federal court noted that, in the absence of an express statute, it "is an elementary maxim that a search, seizure or arrest cannot be retroactively justified by what is uncovered."[14]

Citizen's Arrests

As noted previously, citizens were frequently used to make arrests under common law. In most states, private persons still have the right to make some arrests but this privilege is usually regulated by statute. Thus, in a number of jurisdictions, a citizen has the authority to arrest without a warrant for a felony committed in his presence. Some state laws allow a warrantless arrest by a citizen for either a felony or misdemeanor that occurs in the citizen's presence. Other state laws have narrowed this to include some misdemeanors such as petit larceny. Still others have restricted this power to felony matters only.

Booking Procedures

After an individual is arrested on a felony warrant, he is booked and then arraigned. Booking procedures vary slightly from state to state but the basics include the following:

12. Henry v. U.S., 361 US 98, 80 S Ct 168.
13. Rios v. U.S., 364 US 253, 80 S Ct 1431.
14. Silverthorne Lumber Co. v. U.S., U.S. v. Como, 340 F 2d 891, 251 US 385 (1920) and Nardone v. U.S., 308 US 338 (1939).

1. The prisoner is requested to furnish his name and address to the jailer and the arresting officer advises where the arrest took place and when, the type of crime charged, and whether the arrest was made on a warrant. If information is available to establish probable cause, this information may be briefly summarized.

2. The officer who made the arrest is then required to inform the prisoner of his right to an attorney, and that a lawyer will be provided if he cannot pay for one. The prisoner is also told that he has the right to remain silent, and that if he does make any kind of statement that it may be used against him in a court of law. A notation is then made in the record that the prisoner was advised of these rights.

3. The jailer will then search the prisoner, taking his papers, identification, jewelry, and items of value. The prisoner will then be given a receipt for these items, and be asked to sign it. If the prisoner refuses to sign the receipt, it is witnessed by other jail officials or police officers and is placed in file without being signed. The prisoner should be searched at the jail, even though he may have been given a field search by the officer who made the arrest. The prisoner may be given a complete strip search if he is regarded as dangerous, an escape artist, or one who has been known to carry contraband.

4. The prisoner is then fingerprinted and photographed.

5. The records of the identification division are then searched to see whether other warrants are on file, or whether his fingerprint card has a notation indicating that he is wanted by another law enforcement agency.

6. The prisoner is then told when he will be arraigned and is given information as to the name and address of the court where the arraignment will take place. If the accused is eligible for release on bail, he is allowed to contact a bail bondsman or someone who can help in obtaining bail. The jail or detention holding tank rules are then explained to the prisoner.

7. The prisoner is then locked in a cell, pending arraignment, release on bail, or release to a jail hospital if the facts appear to so warrant.[15]

15. See Paul B. Weston and Kenneth M. Wells, *The Administration of Justice*, 2d ed. (Englewood Cliffs: Prentice–Hall, Inc., 1973), p. 44.

An individual under arrest always has the right to call his attorney from the booking office. In California, the accused is entitled to make two calls. By statute, any public officer or employee who withholds this right to make calls is guilty of a misdemeanor. In California, an officer or official in charge of a prisoner is also guilty of a misdemeanor if he willfully refuses or neglects to allow a licensed attorney to see the prisoner. This does not mean, however, that the lawyer must be allowed to come and go at will; reasonable rules can be set up and enforced to protect both the prisoner and the jail routine.[16]

BAIL AND ALTERNATIVES TO BAIL

In ancient times, the word "bail" meant the delivery of property of any kind from one individual to another. For purposes of our discussion, bail is the delivery of one person to another for keeping. The person delivered is one who has been arrested or committed to prison in a criminal process.

A bail bond is a contract between one accused of crime, on the one hand, and the local, state or Federal Government on the other. Under this contract, the accused is granted a release from custody in return for his promise to appear at the time of trial, or to begin his sentence when already convicted. In the usual situation, the accused is required to deposit money, property, or a bond that will be forfeited to the court if the promise to appear is not kept. The bond is commonly given to the court by a "surety" for the accused. The surety is usually a professional bail bondsman.

As defined by the courts, "bail is the security given for the due appearance of a prisoner to obtain his release from imprisonment. . ."[17]

Stated in other words:

> The taking of bail consists in the acceptance by a competent court, magistrate, or officer, of sufficient bail for the appearance of the defendant according to the legal effect of his undertaking, or for the payment to the state of a certain specified sum if he does not appear."[18]

16. U.S. v. Como, 340 F 2d 891.
17. Sawyer v. Barbour, 300 P 2d 187, 142 Cal App 2d 827.
18. Alabama Criminal Code (1886), Section 4407.

Historical Background

The early English common law did not permit release on bail in felony prosecutions. Bail was accepted by the courts, however, for misdemeanors. By the thirteenth century, bail was taken in felony matters before trial but not during or after trial. When felony bail was granted in those early days, it was allowed at the discretion of the presiding judge of the court, not as a matter of absolute right.

The development of this kind of release arose out of the fact that only a limited number of judges were assigned to the king's courts and the accused might sit in jail awaiting trial for six months, a year, or even longer before the judge "got around" to that part of the country again. If the involved violation was a minor one, the jailed accused might actually spend more time in custody than the maximum penalty imposed upon conviction.[19]

Constitutional Guarantees

Under the common law, the judge had the right to exercise discretion as to whether or not to allow freedom on bail in felony cases. Today, in most jurisdictions in the United States, constitutional or statutory guarantees give everyone the right to bail, unless the crime is one that carries the death penalty.[20] If the crime involved is a capital offense, however, the judge usually has the right to refuse to release on bail when the proof of the crime seems evident, or the presumption of guilt is great.

When the right to bail is absolute, an appellate court is duty bound to grant bail, in the event that it is refused by the lower court. In some states, however, the judge or magistrate still retains the discretion to decide whether the accused shall be released on bail, in noncapital felony cases.[21] In practically all jurisdictions, the defendant has the right to bail in misdemeanor cases.

Why a Bail System?

The constitutional and statutory guarantees in the American system of criminal justice are founded on the assumption that everyone is innocent until proven guilty. Bail is allowed to the ac-

19. U.S. v. Rice, 192 F 720; State v. Pett, 92 NW 2d 265, 253 Minn 429; Thomas v. Oklahoma, 93 P 980, 1 Okla Crim 15.
20. Ex parte Nagel, 167 P 689, 41 Nev 86.
21. New York State is one of the exceptions; bail may be denied in serious felonies that do not carry the death penalty. See People ex rel. Shapiro v. Keeper of City Prison, 49 NE 498, 290 NY 393. See also U.S. v ex rel. Covington v. Coparo, 297 F Supp 203; Section 554 New York Code of Criminal Procedure.

cused, under our constitutional system, to retain this presumption of innocence until guilt has been proven in court. One judge, speaking for many American legal authorities, stated that "refusal of freedom . . . would constitute punishment before conviction, a notion abhorrent to our democratic system."[22]

Then too, the purpose of bail is "to serve the convenience of the accused, without interfering with or defeating the administration of justice."[23] When the accused is innocent, he is able to locate witnesses and develop proof that might not be available to him from his jail cell. Bail also allows him more time to confer with his attorney in preparing his defense.

Even when the accused is not innocent, bail helps him to put his business in order, so that his family may not be a burden on the state while he is in prison. It also relieves the state of the trouble and expense of keeping the accused until trial begins.

Undoubtedly, it is often galling to the arresting officer when an accused is allowed his immediate freedom in spite of overwhelming evidence. The integrity of the legal process can't be maintained, however, unless the accused is granted all the legal preliminaries to which he is entitled.

How the Bail System Works

In theory, bail keeps the accused in the constructive custody of the court although he is not in actual physical custody. Bail is, in effect, a continuation of the arrest, with the bail bondsman as the "keeper" of the accused. The defendant is still under the supervision of the court. Clearly, he has not been granted that absolute liberty which he enjoyed previously.[24]

Stated in other words, the bail bondsman becomes the custodial officer of the accused for the court. He has "the right and duty to arrest him in case he contemplates flight; the court looks to (his) vigilance to prevent the absconding of the defendant."[25]

The courts say that a bondsman has no legal duty to watch or to keep the accused under surveillance. He must, however, produce the defendant, his principal, at the time and place specified in the

22. State v. Konigsberg, 164 A 2d 740, 33 NJ 367.
23. People v. Wilcox, 349 P 2d 522, 53 Cal 2d 651.
24. State v. Bates, 99 A 2d 133, 140 Conn 326.
25. U.S. v. Simmons, 47 F 575.

bond; therefore, he has the right to prevent the accused from leaving the state.[26]

Even though the accused has not taken to flight, the bondsman may arrest his charge, take physical custody, and surrender him to the court in order to relieve himself of this kind of responsibility. This may be done whenever the bondsman chooses and the accused must then remain in jail until he is able to make new arrangements for bail.[27] The bondsman retains this right to protect himself from liability, whether we call this a special kind of criminal arrest procedure or recognize it as a form of legalized kidnapping. In some jurisdictions, statutory requirements state that the accused may not be taken into custody by the bondsman at night or on a Sunday, except in a case of "pressing necessity."

The bondsman may also travel into another state, locate the accused, arrest the latter, and bring him back without the necessity of going through extradition or removal proceedings of any sort. A transportation of this kind does not violate the Federal Kidnapping Statute.[28]

If he needs to gain entrance in order to make arrest, the bondsman is justified in breaking open the door or breaking into the accused's home. He may be successfully sued, however, if he breaks into the home of a third party.

Frequently, a criminal who is wanted by a bail bondsman will be located in a jail or in the custody of police officers in another state. In a situation of this kind, the bondsman can't take the accused from the custody of state officers who have him under arrest. However, a detainer may rightfully be filed by prosecuting officials representing the first state, provided the accused is wanted for "bail jumping."

Regulating the Bail Bond Business

Unless bail bondsmen are alert to their responsibilities, an unwarranted number of accused criminals may flee to far away locations. This poses a number of problems for the courts and peace officers who are responsible for locating and apprehending fugitives. While the bondsman may never be completely sure that the accused will report as promised, he can keep effective control by insisting on adequate monetary security for the risks he takes.

Let's also note that unless the bail bond business is supervised,

26. State v. Wynne, 204 SW 2d 927, 356 Mo 1095.
27. Jordan v. Knight, 35 So 2d 178.
28. Fitzpatrick v. Williams, 46 F 2d 40; Golla v. State, 135 A 137, 355 US 965.

the state may possibly be defrauded. Then too, serious interference
with the orderly handling of criminal prosecutions may occur.
Therefore, the courts have consistently stepped in to regulate the
bail bond business when they felt it necessary. When supervision is
exercised, the courts have ruled that they have inherent powers to
regulate this activity as a necessary adjunct to the court system.

Of course, we find no requirement that the accused must use
the services of a professional bondsman. If the accused has enough
resources, he or she may deposit cash, negotiable securities, or other
assets of equal value to the full amount of the bond. In some jurisdictions, the defendant or his relatives may be allowed to offer title
to real estate in lieu of a cash bond.

Regardless of the kind of bond that may be approved, however,
the accused seldom has enough assets to act as his own surety and
must often turn to a professional bondsman. The traditional arrangement for this transaction requires the accused to pay the
bondsman ten percent of the amount of the bond.

The bondsman, of course, retains the ten percent of the bond
as a fee for doing business and for taking a chance on the prisoner.
Usually, the bondsman also requires additional financial security
from the accused. This may involve a mortgage on his home, business, automobile, or household furnishings or the pledge of a savings account book, stocks and bonds. These items may legally be
taken by the bondsman when the accused fails to appear at the time
ordered by the court.

After agreeing to act for the accused, the professional bail
bondsman must then "justify" or certify to the court that he has sufficient financial worth to pay the court in the event of default.
"Straw bail" means bail offered to the court by persons who do not
possess the needed financial qualifications, but who are willing to
swear that they do possess sufficient financial worth.[29]

The higher courts have consistently stated that the judge who
accepts bail is the sole and only judge of the security that is offered.
The judge decides whether the bail bondsman is a fit and proper
person to qualify.[30] If the security offered appears to be "straw bail,"
the judge may decline to accept it. The appellate courts allow trial
judges to exercise wide discretion in decisions of this kind.

29. Early day bondsmen stood around the entrance to English criminal court buildings
wearing straw in their shoes as a mark of their profession. Some were irresponsible
persons or men of no property, who practiced "going bail" for anyone who would pay
them a fee. The term "straw bail" originated from these individuals who offered
worthless bail.
30. Summit Fidelity & Surety Co. v. Nimtz, 64 NW 2d 803, 158 Neb 762.

Release on "Own Recognizance"

The terms "bail bond" and "recognizance" are often used interchangeably in statutes and by attorneys. Originally, a recognizance was an obligation or bond to the courts. It is still an obligation or formal legal document by which the accused promises to appear; however, it does not require the deposit of money or property with the court.

If the crime involved does not appear to be a particularly serious one or the accused seems to have substantial ties to the community by means of his family or associates, the prisoner may be released on his or her "own recognizance." In effect, then, a recognizance is a form of bail that allows the release of the accused on a solemn promise in writing to the court, without the deposit of money or property.

When Is Bail Set?

The point in time at which bail is set varies from state to state. In some jurisdictions, a specific sum is set by the magistrate at the time that he signs the arrest warrant; the amount of the bond is endorsed on the warrant itself. In jurisdictions where this procedure is followed, the accused may be arrested, taken to the station house, and released on the specified bond without appearing before the magistrate. Thus, the amount of bond is customarily set on a sliding scale, depending on the severity of the criminal charge.

Other jurisdictions make certain that magistrates or bail commissioners are easily available at an office or at home, so that the amount of bond may be set and prompt arrangements can be made for release. A night court may remain open until midnight in New York City, for example, thus providing judicial determination of bail at an unusual hour.

Still other jurisdictions do not provide immediate bail hearings for arrested persons. Periods of up to ten days may elapse in some locations. In isolated instances, bail for some violations is set only upon application of the accused; if not represented by an attorney, the accused may be ignorant of this right or he may not know how to make use of it.

In many locations, the judge or magistrate simply adheres to a fixed schedule, increasing the amount of the bail with the seriousness of the crime charged. Little or no allowance is made for individual differences between defendants, based on the probability that they will appear at the time of trial.

"Station House" Bail

In a number of states, a bail schedule is approved in advance by the judges in the county or district. This arrangement authorizes police officers to set bail at a stipulated figure, so that the defendant and bondsman may post bail and gain immediate freedom for the arrestee. "Station house" bail of this kind is limited to misdemeanor cases in some states.

As a procedure for handling some traffic violations and minor infractions, the station house bail system has much to commend it. Statutes in a number of jurisdictions allow the forfeiture of bail to serve as satisfaction for the criminal charge. If the charge is a serious one, such as drunk driving, however, these statutes require a regular trial.

The Exercise of Discretion in Allowing Bail

When bail must be allowed as a matter of right, the only problem that remains is to set it at a reasonable figure. If the crime involved is a capital offense, such as murder, then the judge is completely justified in refusing to release the accused in "an open and shut case," or in a situation where guilt seems highly probable.

When the judge has the right to exercise discretion, his decision may vary from case to case. Certain standards must be met by the judge, however. The right to bail cannot be denied merely because the accused has never been liked in the community or because he has a reputation for dishonesty. The test is whether bail will provide the appearance of the accused at the proper time in court.

In exercising this discretion, the court considers the conduct of the prisoner prior to the application for release. If the accused immediately surrendered himself to the authority of the court upon learning that he was wanted, this will be a strong consideration for release. When his conduct in jail and as a private individual has usually been above average, this too is considered in the prisoner's favor. The court, however, is justified in refusing to release a prisoner in a discretionary situation when the prisoner has previously jumped bail or failed to report in accordance with court orders.

Ill health of the accused is a considered factor when discretionary power to release on bond exists. If imprisonment is likely to cause a worsening of a diseased condition, this may be a factor in allowing the posting of bond.[31] On the other hand, illness does not

---

31. State v. Bouchelle, 61 SE 2d 232, 134 W Va 34.

guarantee the accused the right to release. If jail medical facilities are sufficient to provide all the care that the prisoner requires, bail may be denied when other factors do not favor release.[32]

Usually, a hearing is scheduled when the granting of bail is a discretionary matter and testimony may be offered by one or both sides. In some cases, witnesses may be subpoenaed by both sides, and they may be questioned by the judge. After a decision has been made, the judge generally will avoid any discussion of his reasons for granting or refusing bail, in order that his comments will not influence the forthcoming trial. In fact, the judge is not required to give his reasons to anyone. Ordinarily an appellate court will not reverse his decision unless the defendant shows that the judge abused his discretion or that the accused would not likely report at the time of trial. The views of the public prosecutor may carry some weight as to whether bail will be allowed but his opinions are by no means conclusive or binding on the judge or magistrate who has discretionary authority.

In those states that do not allow bail in capital cases, when the proof is evident or the presumption great, the question often arises as to whether an indictment conclusively demonstrates that the proof is great. We find a difference of opinion in the courts on this matter. Some decisions hold that an indictment is not conclusive against bail, but the burden does shift to the accused to show no great presumption of guilt or lack of convincing evidence.[33] The return of an indictment for a noncapital felony does not necessarily prevent release on bond.

Granting Bail After Conviction

In some cases, the courts may allow an individual his continued freedom on bail even after conviction. This requires an appeal to a higher court. It is not allowed when the appeal seems to be frivolous. A presumption of innocence no longer exists in this situation, so the accused does not have an absolute right to bail. The courts usually allow release only after appropriate caution. If the crime is serious and there is a fear of other criminal violations, the judge will almost always refuse bail, pending appeal. The danger of flight is usually increased after conviction; this factor, along with prior criminal record, attitudes toward society, and behavior during and after trial are considered by the judge.

32. Petition of Leeper, 245 P 2d 337, 111 Cal App 2d 623.
33. Quillen v. Betts, 98 A 2d 770, 48 Del 93; State v. Jenkins, 57 So 321, 129 La 1019.

If an appeal is made for release following conviction, the appellate courts almost always uphold the judgment of the trial court.[34] Some cases also emphasize the statement that the court must consider whether, under all the circumstances, the convicted person will be present to abide his punishment if the appeal is denied.[35]

Bail Shall Not Be Excessive

Since the passage of the Federal Judiciary Act of 1789, all persons charged with noncapital offenses in federal court must be admitted to bail. This right continues today in the federal law under the Federal Rules of Criminal Procedure, Rule 46 (a) (1). In addition, the Eighth Amendment to the U.S. Constitution provides: "Excessive bail shall not be required . . ."

In the case of *Stack* v. *Boyle,* twelve individuals were indicted in federal court under the Smith Act (Title 18 U.S. Code, Section 2385). The bond set for one of the accused was in the amount of $100,000 and, on appeal, the case was taken to the Supreme Court for a reduction of the bail.

Why the bond was set so high was not clear from the record, but the indictment was returned because the defendants were alleged to be among the ten top members of the U. S. Communist Party, conspiring to overthrow the United States Government. At the time bail was fixed, the Government had presented evidence to show that four other persons previously convicted under the Smith Act in the New York City area had forfeited bail and fled. This was at a time when top Communist Party functionaries in the United States were usually instructed by Moscow to flee to Mexico. However, the FBI could not reveal this for the court record without compromising the identity of key informants in the party.

Since no other evidence was presented, the Supreme Court held in *Stack* v. *Boyle* that it was unconstitutional to fix excessive bail merely for the purpose of making certain that the accused would remain in jail. Ironically enough, the defendants were charged as deadly enemies of the very government whose highest court ordered a reduction of their bail.

In *Stack* v. *Boyle,* the Supreme Court also said:

> The practice of admission to bail, as it has evolved in Anglo-American law, is not a device for keeping persons in jail upon mere accusation until it is found convenient to give them a trial

34. Re Scaggs, 303 P 2d 1009, 47 Cal 2d 416.
35. Sioux Falls v. Marshall, 204 NW 999, 48 SD 378.

... Admission to bail always involves a risk that the accused will take flight. This is a calculated risk which the law takes as the price of our system of justice. We know that Congress anticipated that bail would enable some escapes, because it provides a procedure for dealing with them.[36]

The general rule then, in both federal and state courts, is to try to strike a balance between the "need for a tie to the jurisdiction and the right to freedom from unnecessary restraint before conviction, under the circumstances surrounding each particular case."[37]

One of the features of our court system is that the Supreme Court can settle only the problem that is actually before it. For example, the Court had the power to say in *Stack* v. *Boyle* that $100,000 was excessive bail for one subject under the circumstances. The Court could not say that $50,000 or $25,000 or even $5,000 would be satisfactory bail in this situation. What eventually happened was that the matter was remanded and sent back to a lower court to make a determination of bail that would not be excessive.

One session of the Supreme Court can't speak for the future courts on matters not squarely in issue at the time. The Justices do, of course, speak out on side issues, other than those under consideration. Opinions that go beyond the matters under dispute, are called "dicta" by attorneys. These gratuitous statements or "side bar remarks" do cast considerable light on what the Court may later hold if a similar situation comes before the same Court. Until that actually happens, however, the remarks made by the judges are not recognized as binding.[38]

The excessive bail portion of the Eighth Amendment to the U.S. Constitution (*Stack* v. *Boyle*) has not yet been incorporated into the Fourteenth Amendment, as binding on the states. However, practically all of the state constitutions do contain provisions against excessive bail; the Supreme Court likely will later apply the principle of *Stack* v. *Boyle* to state cases as well.[39] In other words, bail must be tailored to "the probability of the appearance of the accused."[40]

---

36. Stack v. Boyle, 342 US 1, 72 S Ct 1.

37. Spector v. U.S., 193 F 2d 1002.

38. Israel and LaFavre, leading authorities on constitutional law, state that standards for determining what constitutes "excessive bail" have not been fully developed by the Supreme Court. See Jerold H. Israel and Wayne R. LaFavre, *Criminal Procedure in a Nutshell*, (St. Paul: West Publishing Co., 1976), p. 30.

39. State v. Seaton, 103 NW 2d 833, 170 Neb 687; Commonwealth v. Tsouprakakis, 166 NE 855, 267 Mass 496.

40. People ex rel. Sammons v. Snow, 173 NE 8.

This does not mean that a high bail may not be set. High bail is justified if the subject has a bad criminal record and is likely to escape.[41] When the accused is charged with a particularly brutal aggravated assault and it appears that the victim of the attack may die, higher than average bail may be justified. If the victim dies, the accused may face a charge of first degree murder and is, therefore, more likely to flee.[42] Yet, that which is excessive bail for one defendant may be proper for another. Even crimes of the same classification often differ greatly in character, thus causing the perpetrator to be more likely to take to flight.

In another landmark case, *Bandy* v. *United States*,[43] the Supreme Court held that even a modest amount of money may be excessive bail to an accused individual who has little or no property or funds. The Court stated that judges should lean heavily toward release on bond. The Court said, in addition: ". . . there may be other deterrents to jumping bail: long residence in a locality, the ties of friends and family . . . All these in a given case may offer a deterrent at least equal to that of the threat of forfeiture."

In the Bandy case, the Supreme Court did not strike down the established legal principle that bail is not excessive by the mere fact that the accused is not able to raise it.[44] Apparently, what the court meant was that reasonable bail to a rich man may be equivalent to the denial of bail to a poor man who is charged with a like offense. Therefore, a judge who sets bond should look for other factors that will insure the appearance of the accused.

Modern Bail Reforms

Clearly, the ten percent cash fee charged by a professional bail bondsman is lost forever to the accused. Some judges and legal scholars have recognized this as a harsh requirement. As a result, they have instigated some bail reform provisions that have been adopted in the federal courts, as well as in some states. Under this concept, the ten percent cash fee usually paid to the bondsman is given to the court by the accused. If the accused then appears as ordered, the major part of this cash fee is returned to him.

The Federal Bail Reform Act of 1966 also provides that per-

41. Ex parte Lonardo, 89 NE 2d 502, 86 Ohio App 289.
42. State v. McLeod, 311 P 2d 400, 131 Mont 478.
43. Bandy v. U.S., 5 L Ed 2d 218, 81 S Ct 197 (1960).
44. Braden v. Lady, 278 SW 2d 664.

sons accused of federal noncapital crimes are to be released on their own recognizance, on unsecured bond, or on other nonmonetary conditions, where it seems reasonable to assume that the accused will appear as directed. This federal act provides that:

(a) Any person charged with an offense, other than an offense punishable by death, shall, at his appearance before a judicial officer, be ordered released pending trial on his personal recognizance or upon the execution of an unsecured appearance bond in an amount specified by the judicial officer, unless the officer determines, in the exercise of his discretion, that such a release will not reasonably assure the appearance of the person as required. When such a determination is made, the judicial officer shall, either in lieu of or in addition to the above methods of release, impose the first of the following conditions of release which will reasonably assure the appearance of the person for trial or, if no single condition gives that assurance, any combination of the following conditions:

1. place the person in the custody of a designated person or organization agreeing to supervise him;

2. place restrictions on the travel, association, or place of abode of the person during the period of release;

3. require the execution of an appearance bond in a specified amount and the deposit in the registry of the court, in cash or other security as directed, of a sum not to exceed ten percentum of the amount of the bond, such deposit to be returned upon the performance of the conditions of release;

4. require the execution of a bail bond with sufficient solvent sureties, or the deposit of cash in lieu thereof; or

5. impose any other condition deemed reasonably necessary to assure appearance as required, including a condition requiring that the person return to custody after specified hours.

(b) In determining which conditions of release will reasonably assure appearance, the judicial officer shall, on the basis of available information, take into account the nature of circumstances of the offense charged, the weight of the evidence against the accused, the accused's family ties, employment, financial resources, character and mental condition, the length of his residence in the community, his record of convictions, and his record of appearance at court proceedings or of flight to avoid prosecution or failure to appear at court proceedings.[45]

Increasing Bail

Bail may be raised as well as lowered, based on the sound discretion of the judge who has jurisdiction. If an individual is free on bail and makes serious statements to the effect that he is "not going to be tried," the courts have held the judge justified in increasing the amount of bail.[46]

Revoking Bail

Generally, a trial judge has the discretionary right to order a defendant who has been at large on bail into custody during the trial, even though the criminal accusation against the defendant is bailable.[47] When the judge has received reliable information that the accused has attempted to interfere with the trial, tamper with the selection of the jury, or otherwise impede the trial, the judge may direct that the accused must remain in jail until a verdict is reached.

Exoneration of the Bail Bondsman

Normally, a bail bondsman is not exonerated or relieved of his responsibility until the accused submits to trial. The bondsman may be excused, however, under some other circumstances. If the defendant is committed to a state mental hospital or is arrested and held for trial in another criminal prosecution in another state, the judge may excuse the bondsman. Death, serious illness that precludes trial, and some other circumstances may be presented to the judge for an exoneration.

Generally, the defendant's bond terminates when the jury's verdict is reached and the accused is found guilty and is taken into

---

45. Title 18, U. S. Code, Section 3146.
46. Ex parte Calloway, 265 SW 699, 98 Tex Crim 347.
47. State v. Wright, 138 SE 828, 140 SC 363; Adkins v. Commonwealth, 33 SW 918, 98 Ky 539.

the custody of the law. In most jurisdictions the bond continues, in the event of a mistrial, until the matter is actually settled by conviction or release.

Forfeiture of Bail

When the accused doesn't appear in answer to the orders of the court, the judge may order the bond forfeited. Most judges, however, give the bondsman a reasonable opportunity to bring in the accused before ordering forfeiture. Frequently, state statutes allow the bondsman sixty days to present the accused before action is taken by the judge.

Bail jumping is a federal crime as well as a criminal violation in most states. When the accused disappears, this charge is usually brought against the person who flees.

Preventive Detention

The American judicial system has consistently recognized only one reason for keeping an accused person in jail. That is, to prevent him from fleeing. However, European governments frequently utilize preventive detention, based on the belief that the safety of the community will be threatened by the accused's release.

Although preventive detention is somewhat controversial, we find considerable reason to recommend it. Violent and brutal crimes are frequently committed by persons who recently have been released on bail. Some few criminals think that the only way to avoid a prison term is to "kill off" witnesses who may testify against them. In any event, criminals may tamper with witnesses.

Prior to the passage of the Federal Bail Reform Act of 1966, consideration was given to proposed federal legislation providing for preventive detention before trial when a judicial officer found that release conditons would not reasonably assure the safety of individuals in the community. This seems to be a better approach than excessively high bail. However, some authorities on constitutional law feel that an accused person usually may not be legally held in mere preventive custody before trial.

Requiring Witnesses to Furnish Bail

The laws of arrest in most states contain no provision for the detention of a witness who is hesitant to appear at a trial. Of course, the witness may be subpoenaed to appear and held in contempt of

87

court when he fails to do so. As a practical matter, however, a witness who flees to a far away place may not be located in time for a subpoena to be served.

Under the Federal Rules of Criminal Procedure,[48] a witness to a federal crime may be required to "put up" bail if there is a strong possibility that he will deliberately evade testifying. In the event he can't make bail, he must remain in jail until his testimony is needed by the prosecutor. Several states, among them New York and Wisconsin, have statutes that require a material witness to make bail or remain in jail when it is feared that he will flee to avoid testifying.[49]

A number of past court decisions have upheld the constitutionality of statutes requiring witnesses to post bond under such circumstances.[50] In recent years, however, we have seen some abuses of these laws. In some cases, witnesses have remained in jail when unable to make bail, while the accused criminal was at liberty on bond. Some states have solved this problem by holding the witness for a short period of time and obtaining a deposition from him.

The Federal Unlawful Flight Statute

The Unlawful Flight Statute is a federal enactment allowing the FBI to conduct fugitive investigations for persons wanted for state felonies. The same law holds true in New Jersey for persons wanted for high misdemeanors. The wanted person must leave the state to avoid prosecution, flee from the state's penal institution or jail, or flee to avoid testifying as a witness in order for the Unlawful Flight Statute to apply.

The Unlawful Flight Statute, sometimes termed "Flight to Avoid Prosecution or Giving Testimony", is seldom, if ever, filed for the purpose of prosecuting in federal court. It is a device or tool whereby the FBI obtains a federal warrant permitting a federal officer to arrest. After apprehension under the federal process, the U.S. Attorney, or federal prosecutor, routinely dismisses the federal warrant and releases the wanted person to state authorities. A reluctant state witness in a felony prosecution may also be located by the FBI under the provisions of this statute.

48. Federal Rules of Criminal Procedure, Rule 46 (b), and Title 18 U. S. Code, Section 659.
49. See New York Code of Criminal Procedure, Section 618-b and Section 954.20 of Wisconsin Criminal Statutes.
50. Barry v. U.S. ex rel. Cunningham, 279 US 597, 49 S Ct 452 (1928); State ex rel. Howard v. Grace, 18 Minn 398.

It is the flight across a state line that gives the FBI jurisdiction here. Until the wanted criminal or witness has gone into another state, no federal violation exists.

Title 18, Section 1073, of the U.S. Code, provides:

Flight to Avoid Prosecution or Giving Testimony

Whoever moves or travels in interstate or foreign commerce with intent either (1) to avoid prosecution, or custody or confinement after conviction, under the laws of the place from which he flees, for a crime, or an attempt to commit a crime, punishable by death or which is a felony under the laws of the place from which the fugitive flees, or which, in the case of New Jersey, is a high misdemeanor under the laws of said State, or (2) to avoid giving testimony in any criminal proceedings in such place in which the commission of an offense punishable by death or which is a felony under the laws of such place, or which in the case of New Jersey, is a high misdemeanor under the laws of said State, is charged, or (3) to avoid service of, or contempt proceedings for alleged disobedience of, lawful process requiring attendance and the giving of testimony or the production of documentary evidence before an agency of a State empowered by the law of such State to conduct investigations of alleged criminal activities, shall be fined not more than $5,000 or imprisoned not more than five years, or both.

SUMMARY

Whether a conviction is obtained or lost may often depend on whether the officer makes a legal arrest. If the detention is improper, the evidence obtained during the arrest will not be allowed as evidence in court. Almost invariably, the best solution is to obtain an arrest warrant, using this warrant as the legal basis for arrest. In general, an officer has made a proper arrest without a warrant if: (1) the crime was a misdemeanor actually committed in the officer's presence, or (2) the officer has reasonable grounds to believe that a felony has been committed or is being committed by the person being arrested. Under some circumstances, an officer may stop and question an individual, or make a detention, without effecting an arrest. The exact limits of the right to stop and question have not been clearly announced by the Supreme Court. Accordingly, an officer should exercise care in those situations where there is no sound basis for arrest. Every accused has the right to be released on bail, except in those crimes where the death penalty may be invoked. The Supreme Court has ruled that bail cannot be excessive merely because of the nature of the crime or because of community attitudes toward the accused. An unpopular defendant is entitled to bail, as is a popular individual. Bail should be required only to the extent it is needed to hold the accused to answer at the time of trial. Bail should not be set automatically but in accordance with the likelihood that it will prevent the defendant from taking flight. For a poor man, far less bail may be necessary to hold the accused to answer.

QUESTIONS

1. Does a magistrate generally have the power to arrest without a warrant? Explain why, if the answer is affirmative.

2. Explain the circumstances under which a person committing a felony may be arrested without a warrant.

3. What are the requirements for an arrest without a warrant when a misdemeanor has been committed? Does it matter whether the arresting person here is a police officer or a private citizen? Explain.

4. Explain the meaning of probable cause.

5. Explain why a felony arrest must be lawful at the time it is made.

6. What are the rights of a private security guard in making an arrest?

7. Describe the bail process and how it works.

8. Explain the circumstances under which an arrested person has the right to bail.

9. What is the nature of the relationship between the bail bondsman and the accused? Does the bondsman have the right to bring his client into court by force under some circumstances? Explain.

10. Explain the meaning of a release on the prisoner's "own recognizance."

11. When is bail set?

12. What is meant by "station house" bail?

13. Explain when bail may be granted after conviction. Is this a customary practice? Why?

14. What are the tests as to when bail is excessive? Explain how bail may be increased or lowered. What is the legal significance if a court finds bail to be excessive?

15. How may a bail bondsman be exonerated, or relieved, of his obligations to the court?

16. When may a witness be required to furnish bond?

17. Explain the workings of the Federal Unlawful Flight Statute. What is the usual outcome when an individual is arrested on a federal charge of unlawful flight to avoid prosecution?

. . . the prosecuting attorney is the representative not of an ordinary party to a controversy, but of a sovereignty whose obligation to govern impartially is as compelling as its obligation to govern at all; and whose interest, therefore, in a criminal prosecution is not that it shall win a case, but that justice shall be done. . . . he is . . . the servant of the law, the twofold aim of which is that guilt shall not escape nor innocence suffer.

Justice George Sutherland, United States Supreme Court, in *Berger* v. *United States*, 295 US 78 (1935)

chapter six

THE PROSECUTING ATTORNEY

The purpose of this chapter is to outline the duties and responsibilities of the prosecuting attorney. The prosecutor is one of the
key participants in the adversary trial system that is used in the
United States in criminal trials. This material is concerned with how
adversary proceedings work, and the part that is played by the
prosecutor, in federal, state, or local courts.

THE CRIMINAL TRIAL AS AN ADVERSARY PROCEEDING

The court system in the United States is frequently described by
legal scholars as being an adversary proceeding. What this means is
that there are two clearly drawn sides, with both the prosecution and
the defense presenting the facts known to them. The theory is that
each side is in the best position to present those things that are
favorable to their claim of guilt or innocence. Experience indicates
that the truth is more likely to be found when the searchers are
closing in from both sides. If these presentations are properly made,
then the truth should be clearly evident to a fair-minded jury.

The essence of the adversary system is challenge. The survival of our system of criminal justice and the values which it advances depend upon a constant, searching, and creative questioning of official decisions and assertions of authority at all stages of the process.

This adversary presentation cancels out the natural human tendency to jump to a decision without waiting to hear all the facts.

In this adversary-accusatorial trial system that is used in criminal prosecutions in the English and American courts, the judge serves as an umpire between the two sides in the conflict. In the so-called inquisitorial system followed by the courts in a number of European countries, the court and its officers retain complete control over the development and presentation of the trial. The judge there exercises affirmative participation, rather than a neutral role, in the accumulation and presentation of the evidence. A just verdict may, of course, be reached under either system, but American legal scholars believe the judge's role should be an uninvolved one.

The higher, or appellate, courts uniformly agree that in this adversary contest the trial judge must remain basically fair, both to the public's right to be protected against criminality, and to the individual's right to a fair trial. As expressed by one court, integrity is the very breath of justice. Confidence in our law, our courts, and in the administration of justice is our supreme interest.[1]

The adversary system is not a perfect one by any means. If the attorney for one side does not aggressively present his side of the case, then that side is at a disadvantage. It is still, however, the best trial system that has been devised from our English common law heritage.[2]

THE PROSECUTING ATTORNEY

A prosecution is a criminal action or proceeding instituted and carried on in the name of the government before a competent criminal court. This is, of course, with the fixed purpose of reaching a court determination of the guilt or innocence of the accused.[3]

1. Jennings v. Di Genova, 141 A 866, 107 Conn 491.
2. Welcome D. Pierson, *The Defense Attorney and Basic Defense Tactics,* (Indianapolis: Bobbs-Merrill Co., Inc., 1956 [and 1966 Supplement]), p. 39. See also: Ronald L. Carlson, *Criminal Justice Procedures for Police,* (Cincinnati: The W. H. Anderson Co., 1970), pp. 208–210; Barrett, "The Adversary System and the Ethics of Advocacy," 37 *Notre Dame Lawyer,* 479 (1962); Hickman v. Taylor, 329 US 495 (1947) and Arrant v. State, 167 So 540, 232 Ala 275 (1936). U.S. v. Nixon, 417 US 709 (1960).
3. U. S. v. Reisinger, 128 US 398, 9 S Ct 99.

To prosecute is not merely to file papers that begin the action, but to follow the case through to an ultimate conclusion. When the matter comes before a court, the prosecuting attorney performs the functions of a trial lawyer for the people.

In practically all states, the practice of law by one serving as prosecutor or by one holding a judicial position is forbidden. It is simply too difficult to serve the interests of the state and to engage in a private occupation at the same time.

The prosecutor is always an attorney, and in the majority of states this is an elective office. Felonies and other serious crimes are prosecuted by the district attorney or county attorney in most states, while it is the responsibility of the city attorney to handle violations of city ordinances or municipal codes. In some areas, the prosecuting attorney is called the prosecutor of pleas. He may also be called the state's attorney or the attorney for the people.

In some instances, the prosecutor initiates the prosecutive action by preparing an affidavit charging a named person with the commission of a penal offense, upon which a warrant is issued or an indictment or accusation is based. At other times, the criminal complaint may be filed by the investigating police officer. Generally, a warrant cannot be obtained by a police officer without first obtaining the approval, or authority of the prosecuting attorney.

The prosecutor is allowed to use his judgment as to whether a warrant should be obtained. From a practical standpoint, there may be instances when an investigating officer is carried away with his own suspicions. In such a case, the prosecutor serves as a brake on an overly enthusiastic or inexperienced investigator. In other words, he may decline to authorize the issuance of a warrant because he has serious reservations as to whether, as yet, a criminal violation has been reasonably established. He may inform the investigating officer that he will withhold issuance of any criminal process until more proof is obtained. This is a matter of legal judgment, for the prosecutor knows what kind of a case he must have to present in the courtroom. There is no way that any court, grand jury, or other governmental body can force the prosecutor to issue a warrant.

In some cases, the prosecutor may be convinced that a criminal offense has been committed, but he may decline to prosecute as a matter of policy. A typical situation of this kind could involve a relatively minor offense that has become public knowledge, thereby ruining the accused's reputation in the community. The prosecutor may feel that, in this case, the disgrace suffered has been punishment for the crime. In legal terms, substantial justice has already been done.

95

The prosecutor may also be inclined to decline prosecution in a relatively minor case in which the accused suffers indirectly because of injury or loss of a loved one who is the unintended victim of the criminal act. A case of this kind might be one in which the accused buys firecrackers in violation of a city ordinance. The criminal violation may be revealed when one of the accused's small children is burned while handling the prohibited firecrackers.

In many instances, the accused's activities may involve violations of both state and federal laws. If the accused is apprehended by either a state or federal officer, a criminal prosecution may be undertaken in that jurisdiction. The prosecutor in the other jurisdiction will then usually decline to press charges, feeling that all of the accused's activities will be taken into account when sentence is passed. The language usually used by the prosecutor in such a case is that he has declined in favor of the prosecution already undertaken.

There are, of course, occasions when a prosecutor fails to prosecute a case that has real merit. When this happens, a grand jury may indict the accused, who will answer to the court directly.

At times, there are prosecutors who will not authorize prosecution unless the facts seem to spell out "an ironclad case." The charge has sometimes been made that these prosecutors are afraid to lose a case. The prosecutor may be under the impression that it is necessary for him to have a record of almost 100 percent convictions as a stepping stone to higher elective office.

Because of the adversary trial idea, some individuals in the general public are under the impression that the prosecution must do everything possible to obtain a conviction. This is a misconception. The prosecuting attorney has two distinct responsibilities:

1. As the people's representative in the adversary contest in the courts, he must seek to convict those guilty of crime.

2. As the representative of a government that believes in fair treatment for all, he must make certain that the accused is not deprived of a fair trial.

The Supreme Court describes this situation in the following language:

> the prosecutor . . . is in a peculiar and very definite sense the servant of the law, the twofold aim of which is that guilt shall not escape or innocence suffer. He may prosecute with earnestness and vigor—indeed, he should do so. But while he may

strike hard blows, he is not at liberty to strike foul ones. It is as much his duty to refrain from improper methods calculated to produce a wrong conviction as it is to use every legitimate means to bring about a just one.[4]

In the Berger case, the Supreme Court held that a prosecutor can never actively utilize false testimony that could result in a conviction. But the prosecutor's duty goes beyond this. He cannot stand idly by and fail to make an issue of perjured testimony that is offered by a prosecution witness. If he knows, or has reason to believe, that one of his witnesses is lying on the witness stand, he has a responsibility to correct the testimony on the spot or immediately bring the facts to the attention of the judge in charge of the trial.[5]

If the prosecutor fails to take this affirmative action, the courts hold that the accused has not been afforded due process of law. Therefore, he is entitled to a new trial, unhampered by the use of dishonest testimony.[6]

Then too, the prosecutor has a responsibility to reveal evidence that indicates innocence. A typical case of this type might be one in which an individual is being prosecuted for sending a typewritten letter demanding loot in a kidnapping or extortion case. When the prosecutor obtains the letter in question, he has it examined by three experts on questioned documents. Two of these experts are strongly of the opinion that the document was typed on a typewriter known to have been in possession of the accused. The third expert notes similarities between typewriting samples and the questioned document, but he also has some doubts because of some points of possible dissimilarity. When the matter comes to trial the prosecutor is duty-bound to have all of the experts testify. He cannot present only the two experts favorable to his case.

To avoid the possibility of a new trial, the prosecutor must present any substantial defense evidence that he receives while preparing the case for the prosecution.[7] Some courts have gone so far as to say that the prosecutor must reveal evidence favorable to the

---

4. Berger v. U.S., 295 US 78 (1935).

5. Pyle v. Kansas, 317 US 213.

6. Alcorta v. Texas, 355 US 28, 78 S Ct 103 (1957). Exactly what is meant by the term due process is difficult to define. The Fourteenth Amendment to the U.S. Constitution provides ". . . nor shall any state deprive any person of life, liberty, or property without due process of law; . . ." The courts have generally interpreted this to mean a basic or fundamental sense of fairness.

7. Barbee v. Warden Maryland Penitentiary, 331 F 2d 842 (1964).

97

defendant, even though the prosecutor doubts the honesty or accuracy of the evidence.[8] There is good reason for some judges to disagree here, on the basis that doubtful or questionable evidence will only confuse the jury. On the other side of the argument, some legal commentators believe that the jury is entitled to all available information bearing on guilt or innocence, even though this places a considerable burden on the prosecutor.

In cases where the prosecutor actively procures a lying witness, or covers up the witnesses' lies, we have seen that the accused is entitled to a new trial, even without showing that the false evidence harmed his case in any way. It is a different matter, however, if the prosecutor merely knows of the existence of evidence favorable to the accused's case and fails to present it. In the event of a passive failure to disclose, the accused must prove that his case was prejudiced by the nondisclosure before he will be awarded a new trial.[9]

In heavily populated areas, the prosecuting attorney may assign the entire preparation and handling of cases to full-time assistants. In some instances, the state laws provide for the hiring of a special prosecutor to handle a single case that is particularly complicated.[10]

The prosecutor must uphold the law in a consistent manner. He cannot arbitrarily single out some defendants for prosecution, while refusing to prosecute others who violated the law in the same way.[11]

The Supreme Court has given all prosecutors a shield against civil suits brought by the accused in a criminal prosecution. In a case decided in 1976, Justice Lewis F. Powell of the Supreme Court pointed out that prosecutors must be exempt from the harassment of civil lawsuits to ensure that they carry out their duties vigorously and courageously.[12]

---

8. U.S. v. Zborowski, 271 F 2d 661.

9. See Marshall v. U.S., 355 F 2d 999, Brady v. Maryland, 373 US 83 (1963) and Pyle v. Kansas, 317 US 213 (1942).

10. The prosecutor brings a legally trained mind to the job and may authorize prosecution or advise a continuing investigation. His authority to prosecute or to decline to prosecute is seldom questioned by the courts. For additional background, see: John C. Klotter and Jacqueline R. Kanovitz, *Constitutional Law for Poilice,* (Cincinnati: The W. H. Anderson Co., 1968), pp. 293–94; Paul B. Weston and Kenneth M. Wells, *The Administration of Justice,* 2d ed., (Englewood Cliffs: Prentice–Hall, Inc., 1973), p. 73; and R. Gene Wright and John A. Marlo, *The Police Officer and Criminal Justice,* (New York: McGraw-Hill and Co., 1970), pp. 92–94.

11. Oyler v. Boles, 368 US 448 (1962). See also: Jerold H. Israel and Wayne R. LaFavre, *Criminal Procedure in a Nutshell,* (St. Paul: West Publishing Co., 1976), p. 34.

12. Imbler v. Pachtman, decided by the United States Supreme Court, March 2, 1976.

The Prosecutor and the Investigating Officer Must Function as a Team

The prosecutor should be consulted by the investigating officer as soon as it is known that a criminal case is going to trial. In serious cases, it is preferable to keep the prosecutor advised almost from the outset. This is to make certain that proper procedures are being utilized, and that evidence will be admissible.

In major cities, the prosecutor may have such a heavy caseload that it is hard to confer with the police officer in every case. Consequently, there may be instances when the case is not discussed with the prosecutive attorney until a few minutes before the opening of trial.

Experience shows that this is a poor procedure, frequently resulting in the acquittal of a defendant against whom there was considerable evidence. Without written reports of the investigation, followed up by a conference, the prosecutive presentation may be crippled. It is important for the officer to outline the different kinds of evidence, how it was obtained, and his knowledge as to any objections that may be made to the introduction of the evidence.

While there should be complete cooperation between the prosecutor and the investigative agency, the prosecutor should never try to put words in the mouth of the witness. Frequently, a defense attorney may ask whether the investigator has discussed the case with the prosecutor. The implication in this line of questioning is usually that there must have been something sinister in the discussion. The investigator should, of course, be completely truthful in stating whether or not he did have a conference with the prosecuting attorney. The defense attorney will usually turn away from this line of questioning if the investigator points out that he or she did have a discussion with the prosecutor, and that the investigator at that time outlined the detailed evidence to indicate the defendant's guilt.

There are times when the prosecutor may not present the evidence in the way the police believe it should be introduced. For either evidentiary or psychological reasons, the prosecutor may not introduce specific pieces of evidence. This is the prosecutor's decision, based on his ability and experience as an attorney and his knowledge of the judge's procedures for the operation of the court. If it appears, however, that the attorney has forgotten a key piece of evidence, the investigator should point this out.

The handling of a trial should never be allowed to become a sore spot between the investigative agency and the prosecutor, as cooperation is essential to good law enforcement and criminal justice. If there is any question, the prosecutor should accept the responsibility of challenging the evidence produced by the investigating officer. The purpose of this is to make certain that a competent and thorough investigation has been conducted, as well as to help the prosecutor anticipate all of the defense claims that may be raised to cast doubt on the evidence.

JUSTICE MAY NOT ALWAYS BE SERVED BY PROSECUTING

Not all persons who are technically guilty of violating the law are prosecuted. Sometimes there are good reasons for this. Frequently, there are noticeable dissimilarities in the motivations that drive different individuals to commit the same crime. Also, from an ethical, moral, administrative, or practical point of view, there are often great differences in activity that is branded as criminal.

When considering the facts in a specific case, the prosecutor may ask, "What is the social objective that requires prosecutive action in this case?" For example, the purpose of nonsupport laws is to force parents to accept responsibility for the support of their dependents. If an errant father has been located and has already begun to send support money to his family, then the law's purpose has been accomplished. A jail sentence at this stage would deprive the family of their breadwinner. When facts of this kind are presented to him, the prosecutor may feel that criminal prosecution is not justified. A month later, if the errant father has again run away and deserted his small children, the prosecutor is no longer justified in withholding prosecution—it is obvious at this point that the father will not learn until legal action is taken.

The prosecutor must consider the overall picture. Then, he must use his discretion as to whether an apparently guilty individual should be charged and brought to trial.

It is a different matter, however, for the prosecutor to fail to prosecute because he is not sympathetic with the law in question. In larger cities a prosecutor may fail to take action against pornography because he feels the problem is going to continue. This is a failure on the part of the prosecutor to do the job for which he was elected. The prosecutor's judgment extends to specific violations, not to specific classes of laws.

THE ATTORNEY GENERAL OF THE UNITED STATES

The Attorney General of the United States is the head of the U.S. Department of Justice and is a member of the President's Cabinet. He is in charge of all legal matters for the executive branch of the United States Government, being in charge of both civil and criminal problems before the courts. The Attorney General's chief assistant has the title of Solicitor General. The latter official appears on behalf of the government in all cases before the Supreme Court in which the government has a strong interest. Appointed by the President, the Attorney General furnishes legal advice to high officers of the government, including the President.

The United States Attorney is an assistant to the Attorney General, the former serving in a specified district, handling both criminal prosecutions and civil matters. In federal criminal cases with unusual prosecutive angles or matters of unusual public interest, the Attorney General may send lawyers from his staff in Washington, D.C. to assist the local United States Attorney in the preparation and trial of the case.

The State Attorney General

All state governments have a chief legal officer, who is usually called the State Attorney General. He gives legal advice to state officials and represents the state in matters of interest in the courts. He may protect the public at large through the efforts of investigators and attorneys in a Consumer Fraud Council. He may seek to expose and combat crime at large and criminal rings, while the district attorney or county attorney prosecutes specific violations.

In most states, the Attorney General has the authority to provide seasoned attorneys who can step in to assist the regular prosecutive official who is in need of trial court experience. His duties, at the state level, are similar to those of the Attorney General of the United States at the federal level.

The Trial Judge

The trial judge stands between the two sides in the adversary trial system. His duties will be discussed in more detail in our study of the courts. For our purposes here, though, we should consider the interplay between the judge, the prosecutor, and the defense attorney.

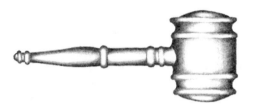

As a public officer, the judge is charged with the responsibility to administer justice in the court system. He presides over the trial and directs all phases of it. The judge is paid by the government but he owes allegiance neither to the prosecution nor to the defense. His only responsibility is to the criminal justice system.

It is the judge's job to decide questions of law. In situations in which the facts are to be decided by a jury, the judge instructs the jury as to the law which is applicable and points out to the jury members the exact questions for their determination. The judge also pronounces the sentence, or enters the judgment of the court.[13]

In early day England, the judges in some of the king's courts were called justices. This title is still used today. In the United States, judges in both federal and state courts of high rank are called justices. These justices usually preside over appellate courts.

If the court is one that is staffed by several justices, the administrative head of the court is usually called the Chief Justice. He assigns duties and responsibilities to the other justices, as well as to himself. The title of "justice" may also be used to designate a lower court judge, called the justice of the peace.

It is a definite advantage in his work if a judge is also a lawyer. Today, the judges in all of the federal courts and in all of the higher state courts must be attorneys. This is usually required by legislative enactment. Not too many years ago, however, some highly placed judges did not have a formal legal education.

In some states, a judge of an inferior court, such as a justice of the peace, may serve on a part time basis, practicing law when he is not otherwise occupied. Generally, however, no judge of any kind can practice law in the courts in which he serves as a judge. Except for some inferior state courts, the position of judge is a full-time job.

13. Welcome D. Pierson, *The Defense Attorney and Basic Defense Tactics,* (Indianapolis: Bobbs-Merrill Co., Inc., 1956 and [1966 Supplement], pp. 7–72.

The judge must be impartial under all circumstances. If he has any family connections or business relationships with any of the parties, the judge must disqualify himself. This means that he cannot preside at the trial but must step down from the bench and allow a disinterested judge to try the case. The judge is expected to take this action without being asked by either party. A new trial will be granted before a new judge if the higher courts believe there is substance to a claim of prejudice on the part of the judge.

A judge cannot be brought to account for any decision he makes. If it were otherwise, the courts would be subjected to all manner of political pressures. In the absence of outright fraud, a judge cannot be questioned for the correctness of his rulings, and he cannot be sued unless there is a clear case of bribery or a payoff.

There would be absolute chaos if the judge did not have the power to run his own court. This authority is never questioned by the higher courts unless it is obvious that the judge is so highhanded that the trial is unfair.

The higher courts take the attitude that a case could drag on forever unless the judge is allowed to run the court in a businesslike way. He must, of course, give the accused "his day in court." However, he is not required to tolerate deliberate delay or confusion by the defense attorney or the defendant.

In the final analysis, the accused will not be allowed to complain of the action of the trial judge unless there is a clear showing of bias against the accused.[14]

SUMMARY

The court system in the United States operates on an adversary basis, with both the prosecution and the defense presenting those facts most favorable to their claims of guilt or innocence. The prosecuting attorney handles the case for the government. He presents the evidence which indicates the guilt of the accused. While he is expected to prosecute vigorously, he must do so fairly. It is his job to see that the guilty are convicted and that the innocent are given their freedom. The prosecution must, therefore, advise the defense if

14. See the statement of the judge's duties in the dissenting opinion of Justice McReynolds in the Supreme Court case of Berger v. U.S., 255 US 22 (1921). Legal authorities agree that the judge must be fair to both sides. Goldstein v. U.S., 63 Fed 2d 609; Gilglio v. Valdez, 114 So 2d 305; State v. Levy, 113 P 2d 306; Veal v. State, 268 SW 2d 345.

evidence is uncovered that tends to prove innocence. This is a one-way obligation, however, as the defense has no burden to disclose evidence of guilt. The prosecutor does not merely file papers against the accused. He follows the case through to a logical conclusion. The prosecutor prepares the case; explores the testimony that can be furnished by individual witnesses, including investigating police officers; and presents the matter and makes motions in court. He also argues the government side of the case during the trial. The police officer should consult the prosecutor as soon as it is known that a case is going to trial. If the prosecutor feels that the evidence is insufficient to prove all elements of the case, or that justice would not be served in a trial, he can refuse to initiate prosecution. The prosecutor has complete discretion here. If he feels the case is so weak that a conviction may not be obtained, the prosecutor can indulge in plea bargaining, accepting a guilty plea to a reduced charge. Plea bargaining works on the theory that a half a loaf is better than none.

QUESTIONS

1. Why is an adversary trial system likely to bring out the truth at the time of trial?

2. How is this adversary procedure different from the so-called inquisitorial system followed by most European countries?

3. How would you describe the judge's role in the adversary contest?

4. Can the prosecuting attorney blindly close his eyes to evidence that would tend to clear the accused?

5. May the prosecutor be forced to prosecute when he doubts that the case has merit?

6. Is the prosecutor responsible for having a good conviction record, or making certain that just decisions are reached by the criminal courts? Why?

7. May the prosecutor ignore perjury by a prosecution witness?

8. What are the basic duties and responsibilities of the Attorney General of the United States?

9. Are responsibilities of the State Attorney General similar to those of the Attorney General of the United States?

10. May the State Attorney General's office extend prosecutive help to the local prosecutor's office? If so, under what circumstances?

. . . traditional right to freedom before conviction permits the unhampered preparation of a defense and serves to prevent the infliction of punishment prior to conviction. Unless this right is preserved, the presumption of innocence, secured only after years of struggle, would lose its meaning.

Justice Robert Jackson, United States Supreme Court, in concurring opinion in *Stack* v. *Boyle*, 342 US 1 (1951)

chapter seven
THE DEFENSE ATTORNEY

The purpose of this chapter is to outline the duties and responsibilities of the defense attorney in the criminal justice system. The functions of the paid attorney, the responsibilities of the public defender, the role of the legal aid society attorney, and the duties of the court-appointed defense attorney will be discussed.

In addition, this chapter will outline the right of the accused to an attorney. The extent and limits of this right and the privilege of acting as one's own attorney will also be explored.

PROCEDURAL RIGHTS AS "TOOLS" FOR THE ACCUSED AND HIS ATTORNEY

Procedural rights under the law are not an end in themselves. They are "tools" used to prevent the arbitrary exercise of power by individuals in governmental positions. The approach used by the United States Supreme Court in deciding cases has long been to make certain that these procedural rights were made available to the accused in every criminal prosecution.

In every case decided by the Supreme Court, the accused is entitled to have his case judged according to the written law and not according to his financial worth, his accomplishments, or his standing in society. Under the interpretations of the Court, the U.S. Constitution requires substantial equality and fair treatment. All of this is meaningless if an accused who may have committed an exceptionally brutal or repugnant crime is unable to find a competent lawyer who will defend him. His opportunity to have his day in court may be seriously hampered if this kind of prejudgment is allowed. Criminal justice procedure in the United States is intended to prevent this kind of problem.

THE DEFENSE ATTORNEY AND HIS ROLE

Legal authorities sometimes state that both the prosecuting attorney and the defense attorney are officers of the court. Technically, this may be true, but in actual practice there are important differences between these two classes of attorneys.[1]

Members of the public sometimes state that a defense lawyer will take advantage of any loophole or legal technicality in order to free his client. This kind of thinking may be difficult to reconcile with the statement that the defense attorney is himself an officer of the court.

It is inexcusable for an attorney to be dishonest or unethical. However, the defense attorney's position should be examined for what it is—he is a part of the adversary system, a trial procedure that requires the defense lawyer to present those things that are most favorable to his client's claims.

From one viewpoint, the defense attorney has no real duty to his client. Rather, he is responsible to the legal system and to the court. His job is to represent the accused zealously but within the bounds of honesty and of the law. If he feels it is necessary, he can decline to bring out those facts that might convict his client. However, he can never bring out evidence that he knows to be untrue. He also has the responsibility to point out whatever holes there may be in the evidence presented by the prosecution. Some defense attorneys do, however, get carried away in their effort. The defendant has the right to have all his rights protected but the attorney should not deceitfully represent his client as a fallen angel who should be returned to freedom on the street, through perjury or a false alibi.

The defense lawyer is duty-bound to represent the accused in the most favorable light, even though he may personally feel that his client is a reprehensible individual, deserving of severe punishment. At the same time, the defense attorney believes that conviction should not result until after a fairly conducted trial in which the prosecution has proved guilt beyond a reasonable doubt, and the accused has been afforded all his legal rights.[2]

1. Monrad G. Paulsen, *The Problem of a Criminal Defense*, American Law Institute, 1961, pp. 2–46 and pp. 59–85.
2. See the opinion of Justice Robert Jackson, Watts v. Indiana, 338 US 49 (1949).

Stated in other terms, it is the function of the judge and the jury to weigh the two presentations and to find guilt or innocence. It is the defense attorney's obligation to make the prosecution prove the guilt of his client, every step of the way.

The accused has the right to reveal any kind of confidential matter to an attorney while seeking legal aid, whether the attorney has been hired or has agreed to represent the accused or not. When the accused does this, he is not running the risk that confidential revelations will be revealed and used against him.[3] This attorney-client relationship, or privilege, is as old as the common law of England.

There is no legal way for any court or government body to make the attorney reveal this type of information. In the unlikely possibility that the attorney should reveal it, the courts would not allow it to be used as evidence.

If, however, proof shows that the attorney persuaded the client to take the witness stand and testify falsely after making an admission of guilt to the attorney, then the defense attorney is subject to prosecution and may be disbarred. This is the crime of subornation of perjury.

It is improper for a lawyer to represent a group engaged in the violation of the law for the purpose of advising the members how to break the law and at the same time escape it. This would make the attorney a principal in the crime! A lawyer must see to it that anyone accused of a crime, no matter how serious or flagrant, has a fair trial. The attorney may present all available defenses but he may not cooperate with criminals in planning violations of the law. There is a sharp distinction between advising what can lawfully be done and advising how unlawful acts can be done in a way to avoid conviction.[4]

Unlike the prosecution, the defense attorney has no obligation to reveal any evidence that is favorable to the other side. He has no duty to disclose anything. In fact, the defense attorney is not required to produce any evidence or testimony if he feels that this is the best strategy for his client. As we will see in another section, the prosecutor is not allowed to infer that this failure to testify is an indication of guilt.

The defense attorney will be subject to discipline by the courts and by the bar association if he knowingly allows the accused or one of his witnesses to commit perjury. An attorney for either side may

3. Sitton v. Peyree, 241 P 62, 117 Ore 107.
4. Ronald L. Carlson, *Criminal Justice Procedures for Police*, (Cincinnati: The W. H. Anderson Co., 1970), p. 209; and R. Gene Wright and John A. Marlo, *The Police Officer and Criminal Justice*, (New York: McGraw-Hill and Co., 1970), pp. 95–97.

be prosecuted and disbarred if he deliberately seeks to obtain false testimony to be used in court, for this is the crime of subornation of perjury. However, the defense attorney cannot be prosecuted for the false testimony of his client, unless it can be proved that the defense attorney knew of this falsity.[5]

THE PUBLIC DEFENDER

Many localities still use a system in which members of the local bar serve in rotation to represent accused persons who are unable to pay. This is a part of the attorney's obligation to the court system.

Many other localities utilize a public defender, a county official who is paid to defend penniless persons accused of crime. Usually, this operates on a county by county basis.

The public defender system originated in Los Angeles, California, in 1915, and has spread into most states. The duties of this official, as set out in the California Government Code are as follows:

> The board of supervisors of any county may establish and maintain the office of public defender for the county. Any county may join with one or more counties to establish and maintain the office of public defender to serve such counties.
>
> . . . In counties of the first, second and third classes, the public defender shall devote all his time to the duties of the office and shall not engage in the practice of law except in the capacity of public defender.
>
> . . . he shall defend, without expense to the defendant, any person who is not financially able to employ counsel and who is charged with the commission of any contempt or offense triable in the superior, municipal or justice courts at all stages of the proceedings, including the preliminary examination . . . and shall prosecute all appeals to a higher court or courts of any person who has been convicted, where, in his opinion, the appeal will or might reasonably be expected to result in the reversal or modification of the judgment of conviction.[6]

The court has the final say as to whether or not the accused qualifies as an individual who may use the services of the public defender. In some states, an individual who claims that he cannot

5. "Like the court [judge] itself, an attorney is an instrument or agency to advance the ends of justice." 7 *American Jurisprudence* 2d, p. 45. People ex rel. Karlin v. Culkin, 248 NY 465, 162 NE 487, 60 ALR 851.
6. California Government Code, Sections 27700, 27705, 27706a.

pay for an attorney is required to fill out a lengthy financial statement, giving written consent to authorities to examine the latest copy of the accused's income tax return. This, of course, is to determine whether the applicant for free legal services has secret financial means. If the accused makes a false claim and investigation reveals that he has the ability to pay for a lawyer, he may face an additional charge of perjury.

HOW AN ATTORNEY MAY BE HELPFUL TO THE ACCUSED

We have seen that criminal trials in the United States are described by the courts as being "of an adversary nature." The courts usually say that both the prosecution and the defense must bring out the available facts that indicate guilt on the one hand, and innocence on the other. If this is done in a searching, probing way, then eventually the truth will be evident to a jury. Over hundreds of years the courts have worked out rules of evidence to make certain that the evidence presented has reasonable guarantees of accuracy and truth. Then too, the defense has the right to challenge whatever proof is offered to show guilt. The object of the courts in all this has been to work out a reliable guilt-determining process.

The court usually feels that a person who is unskilled in the rules of law may not be able to present his own case in the most favorable light. If a man has no attorney, the tensions of a trial, with life or liberty at stake, might alone make him completely unfit to give his explanation properly or completely.

The courts have consistently said that an innocent man is much more likely to be overwhelmed than an offender who is hardened in guilt. If confined to jail, deprived of access to family and friends, and confused by the complexities of the trial process, the accused may not be able to present his side of the case. In short, he may be incapable of providing the challenges that are indispensable to the operation of the adversary system.

As said by Justice Sutherland of the Supreme Court:

> The right to be heard would be, in many cases, of little avail if it did not comprehend the right to be heard by counsel. Even the intelligent and educated layman has small and sometimes no skill in the science of law. If charged with crime, he is incapable, generally, of determining for himself whether the indictment is good or bad. He is unfamiliar with the rules of evidence . . . He requires the guiding hand of counsel at every

step in the proceedings against him. Without it, though he may not be guilty, he faces the danger of conviction because he does not know how to establish his innocence.[7]

HOW THE RIGHT TO AN ATTORNEY DEVELOPED

By modern day standards, the early English courts gave harsh treatment to persons accused of crime. It is true that a person accused of a misdemeanor has been entitled to a lawyer for hundreds of years. However, the same right was not given to a person charged with a felony. The early English judges and legal writers contended that the courts had been set up to function in felony cases, both for the government and for the accused, providing ample safeguards for the individual charged.

There was a considerable buildup of pressure from public officials and social reformers to change this practice, and in 1688 a law was passed giving persons charged with treason the right to an attorney. It was not until 1836, however, that English courts allowed an attorney for persons accused of other felonies. It had been the practice of some of the English judges somewhat earlier to let hired attorneys come into the jail for conferences with their clients. During these jail sessions the lawyers briefed their clients as to what questions should be asked of witnesses for the prosecution, and what strategy should be used by the defendant in conducting his own defense.[8]

When the colonists came from the Old World to America, many were influenced by the oppressions that they had seen in the governments of Europe. Accordingly, there was strong feeling in favor of allowing an accused the right to an attorney.

THE RIGHT TO AN ATTORNEY AS SET OUT IN THE U.S. CONSTITUTION

The Sixth Amendment to the U.S. Constitution provides that: "In all criminal prosecutions, the accused shall enjoy the right . . . to have the Assistance of Counsel for his defense."[9]

7. Powell v. Alabama, 287 US 68 (1932).
8. See Klotter & Kanovitz, *Constitutional Law for Police,* (Cincinnati: The W. H. Anderson Company, 1968), p. 235.
9. The term "counsel" here means the same as lawyer, attorney, or legal counselor. These words are generally used interchangeably by the courts and lawyers in the United States. People v. Taylor, 138 P 762, 56 Colo 441.

The way this provision has been construed by the courts is that an individual accused of crime has the "right to be heard and to be assisted by counsel in his defense." In other words, there are two separate rights here for the accused:

1. that of legal help in getting the defense ready: the planning of strategy and the calling of defense witnesses, and

2. that of having a member of the bar speak to the court and jury as the accused's "mouthpiece," and in making legal arguments and handling the cross examination of witnesses.[10]

In addition to the right of an attorney that is set out in the U.S. Constitution, many state constitutions include such a provision. For example, the constitution of New York State specifies that the accused is "allowed" an attorney, while that of Connecticut gives the accused the "right to be heard by himself and by his counsel."

The Right to a Lawyer in Federal Cases, Even if Unable to Pay

For many years the federal courts took the position that a person accused of a noncapital felony had permission to obtain an attorney if he could pay for one. In other words, the approach of the courts was that the accused was "allowed" to have someone represent him. There was, however, no requirement that the courts had to provide counsel for one who could not pay for legal services.

In 1938, in the case of *Johnson* v. *Zerbst,*[11] the Supreme Court extended the right to an attorney to any serious prosecution undertaken in the federal courts. In this case, two individuals had been convicted for passing counterfeit bills. One of these defendants had been represented by a lawyer at the time of arrest but had not been able to pay for an attorney at the time of trial. After serving part of his sentence, the convicted man filed a writ in federal court. The Supreme Court said that it was the responsibility of the federal trial court to make certain that the accused was given a lawyer, whether or not the accused could pay.

10. As stated in Powell v. Alabama, 287 US 68, the right to assistance in preparing for trial is equally as important to the accused as the right to representation during the trial itself. See also Jerold H. Israel and Wayne R. LaFavre, *Criminal Procedure in a Nutshell,* (West Publishing Co., St. Paul, 1976), pp. 47, 48.
11. Johnson v. Zerbst, 304 US 458 (1938).

In the language of the Court:

> If the accused . . . is not represented by counsel and has not
> competently and intelligently waived his constitutional right,
> the Sixth Amendment stands as a . . . bar to a valid conviction.

Development of the Right to
an Attorney in State Felony Cases

Another case that became well known to legal authorities was
Powell v. *Alabama*,[12] a state prosecution in which the death penalty
was being sought in 1932. This matter also reached the Supreme
Court on appeal, and it was held that the accused had been deprived
of his rights because the trial court had not assigned the accused an
attorney at the outset of the prosecution.

The Supreme Court did not decide this case on the basis that
the United States' Sixth Amendment should be extended to the
states, but on the basis that failure to get an attorney had been a
failure to give a fair trial, under the due process clause of the
Fourteenth Amendment.

In part, the Fourteenth Amendment provides: " . . . nor shall
any State deprive any person of life, liberty, or property, without due
process of law."

Exactly what is meant by the term "due process" has never been
fully clarified by the Supreme Court. From statements that have
been made in cases before the Court, it appears that the deprivation
of due process in a criminal prosecution is any action in the trial
court that does not allow the accused his "day in court" or "give him
a free opportunity to refute or explain away the criminal charges
that have been made." In other words, the term "due process" is
difficult to define but it refers to "that which is eminently fair—that
which is fundamental and essential to the processes of a fair trial."
"Due process involves the right to be heard by testimony or otherwise, and to have a clear chance to dispute or controvert, by proof,
every material fact which bears on the criminal allegation."

THE ACCUSED'S RIGHT TO A LAWYER
IN ALL STATE FELONY CASES

For a long time, the courts have agreed that no state could deny a
defendant the right to go out and hire his own attorney. In *Powell* v.

12. Powell v. Alabama, 287 US 45 (1932).

Alabama, it was settled that the state had to furnish a penniless defendant an attorney if the state was asking the death penalty. It continued to be the law, however, that a state was not required to furnish a lawyer for a penniless person accused of a noncapital felony, unless some very special circumstances, such as the youthfulness of the accused, made legal assistance essential to a fair trial.

The leading case in this regard was *Betts* v. *Brady*,[13] in which the Supreme Court stated in 1942 that refusal to appoint an attorney for the accused in a routine state felony prosecution was not so "offensive to the common and fundamental ideas of fairness" as to involve a denial of due process. In other words, the due process clause of the Fourteenth Amendment did not require the appointment of a lawyer, unless there were some special circumstances that made the trial an unfair contest.

In 1963, a case with facts almost identical to *Betts* v. *Brady* was appealed to the Supreme Court, squarely overruling the law that was thought to be settled in this area of criminal procedure. The new decision was *Gideon* v. *Wainwright*,[14] a case which has been heavily publicized.

The facts in this case were that a man named Gideon had been charged with breaking into a pool room for the purpose of committing a misdemeanor inside. Under Florida law, this type of breaking and entering constituted a felony. "Appearing in court without funds and without lawyer," Gideon asked the court to appoint counsel for him, . . ." When the request was refused, an appeal eventually reached the Supreme Court.

The case was decided on the basis of the Fourteenth Amendment, rather than the rights set out in the Sixth Amendment. Justice Black of the Supreme Court wrote the opinion for the majority:

> The right of one charged with crime to counsel may not be deemed fundamental and essential to fair trials in some countries, but it is in ours. From the very beginning, our state and national constitutions and laws have laid great emphasis on procedural and substantive safeguards designed to assure fair trials before impartial tribunals in which every defendant stands equal before the law. This noble ideal cannot be realized if the poor man charged with crime has to face his accusors without a lawyer to assist him.

13. Betts v. Brady, 316 US 455 (1942); Rollin M. Perkins, *Criminal Law and Procedure* 3d ed., (Brooklyn: The Foundation Press, 1966), p. 861.
14. Gideon v. Wainwright, 372 US 335 (1963).

The Defense Attorney

The Supreme Court's action here, in directly overruling *Betts* v. *Brady,* can be described as an example of "judicial legislation," or judge-made law—a court decision that construes away the original intent of a constitutional provision or statute, or finds in that statute meanings that the original framers never intended.

Judges both lead and respond to the values of the nation. It may well be that by the time the Gideon case was decided, the social attitudes in the United States had changed to such a point that public opinion favored the appointment of a lawyer for every indigent accused of a felony in any court.

In a situation of this kind, many feel that a deficiency in the machinery of justice, if in fact such a weakness existed, should be corrected by the passage of a statute by Congress. These critics feel that it is a mistake to allow the Supreme Court to alter law that has been relied on by the trial courts for a number of years.

Apparently, however, there was a feeling on the part of the majority in the United States Supreme Court that "there can be no equal justice where the kind of trial a man gets depends on the amount of money he has."[15] This was described by Supreme Court Justice Tom Clark as a "new fetish for indigency."[16]

What Kind of an Attorney Must Be Furnished?

The accused is entitled to the attorney of his choice, but only if he can pay the attorney. The lawyer has a right to refuse, unless he is appointed to serve by a court. Also, the defendant does not have a right to insist on a specific attorney, if this man is not available, or if it would unnecessarily impede or obstruct the court to wait until he is available.[17] The attorney is not required to lower his fees to accommodate a defendant.

When the courts say that an accused is entitled to an attorney, they do not mean that he can have a friend or acquaintance speak for him. The counsel must actually be an attorney.

Sometimes it is subsequently found out that the attorney who represented a defendant was not licensed to practice law in that jurisdiction. The courts are divided here; but it seems to be generally

15. Griffin v. Illinois, 351 US 12 (1956).
16. Douglas v. California, 372 US 353 (1963).
17. People v. Robinson, 222 Cal App 2d 602, 35 Cal Reptr 344.

held that if a man in question was actually an attorney, that this would suffice, even though he had no license that made him a member of the bar in that particular area.[18]

When the attorneys in a particular jurisdiction are appointed to serve indigents in rotation, the accused who cannot pay may be represented by the least experienced member of the bar or by the most talented criminal lawyer in the state. It should also be noted that the lawyer he draws will probably be a general practitioner who spends most of his time on civil cases, as most law practice centers around noncriminal matters.

Since the courts regulate the practice of law, no attorney can refuse to take his turn. This is one of the free services that is rendered to the public, and it may be very costly in lost time for the attorney.

As we have seen, some states require members of the bar to represent indigent criminal defendants, with all members of the bar taking these cases in turn. In recent years there has been a trend toward having the state give payments to attorneys who are required to assist these indigent defendants.

In most states where the bar members serve, the accused who claims that he cannot pay for an attorney is required to fill out an affidavit, swearing under oath that he does not have the money or property to afford a lawyer. If he swears falsely in this regard, the accused may be charged with perjury. As a practical matter, however, the machinery to investigate his claim of poverty is often inadequate.

Duties of the Appointed Attorney

A lawyer who is appointed by the court to represent an indigent is under the same obligation to his client as a lawyer who is furnished a regular fee.[19] He must put forth his best efforts on behalf of his client, giving his undivided loyalty to the accused. If it is apparent in the early stages of the trial that the accused's rights will not be protected by the court-appointed attorney, then the defendant is entitled to have the lawyer replaced.[20] In any event, a lawyer who does not properly serve in a situation of this kind must answer to the wrath of the judge.

18. People v. Cox, 146 NE 19, 12 Ill 2d 265; State v. Russell, 53 NW 441, 83 Wis 330.
19. Kent v. Sanford, 121 F 2d 216 cert denied (Further appeal denied), 315 US 799.
20. MacKenna v. Ellis, 368 US 877; U.S. v. Gutterman, 147 F 2d 540.

The Appointment of an
Incompetent Attorney

In general, the courts will not grant a new trial, based on proof that errors were overlooked by the attorney of the client's own choice. In addition, errors in the attorney's judgment, improper advice, or lack of preparation cannot be used to get a second trial. If, however, the attorney's representation of the accused is so lacking in presentation that it is nothing more than a mockery of justice, then the judgment will be declared void and a second trial granted.[21]

Accused individuals are not guaranteed the right to court-appointed attorneys who do not make mistakes, however. The accused is "stuck" for whatever mistake his lawyer makes, "if they are the kind of errors that are common to all human efforts."[22]

Tardy Appointment of an
Attorney by the Court

An attorney must be appointed for an indigent in sufficient time to allow the lawyer to prepare the case. If sufficient time has not been given, then the defendant has been deprived of his rights without due process of law.[23] Just how much time must be allowed will vary from case to case. Appointing an attorney on the day of the trial has been held to be equivalent to no counsel at all. Three days, however, has been held to be sufficient time, where there was no indication that the defense could have done anything more and where it was apparent that the accused was well-represented by his attorney.[24]

At What Stage of the Prosecution
Must an Attorney Be Provided?

Once it was decided that an attorney is required at the time of trial, the next question was when this right must be given. *In a series of widely publicized cases, the Supreme Court has held that the right to a lawyer extends to every stage of the prosecution.*

In *Hamilton* v. *Alabama*,[25] it was held that the accused was entitled to an attorney as early as the arraignment. In *White* v.

21. Lotz v. Sacks, 292 F 2d 657.
22. Rivera v. U.S., 318 F 2d, 606.
23. Reece v. Georgia, 350 US 85.
24. French v. State, 161 So 2d 879; Avery v. Alabama, 308 US 444.
25. Hamilton v. Alabama, 368 US 52 (1961).

Maryland,[26] the Supreme Court extended this right back to the time of the preliminary hearing. In *Escobedo* v. *Illinois,*[27] the right to an attorney was extended back to the time of the prearrest request of the accused to consult with his lawyer. In the equally celebrated case of *Miranda* v. *Arizona,*[28] the Supreme Court held that the interrogating police officer must warn a suspect that he has the right to an attorney and the right to remain silent, before questioning can begin. Judging from the decisions in these cases, it is apparent that an individual who is to be questioned must be advised of his rights as soon as any suspicion is directed at him.

In still another 1967 ruling, the Supreme Court held that juveniles also have the right to an attorney in criminal actions. Until the Gault case, some states had regarded some actions against juveniles as being custodial in nature, rather than as a criminal prosecution that required the services of an attorney.[29] The practical effect of this decision was to extend the right to an attorney to both the juvenile and his parent or guardian.

THE ACCUSED'S RIGHT TO STAY IN TOUCH WITH HIS LAWYER

If the right to an attorney is to be effective, then the accused must have the right to communicate and consult freely with his lawyer prior to trial, as well as during the trial. Details involving when and where consultations between prisoners and their lawyers may be conducted will vary with the circumstances of each case. Conferences with attorneys are within the discretion of the officer charged with custody of the prisoner, but this discretion must not be abused. It is subject to review by the courts. Clearly, a jail prisoner is not entitled to see his lawyer every hour on the hour. He must, however, be given enough time to prepare his defense. This may require a number of conferences. The prisoner, of course, does not have the right to interviews in a part of the jail where it may be possible for security to be breached. Nevertheless, he must be given ample time for conference, a place to write, and the opportunity to telephone the attorney at regular times.

26. White v. Maryland, 373 US 59 (1963).
27. Escobedo v. Illinois, 378 US 478 (1964).
28. Miranda v. Arizona, 384 US 436 (1966).
29. In re Gault, 387 US 1 (1967).

The Defense Attorney

The hours of interview must be at reasonable times, and interviews must conform to custodial regulations. Refusal to allow an interview to be conducted, except in the presence of the sheriff, has been held to be sufficient cause for dismissal of charges. Eavesdropping or secret recording by a jail employee or police officer would also be a deprivation of the right to an attorney.[30]

In *People* v. *Zammora,* the accused was forced to sit at a separate table from his attorney and could not readily communicate with his attorney at the time of trial. It was held that the accused had been deprived of his rights.[31]

The Right to Defend Without an Attorney

Occasionally, a defendant wants to act as his own defense attorney. Sometimes this is mere egotism. At other times the accused believes that no one else can match the intensity of the feelings that he or she wants to get across.

The federal courts have long allowed an accused person to act as his own lawyer, "provided he knows what he is doing and the choice is made with eyes open."[32] In state trials, the right of the defendant to represent himself is provided in the constitution of some of the states.[33] Until 1975, the courts in some states did not allow the accused to do without an attorney, even when the judge believed that the accused had a thorough understanding of the advantages of an attorney and understood the risks in dispensing with legal assistance.[34]

Many courts look with disfavor on the idea that a man may act as his own attorney. Many authorities feel that the layman may not understand all the fine points of legal procedure. In addition, the accused may be so emotionally involved that he cannot think as objectively as a defense attorney whose liberty is not at stake. In fact, lawyers sometimes quote the old legal saying that "an attorney who acts as his own lawyer has a fool for a client!"

30. State v. Cory, 382 P 2d 1019, 62 Wash 2d 371. Also, see State ex rel. Tucker v. Davis, 130 P 962. See also Klotter & Kanovitz, *Constitutional Law for Police,* (Cincinnati: The W. H. Anderson Co., 1968), p. 234.
31. People v. Zammora, 152 P 2d 180, 66 Cal App 2d 166.
32. Adams v. U.S., 317 US 269.
33. See the constitutions of Connecticut, Delaware, Massachusetts, Pennsylvania, and New Hampshire, for example.
34. People v. Sharp, 103 Cal Reptr 233, 499 P 2d 489.

In *Faretta* v. *California,*[35] decided in June 1975, the Supreme Court held that an accused has an absolute constitutional right to defend himself without a lawyer when he voluntarily and intelligently elects to do so. The Supreme Court pointed out that:

> It is undeniable that in most criminal prosecutions defendants could better defend with counsel's guidance than by their own unskilled efforts. But where the defendant will not voluntarily accept representation by counsel, the potential advantage of a lawyer's training and experience can be realized, if at all, only imperfectly. To force a lawyer on a defendant can only lead a defendant to believe that the law contrives against him. . . . And although he may conduct his own defense ultimately to his own detriment, his choice must be honored . . .

The Supreme Court did indicate, however, that the holding would not be the same if the accused did not have the basic intelligence to weigh the alternatives and understand the consequences of going to trial without an attorney. The Supreme Court also said, in an aside, that the right of self-representation would not be allowed as a method for a disruption of the trial[36] and that a "standby counsel" could be appointed by the court if the accused had a change of heart during the conduct of the trial.

Generally, a trial in which the defense is conducted by the accused is handled the same as if it had been directed by counsel, except that the judge may apply some of the technical rules less stringently.[37] The trial must always be handled under reasonable rules adopted by the court for orderly conduct.

The Defendant's Right to Conduct Part of the Defense

In the past, almost all courts have agreed that the accused should not be allowed to conduct only certain parts of his defense while delegating other parts to a defense attorney.[38] There may now be some doubt on this angle, as a result of the Faretta decision.

---

35. Faretta v. California, United States Supreme Court Cause Number 73-5775, decided June 30, 1975.
36. See People v. Burson, 143 NE 2d 239, 11 Ill 2d 360.
37. State v. Owens, 117 SE 536, 124 SC 220; Dietz v. State, 136 NW 166, 149 Wisc 462.
38. People v. McFerran, 211 Cal App 2d 4, 26 Cal Reptr 914.

WAIVER OF THE RIGHT
TO AN ATTORNEY

All courts agree that an accused may waive his right to an attorney. This must be done in a proper way, however, and the trial court which allows the waiver has a protective duty toward the accused. First, the court must make certain that the defendant understands the nature of the criminal charge that has been made against him. Then too, the judge must make certain that the accused realizes the pleas and defenses that may be available to him, the elements of the offense, and the full extent of the punishment that may be imposed upon him. In addition, the accused must be made to realize that he has the right to a lawyer, if he so desires.

All of this information is brought out by the judge or magistrate, who calls the defendant before him and questions him in great detail as to his understanding of these matters. Unless it is clear that the accused has a good understanding of each of these requirements, the judge will not accept his waiver.

If the defendant later claims that he was not fully aware of what was happening, the appellate courts consider a number of factors. These include his age, background, education, mental condition at the time, his experience, and the kind of conduct that he exhibited at the time of the claimed waiver.[39]

The Right to an Attorney for
One Accused of a Misdemeanor

We have observed that over the years the Supreme Court has extended the right of an indigent to an attorney in state prosecutions. First, the right was granted in cases where the accused was subject to a possible death penalty. Then, it was granted to any indigent in any felony prosecution in state court. But what about the right of the indigent to be represented where the criminal charge is a misdemeanor or a lesser grade of offense, such as a traffic violation?

The Sixth Amendment says that "In all criminal prosecutions the accused shall enjoy . . . the Assistance of Counsel." It is necessary to determine exactly what constitutes "criminal prosecution."

In the case of *Evans* v. *Rives*,[40] the federal court pointed out

39. Aiken v. U.S., 296 F 2d 604.
40. Evans v. Rives, 126 F 2d 633 (1942).

that the Constitution made no distinction between loss of liberty for a short period or for a long one. In *Harvey* v. *Mississippi,*[41] another federal case, the court held in effect that the constitutional right to an assigned attorney extends to a petty offense, with a maximum penalty of 90 days imprisonment. However, neither of these federal cases reached the Supreme Court.

In *People* v. *Letterio,*[42] though, the New York State courts upheld a conviction for ten moving traffic violations, even though an attorney was not supplied to the accused. The court pointed out that "There are, historically, certain minor transgressions which admit of summary disposition." What the New York court was saying was that you must draw the line somewhere, and that the courts must be practical. They cannot supply a lawyer for every minor traffic violation.

Just how far the Supreme Court will go in providing an attorney for indigents in misdemeanor cases or lesser offenses is still in doubt. When, and if, this does come before the Court, a number of legal scholars believe that some practical limits must be worked out. They point to the limit on the time of judges, the cost in lawyer manpower, and the amount of funds available to the courts.

THE RIGHT OF INDIGENTS TO AN ATTORNEY ON APPEAL

In *Douglas* v. *California,*[43] the defendants were tried and convicted in California state court. The procedure in California called for the California District Court of Appeal to then make an independent investigation of the record and determine whether it would be of advantage to the indigent defendants or helpful to the appellate court to have counsel appointed. This independent investigation was made and the appellate court ruled that there would be no advantage to the defendants to have an attorney appointed for them. This matter was then appealed to the federal courts, on the claim that constitutional rights had been denied. The Supreme Court then held that the defendants had an absolute right to an attorney on appeal. The full extent of this ruling is still a matter of conjecture to experts in constitutional law. It seems likely, however, that the states will be

41. Harvey v. Mississippi, 340 F 2d 263 (1965).
42. People v. Letterio, 213 NE 2d 670, 16 NY 2d 307 (1965).
43. Douglas v. California, 372 US 353 (1963).

required to furnish attorneys whenever there is an appeal by an indigent convict.

One of the problems that must be faced by the courts in the future is that an extremely high percentage of the appeals filed by convicted prisoners are without any basis. It costs nothing for the indigent to appeal and he always has an outside hope that he may get a new trial. If this should happen, the witnesses and the evidence originally used to convict him may now be scattered or unavailable. Requiring an attorney to be provided for each of these indigent appeals may place such a burden on the legal profession that the Supreme Court may be pressured into furnishing attorneys only when there seems to be some real basis for an appeal.

The Defendant's Right to Be Advised of Accusatory Information

It is basic law in all courts that the offense charged against an individual must be charged with all necessary certainty and clearness to inform the defendant of the crime of which he stands accused. The charge must be presented in sufficient detail to allow him to prepare his defense.

Also, the defendant must be informed of the accusation against him a reasonable amount of time before he is actually put on trial. The accused is also entitled to inspect the accusatory pleading before deciding whether to plead innocent or guilty.

In many jurisdictions, statutes or constitutional provisions give the defendant the right to a copy of the indictment or information against him. Some statutes require that a copy be given to the accused if he is in custody. If he is not being held in jail, he must pay a small fee for the copy.

THE LEGAL AID SOCIETY OR LEGAL AID FOUNDATION

Legal aid societies, or legal aid foundations, are to be found in many communities throughout this country. The goal of these societies is to provide quality legal services to those who are too poor to pay. The lawyers who serve these societies function exactly as they would for a paying client.

Historically, legal aid societies developed from the individual efforts of a few attorneys who realized that people may need money if a lawyer is necessary to protect their rights. Legal aid societies have functioned for more than fifty years in the larger cities, especially in the neighborhoods of established law schools.

Legal aid societies do not normally charge fees. In some areas the recipient of aid may be asked to pay whatever amount he can afford.

In some locations, the legal aid society provides assistance to poor individuals in either civil or criminal matters. This includes service as a defense attorney for the accused criminal who is unable to pay. If, however, there is a public defender's office in the area, the legal aid society restricts its services to civil matters only.

Usually, a central administrative office of the legal aid society handles the development, planning, operations, and administration of the organization. The Legal Aid Foundation of Los Angeles, for example, utilizes a central administrative office, with contact offices scattered throughout the neighborhoods where needy people reside.

The lawyers who provide free legal services are assigned to specific cases, under the coordination of a paid general counsel or attorney. In donating their services, these attorneys participate as a public service.

Volunteers figure prominently in an organization of this type. Frequently, young law students contribute clerical help, assist in interviewing those who seek help, and perform some administrative duties. An auxiliary, made up of lawyers' wives, may also perform many kinds of nontechnical assistance.

The eligibility of an applicant for legal aid is usually determined by the guidelines laid down by the individual society. Applicants who appear able to pay a fee are referred to a private attorney through the county bar association or through other legal referral services.

In the past, some funds for the operation of legal aid societies have come from the United Way, from the Legal Service Division of the Federal Office of Economic Opportunity, and from contributions made by the general public. Auxiliary groups of lawyers' wives have often been effective in raising funds.

In general, legal aid societies have been helpful, high-minded organizations, making a commendable effort to help those in need. There are some political implications almost any time federal funds are made available to local civic or political groups. Most legal aid societies that handle criminal cases make a substantial contribution to the administration of criminal justice.

125

The Defense Attorney

SUMMARY

Legal scholars sometimes say that both the prosecuting attorney and the defense attorney are officers of the court. It is clear, though, that the defense attorney is not held to the same standards as the prosecutor. As we know, the prosecutor must take all affirmative steps to make sure that justice is done to an accused man or woman. However, the defense attorney is not required to present any evidence except that which is favorable to the accused. In fact, the defense attorney can refuse to present any evidence, if he believes that this is the best strategy for the client. The obligation of the defendant's lawyer is to make sure that every available defense and every applicable right is used in the accused's behalf. The relationship between the defendant and his lawyer is confidential and the attorney never has the right to violate this confidence. The accused must be told that he has the right to an attorney, even if he is unable to pay for representation. In some areas, members of the bar are required by the courts to represent indigent defendants to the best of the attorney's ability. In other sections of the United States the accused who is unable to pay may be represented by a lawyer assigned by the legal aid society, or by the public defender's office. The defense attorney will be subject to discipline by the courts and by the bar association if he knowingly allows the accused or one of the witnesses to commit perjury. The attorney commits a crime by deliberately seeking false testimony. As a practical matter, however, this may be very difficult to prove.

QUESTIONS

1. What is the attorney-client privilege (or relationship)? Is this privilege for the benefit of the accused? Is it for the accused's attorney? For both? Explain.

2. Does the attorney-client relationship apply, even if the accused does not hire or use the lawyer that he interviewed when he was seeking an attorney?

3. Does the defense attorney ever have a duty to disclose information that will hurt or expose his client's case?

4. Is there a distinction between advice from the defense attorney as to what can lawfully be done, and advising how unlawful acts can be committed in a way to avoid conviction? Is a crime

involved in the attorney's activities in either instance? What is the name of the crime?

5. How does the public defender system work?

6. Under what circumstances may the legal aid society furnish an attorney for an accused defendant?

The awful instruments of the criminal law cannot be entrusted to a single functionary. The complicated processes of criminal justice are therefore divided into different parts, responsibility for which is separately vested in the various participants upon whom the criminal law relies for its vindication.

Justice Felix Frankfurter, United States Supreme Court, in *McNabb v. United States,* 318 US 332 (1943)

chapter eight

STATE AND FEDERAL REGULATORY AGENCIES

A number of state and federal regulatory agencies handle highly specific regulations and laws. Usually, this is because the laws involved are somewhat unique and investigation and enforcement may be difficult without specialization.

The purpose of this chapter is to examine some of the typical responsibilities and problems encountered by these regulatory agencies.

ALCOHOLIC BEVERAGE CONTROL

Most states utilize a specialized department or bureau to handle the licensing and control of the sale and consumption of alcoholic beverages. California, for example, set up a Department of Alcoholic Beverage Control in 1955, by constitutional and statutory enactments. The stated purpose of the California Alcohol Beverage Control Department (ABC) is:

> an exercise of the police powers of the State for the protection of the safety, welfare, health, peace and morals of the people of the State, to eliminate the evils of unlicensed and unlawful manufacture, selling, and disposing of alcoholic beverages, and to promote temperance in the use and consumption of alcoholic beverages.[1]

1. Article XX, Section 22 California Constitution and Section 23001 Business and Professions Code.

To further this cause, the California ABC licenses and regulates the manufacture, sale, purchase, possession and importation of alcoholic beverages within the state, subject to the laws of the United States. Agents of the ABC enforce the law by investigating the moral fitness of applicants for bar licenses, and, after the license is granted, by enforcing appropriate statutory requirements.

For example, drinks may not be served to persons under the minimum drinking age of twenty-one years. If complaints of a possible violation are received, an investigation is conducted. If facts are developed indicating substantial evidence, an accusation is filed against the licensee. This usually leads to discipline or suspension of the license.

ABC agents serve the public by ensuring that only the true party in interest is licensed, and that once granted, the licensee operates under the provisions of the law while serving the public. An agency such as the ABC is a service agency, extending aid both to the public and the licensees, endeavoring to enforce the law fairly and impartially. Most states have an agency that operates in similar fashion to the California Alcoholic Beverage Control Department.

PUBLIC UTILITIES COMMISSION AND STATE RAILROAD COMMISSION

Many states have either a Public Utilities Commission or a State Railroad Commission. Originating because of the need to regulate railroad traffic, the California Railroad Commission eventually changed its name to the Public Utilities Commission.

These agencies usually handle the regulation and licensing for railroads, passenger busses, trucks, airlines, and vessels transporting freight or passengers within the state. Carriers which are considered "for hire" are also included. On the federal level, the Interstate Commerce Commission (ICC) regulates transportation between the states.

These commissions usually have responsibility for regulating the sale, distribution, and usage of public utilities, including gas, electric, telephone, water, steam heat utilities, and sewage collection companies. The firms that produce utilities usually have a monopoly and the public would be subjected to excessive rates if regulation was not undertaken.

It is the duty of these commissions to provide adequate service to the public at rates that are fair and reasonable, both to customers and to shareholders of the public utility. Present rates are presumed to be fair and reasonable until proved otherwise. If an application for an increase in rates is filed, the burden of proof is always on the utility company to show that additional revenue is needed to provide a fair return.

Public hearings are held and evidence is introduced by the company. The witnesses who present this evidence may be cross-examined and their claims disputed by members of the public or by representatives of the Public Utilities Commission. The commission then obtains facts and studies by engineers, accountants, rate experts, and others with specialized knowledge. When all the evidence has been heard, the commission takes the case under advisement. After due deliberation, a decision for or against a rate increase is made.

These commissions set up regulations for the use of public highways and transportation facilities. They also take steps to see that companies do not take advantage of persons needing transportation or access to public utilities.

Some of these commissions, such as the Texas State Railroad Commission, regulate the conservation and production of oil fields and natural gas, coal mining, and the removal of natural resources. Oil reserves, for example, may be rapidly depleted by producing all the oil that can be pumped. By regulating production, the eventual recovery from an oil field may be increased considerably.

FEDERAL COMMUNICATIONS COMMISSION (FCC)

The Federal Communications Commission (FCC) regulates interstate and international communications by means of television, radio, wire (telegrams and telegraph), and submarine cable. The commission assigns bands of radio frequencies to radio services and individual broadcasting stations. The commission also licenses and regulates radio services and radio operators. In addition, the commission regulates common carriers involved in interstate and international communications by telephone and telegraph. Another activity of the FCC is to promote safety through the use of radio on land, by ships at sea, and by commercial and private planes.

The commission can hold hearings and discipline or regulate those users who do not conform to statutory law or administrative regulations that have the force of law. The FCC allocates bands of frequencies to nongovernment communications services and assigns frequencies to individual radio and TV stations. The FCC also licenses and regulates stations and operators. This agency assigns

131

radio telephone circuits and facilities that are used by common carriers such as trucks, microwave facilities for the telephone company, and other communications systems.

The FCC is charged with the domestic administration of telecommunications provisions of international treaties and agreements. Airliners in interstate traffic fall into this category.

At various times, the FCC has been handled by the U. S. Department of Commerce, the Post Office Department, the Interstate Commerce Commission, and the Federal Radio Commission. Since 1934 the FCC has been an independent federal agency, reporting directly to Congress.

FEDERAL AVIATION ADMINISTRATION

As early as 1926, a federal law called the Air Commerce Act directed the United States Secretary of Commerce to promote air commerce, regulate it in the interest of safety, and promote aids to navigation. From that date on, pilots and aircraft have had to be inspected and certified by the Federal Government. This certification qualified both pilots and aircraft to fly. This series of laws has been revised several times in the last half century.

World War II spurred the development of aviation. By the end of the war, airlines were expanding in all directions and technological resources had made great strides. With the development of jet engines, the commercial airlines became the most important factor in the transportation industry.

The Federal Aviation Administration is charged with the regulation and administration of both commercial traffic and private aircraft. Flight schools, ground schools, and mechanic's schools are certificated, as are the instructors who teach in them. Pilot proficiency is checked regularly and planes are not allowed to fly unless they are deemed airworthy. Airways and airports are also controlled and regulated. The Federal Aviation Administration (FAA) conducts a comprehensive health program to make sure that the nation's air traffic controllers are physically and mentally fit.[2]

The FAA also conducts research to enhance safety through improvements in design, utility, and efficiency of the airspace system and aircraft. Much of this regulation and enforcement is highly

2. *Federal Aviation Administration*, (Washington, D.C.: United States Government Printing Office), 1971.

132

technical in nature. It is handled by technically trained officials and inspectors hired by the FAA, and is outside the scope of regular police officials or officers.

FEDERAL SECURITY AGENCIES

The Federal Bureau of Investigation (FBI) handles the bulk of federal criminal violations. In addition, the FBI has jurisdiction over federal security violations within the United States. This includes foreign espionage conducted inside this country, sabotage, and the investigation of individuals or groups that are alleged to be subversive, or acting as secret agents of a foreign power.

The Central Intelligence Agency (CIA) has jurisdiction to handle espionage, sabotage, or subversive activities outside the territorial limits of the United States. If an investigation involves angles inside the United States as well as activities outside, then the FBI and CIA coordinate their individual investigative activities.

STATE REGULATORY AND LICENSING BOARDS

Innocent people may be harmed if an unqualified individual claiming to be a medical doctor prescribes dangerous drugs without regard for the consequences. As early as 1879, the California State Legislature set up a Board of Medical Examiners. Eventually, regulatory and licensing boards were set up to protect the public in other fields. The state took the position that only those firms and individuals who possess the necessary education and demonstrated skills to perform their services should be licensed.

There are now over a million individuals in the professions in California. They work in over 100 occupations as varied as auto repairmen, building contractors, beauticians, private investigators, and tax preparers. The demand for better protection of the consumer has so increased that it has become necessary to regulate the practice of all these varied occupations.

Licensing Boards of the California Department of Consumer Affairs have the authority to determine the qualifications of applicants for licenses, to give examinations, to issue licenses, and to regulate these occupations by means of inspections, investigations, and formal disciplinary action.

In most states, the bureaus charged with responsibility in these

133

areas are: the Department of Consumer Affairs, the State Department of Registration and Education, the Consumer Affairs Council, and the Department of Professional and Vocational Standards.

In Illinois, the State Department of Registration and Education revoked forty-seven professional licenses and suspended fifty-one others in the thirteen months prior to August 1975. For example, the Illinois department revoked the licenses of four pharmacists and suspended ten others during that period. All of those disciplined were involved in some degree in operating pill mills—selling drugs illegally over the counter. Two medical doctors had their medical licenses revoked and two others had their licenses suspended when they were convicted of crimes or involved in malpractice resulting in death or bodily injury to patients Accountants who manipulated books for embezzlers or swindlers were also the subjects of revocation procedures.

STATE LABOR COMMISSION; STATE COMPENSATION

All states have a state labor commission or authority which is charged with protecting workers from dangerous or unwarranted hazards. State labor laws guarantee all workers certain basic rights.[3] These include: prompt and full payment of wages; fair and impartial treatment by the employer; certain rights while being hired; and fair treatment to discharged employees, or those who want to leave.

Most states have very specific laws relating to the time, place, and manner of payment of employee wages. Employers who fail to comply to these laws must pay penalties. These penalties may be both civil and criminal in nature. Other labor laws regulate minimum wage scales, provide benefits to employees injured or killed in the course of their employment, and set standards for leaving the job.

The investigation and enforcement of these laws relating to labor are usually handled by investigators and boards of the state department of labor, the state department of industrial relations, the State Compensation Commission, and similar boards. The criminal provisions of these laws are seldom, if ever, handled by regular police officers.

---

3. *Facts for the California Employer,* published by State of California, Division of Labor Standards Enforcement, State Department of Industrial Relations. See also *State Labor Law* and *Worker's Compensation Insurance,* published by the same department, State of California.

THE DEPARTMENT OF MOTOR VEHICLES (DMV)

Although there are some variations in the name, all states have a Department of Motor Vehicles (DMV). This agency performs a number of vital functions in regulating and controlling the usage of automobiles.

The invention and improvement of the so-called "horseless carriage" was a noteworthy development. Speedy individual transit was welcomed but serious concern soon moved in beside enthusiasm for the motor vehicle. Without government controls, it was apparent that the new device would become a monster on wheels. Early lawmakers tried to reduce the tragedies that resulted from misuse of vehicles while still allowing people to enjoy the benefits of the open road. As a result, state legislatures began the licensing of automobile drivers.

The present-day DMV is a regulatory agency, testing drivers and granting or withholding the privilege of driving on the state's roads and highways. This regulation of drivers protects the lives of every other individual who operates a motor vehicle. All drivers have to prove their ability in order to obtain a license.[4]

The power of the DMV to suspend a driver's license has been challenged but has been uniformly upheld by the courts. Most states have also compiled considerable information about the negligent driver and have been empowered by state statutes to require driver attendance at corrective schools where warranted. They can also place other restrictions on driving.

The free movement of passenger cars across state lines has been encouraged under a set of reciprocity laws. One state grants outside motorists the right to move freely on its highways, provided these individuals have been properly registered in another state. This reciprocity requires no additional fees or taxes in the state where the travel is done. Today, almost all states have reciprocity agreements with other states and some Canadian provinces.

The regulation of vehicle ownership is another valuable service performed by the DMV. Records of this agency establish ownership and provide protection in cases of theft, fraud, or other actions that could lead to loss of property. For example, in California every vehicle is registered in DMV files in three ways: by license plate number, by registered owner's name, and by engine or serial

4. See *California's DMV*, published by State of California Department of Motor Vehicles, 1971.

135

number. A history of each vehicle is maintained, including former owners, legal and registered owners, and a record of engine or body modifications. This data is centrally located in a master file in Sacramento.

A stolen or abandoned car can be identified within minutes from any point in the state by teletype, radio, or telephone. A network of computers ties directly into the DMV records. In some states an automobile license plate can be transferred to the owner's new car, but in California and a number of other jurisdictions the plate remains with the vehicle until it is junked.

SUMMARY

There are a number of state and federal regulatory agencies that handle highly specialized laws and regulations. It is usually simpler for administrators and criminal investigators of these agencies to cooperate in a common endeavor than to call in regular law enforcement officials. These regulatory agencies therefore handle the criminal law problems that arise from their administrative regulations. Law enforcement officers should have a broad knowledge of the powers, responsibilities, and criminal violations that should be referred to these agencies for handling.

Practically all states look to the Department of Alcoholic Beverage Control (ABC) for the licensing of bars and liquor sales agencies. The ABC is also responsible for the criminal enforcement of laws concerning the sale, manufacture, and disposal of alcoholic beverages. Similarly, the states utilize a Public Utilities Commission or State Railroad Commission, Consumer Affairs Council or State Department of Registration and Education, State Labor Commission or State Compensation Commission, and Department of Motor Vehicles. On the federal level, the Federal Communications Commission, Federal Aviation Administration, and other agencies regulate individual problems.

QUESTIONS

1. List the names of five state and federal regulatory agencies in your area. Do all agencies have their own agency enforcement officers?

2. List the classes of information usually available from your state Department of Motor Vehicles.

3.   Most states look to a State Department of Alcoholic Beverage
      Control for licensing of bars and liquor sales agencies, as well
      as enforcement of laws concerning the sale, manufacture, and
      disposal of alcoholic beverages. What are the advantages to a
      system of this kind? List any disadvantages that may develop
      from this system, or explain why you feel there are no
      disadvantages.

4.   What types of criminal violations are usually handled by the
      State Labor Commissioner or Labor Department? List the types
      of criminal violations usually investigated and handled by the
      five state and federal regulatory agencies listed in question 1.

. . . the judiciary . . . is the balance wheel of
the entire [justice] system, preserving an
adjustment between individual rights and
governmental powers.

**Justice Willis Van Devanter, United
States Supreme Court, in *Evans* v.
Gore, 253 US 245 (1920)**

chapter nine

THE COURTS

The purpose of this chapter is to describe how the state and federal court systems are set up. The duties and responsibilities of the courts and court officials will be explained. This chapter will also explore how matters reach the courts, the workings of the courts, how criminal matters are tried, and how appeals are taken to a higher court.

HOW THE COURTS DEVELOPED AS PART OF THE JUSTICE SYSTEM

Thousands of years ago men learned that they could survive individually only by living under the structure of an organized government. The courts have long been a part of this governmental framework. We can define a court as an agency set up by government to define and apply the law, to order its enforcement, and to settle disputed points on which individuals or groups do not agree.

All of the procedures in the administration of justice revolve around the court system. If an individual is believed to have violated the law, the concern is to bring that person before the courts in a proper manner, to provide him a trial in court, and to follow through with the disposition or judgment made by the court.[1]

1. Roscoe Pound, *Justice According to Law*, (New Haven: Yale University Press, 1952), pp. 89–91.

In primitive law, the government had two basic purposes: to preserve the peace and to prevent the use of force by one person against another individual or that individual's property. The system in ancient England was to make a personal complaint to the king that one's person had been injured or that his property had been harmed. Over a period of time there were so many of these complaints that the king could not hear them all, so he set up personal representatives or judges throughout the country to dispense justice.

In time, there was a separation between criminal law and civil law. Criminal law deals with activities that work to the injury of society in general, and the civil law, or law of torts, deals with personal or property injury.

Today, criminal courts decide cases brought by the state or federal government against persons thought to be guilty of crime. Modern civil courts try cases brought by one individual or company against another individual or company, seeking a money award or a court injunction (order) prohibiting further injury.

There is still an affinity between the criminal law and the civil law. Both types of law deal with wrongs. In a number of cases an act may be a wrong both to the state as a criminal violation, and to a specific individual as a civil wrong.

AUTHORIZATION FOR SETTING UP THE COURT SYSTEMS

The authorization for setting up the federal courts is set forth in the United States Constitution, Article III, Section 1:

> The judicial power of the United States, shall be vested in one Supreme Court, and in such inferior Courts as the Congress may from time to time ordain and establish. The Judges, both of the supreme and inferior Courts, shall hold their Offices during good behavior, and shall, at stated times, receive for their Services a Compensation which shall not be diminished during their Continuance in office.

In addition, the Constitution provides for the appointment of judges by the President, with the consent of the Senate. The term "good behavior" means that appointments are virtually for life, since a federal judge can be removed from office only by an impeachment trial.

The framers of the Constitution set up only a broad outline as to how the courts should be established, making no claim that they had the moral right or all-seeing wisdom to set up strict limitations. The Constitution did specify that there would be a Chief Justice, but said nothing about the qualifications of the judges and the size of the court. There are nine judges on the court at the present time, and in the past the number has been six, seven, and ten. The number of judges on the United States Court of Appeals varies with the nature and number of the cases to be handled. Generally, one judge hears a case in a federal district court, while three circuit judges hear cases in a court of appeals. Judges of the Supreme Court are usually referred to as Justices.

The Constitution provision against decreasing a federal judge's salary was designed to preserve the independence of the judicial department from Congressional control.

Each of the fifty states has a court system established by the state constitution to enforce the criminal laws, or penal code, of that particular state. There are minor differences between practically all of the states, but most of the state courts fall into two broad classifications. The majority of the states are organized into a three-tiered system, similar to that of the federal government. How these systems work will be considered in a subsequent part of this chapter.

THE FUNCTIONS OF THE COURTS

A court of *first instance*, or a court of *original jurisdiction*, is the court that has the right to hear the case when it is first brought. These are other names for the *trial court*.

There are two completely separate court systems in the United States. One is maintained by the Federal Government and the other by the individual states, but both have trial courts and appellate courts.

A trial court almost always utilizes only one judge who applies the law to the particular case. He is assisted by a jury in deciding matters that may be in dispute. The facts are determined on the basis of evidence presented in court. The *judge* and the *court* are terms that may be used interchangeably in referring to the trial court judge.

A court of record is one that uses a court reporter, or stenographer, to take down the exact words said during the trial. This includes the testimony of witnesses, the statements and motions

141

made verbally by the attorneys, and the comments and verbal instructions of the judge. All of this is called the transcript of the trial, and it serves as a basis for claims of error to the appellate court. The appellate court reviews this record to determine whether the trial was fairly conducted. Most so-called lower, or inferior, courts, such as magistrate's courts, police courts, and justice of the peace courts do not maintain a stenographic record as to what occurred during the trial.

APPELLATE (REVIEW) COURTS

If the accused in a criminal trial can show that he was not given a fair trial, or if he has grounds to feel that he was wrongfully convicted, then he may appeal to a higher court. The higher court may be referred to as a review court.

The appellate court can let the conviction stand, if the decision seems to have been reached in a fair manner. The appellate court can also order the release of the convicted person, under some circumstances, or order a new trial in certain other situations.

This authority of the higher ranking court, or court of appeal, is usually called appellate jurisdiction. These higher courts will usually handle appeals from trial courts over a wide territorial area or from a large metropolitan area.

There is no jury at the appellate level, and all decisions here are limited to errors of law—that is, to incorrect applications of the law by the trial court judge. A higher court will not review disputes or mere conflicts of the facts that appear from the evidence. Neither will the appellate court weigh the facts presented by one side against those presented by the other. It must be shown, however, that sufficient credible facts were presented in the evidence for a jury to have concluded that the accused was guilty, if the decision was based on that evidence.

In all criminal courts, the person convicted has the right to appeal, provided he can spell out some reasonable grounds to indicate that he was wronged or unfairly convicted. The prosecution, however, has a very narrow right of appeal in most states.

It should also be noted that appellate courts do not reverse a case, thereby allowing a new trial, for every error. As a general rule, the convicted individual must be able to show that a different result might have been reached had the trial court not allowed the pre-

sentation of the improper evidence. A harmless error will not result in a new trial.

The appellate court may examine all or part of the written record, or transcript, of what happened at the trial. The court will then render a written opinion, which will affirm or strike down the trial court's conviction. Reasons for the decision of the appellate court are also included in the opinion.

If it is found that some of the damaging evidence against the accused should not have been permitted during the trial, the appellate court will "reverse and remand" the matter. This means that the case will be sent back to the trial court for a completely new trial. In the second trial, the prosecution will not be allowed to use the tainted evidence. If, after the tainted evidence is removed, there is not sufficient evidence on which a jury can reasonably convict the accused, then the appellate court will "reverse" the case without a new trial. The court will then order the acquittal, or release, of the convicted individual.

The granting of a new trial by an appellate court puts the parties in the same position as if no trial had been held. All the evidence must be introduced again, and the parties and attorneys are not allowed to make any reference whatever to the former trial.[2]

Some Judicial Philosophy

The courts state that it is their aim to prevent crime through the operation of the judicial process. Congress and the state legislatures pass laws, and it is then the business of the courts to interpret and enforce those laws. The purpose of the system is to assure all citizens of the right to life, liberty, and the pursuit of happiness, while protecting them from the criminal activity of other persons.

It is also the duty of the courts to protect the individual against tyranny. There are times when the facts so clearly indicate guilt that it seems a waste of time to hold a trial. It must be remembered, though, that not one bit of guilt can attach to anyone until the accused has had his day in court and the proof shows more than reasonable doubt. The court must therefore protect individual lib-

2. See "Appeals by the Prosecution" in John C. Klotter and Jacqueline R. Kanovitz, *Constitutional Law for Police,* (Cincinnati: The W. H. Anderson Co., 1968), p. 268. Only three states—Connecticut, Vermont, and Wisconsin—have statutes conferring on the government a right of appeal substantially equal to that of the accused. Conn. Gen. Stat. Rev., S. 54–96 (1959); Vt. Stat. Ann. tit. 13, S. 7403 (1959) and Wisc. Stat. Ann., S. 958.12(1)(d) (1958).

erties, as "the history of liberty has largely been the history of observance of procedural safeguards."[3] The courts must strike a balance, then, in striving to protect the general public and the accused from tyranny while still holding the individual responsible for his own acts.

In a developed legal system, the judge must keep two factors in mind when working on a case. First, he must try to attain justice in that particular case, and second, he must attain this justice in accordance with acceptable legal principles. Under the English and American legal doctrine known as *stare decisis,* a judge decides a case in light of principles evolved from earlier decisions. There is an overriding policy in Anglo-American law for the courts to preserve stability. This is so that lawyers and ordinary citizens alike can know that they are conducting themselves within the law, and can understand and anticipate what is expected of individuals and institutions.

STRUCTURE OF COURT SYSTEMS

The Federal Government has a three-tiered, or three-level court structure. The federal district courts are the federal courts of original jurisdiction, handling criminal trials and civil matters that get into the federal system.

The United States Courts of Appeals have review or appellate jurisdiction over a circuit of United States District Courts. Most circuits include lower courts from several states. Cases are generally heard by three or more judges, with three being the usual number assigned. On each of these courts, a senior judge is designated as chief judge. In addition to appeals from the United States District Courts, the United States Court of Appeals may accept appeals from federal administrative agencies and federal regulatory commissions.

While there are nine Justices on the United States Supreme Court, six of these judges may constitute a quorum, with no less than four concurring to reach a valid decision.

The United States Supreme Court has both original and appellate jurisdiction, and is the only federal court in the system that has both kinds of authority. As to original jurisdiction, the Supreme Court has the power to hear disputes: (1) between two or more states, (2) between the Federal Government and one or more states, (3) cases involving certain foreign diplomatic officials, and (4) mat-

. Justice Felix Frankfurter of the United States Supreme Court, speaking for the majority in McNabb v. U.S., 318 US 332, 63 S Ct 608 (1943).

FEDERAL COURTS

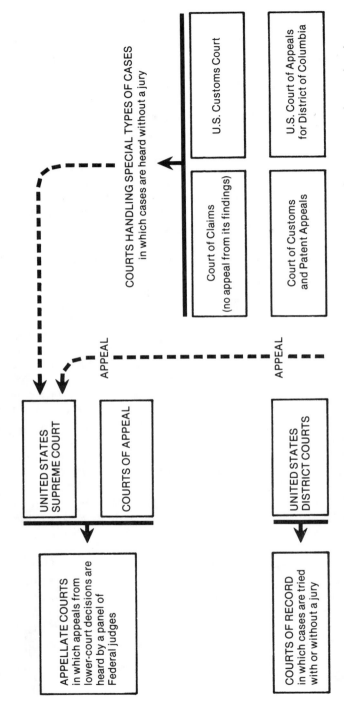

COURTS HANDLING SPECIAL TYPES OF CASES
in which cases are heard without a jury

Court of Claims
(no appeal from its findings)

U.S. Customs Court

Court of Customs
and Patent Appeals

U.S. Court of Appeals
for District of Columbia

UNITED STATES
SUPREME COURT

COURTS OF APPEAL

APPEAL

APPEAL

UNITED STATES
DISTRICT COURTS

APPELLATE COURTS
in which appeals from
lower-court decisions are
heard by a panel of
Federal judges

COURTS OF RECORD
in which cases are tried
with or without a jury

Figure 9–1   The Structure of the Federal Courts. (At the present time there are eleven United States courts of appeal and eighty-eight United States District Courts in the federal system.)

ters in dispute between a state and a foreign country or one state and the resident of another state.

The United States Supreme Court has appellate jurisdiction over cases tried in the lower federal courts. The Supreme Court also has appellate jurisdiction over the highest state courts when questions of the U.S. Constitution are involved.

In addition to the federal district courts, there are some other federal courts that handle specialized matters. These include the Court of Claims, the U.S. Customs Court, and the Court of Customs and Patent Appeals. For all practical purposes, most criminal prosecutions in the federal system begin in the federal district courts.

It should be realized, however, that the framers of the U.S. Constitution did not seek to restrict the courts for future generations. They had the good sense to know that the needs of society would change. The words of the Constitution were as specific as they could be in setting up general principles, but it was left to the Supreme Court as to how constitutional guidelines should be interpreted in future situations. Accordingly, the Supreme Court may reverse a decision that has been settled law for several generations. This does not happen because the Court is unaware as to what the law has been, but rather, because the Court has become aware of changing social needs and pressures.

In speaking of this flexible approach, Chief Justice Hughes of the Supreme Court once remarked that the Constitution means what the Supreme Court says it means at that given time. In a somewhat similar vein, President Woodrow Wilson remarked that the Supreme Court is somewhat like a constitutional convention in continuous session.

In recent years, only disputes between the states have come to the United States Supreme Court on original jurisdiction. Most cases arise under the Court's appellate jurisdiction, after they have been carried through a United States Court of Appeals or the highest state court having jurisdiction to hear a criminal case. Congress has specified that the Supreme Court should hear all cases in which a lower federal court has held any state or federal law unconstitutional, or in which a state court has upheld a state law against the claim that it violated the U.S. Constitution or a federal law.

Since 1925, other matters have reached the Supreme Court on a writ of *certiorari*.* An embittered defendant may petition the Court for a writ, and the case will be heard if four Justices feel that the case

*See Glossary.

has merit. Most appeals that are accepted fall into one of the following categories:

1. Cases that involve a substantial constitutional question;
2. Matters of sufficient national importance;
3. Situations in which there are conflicting decisions of the lower courts; or
4. An important private right is involved.

By withholding or granting *certiorari,* the Court controls the number and kind of cases that will be considered. If approval is granted, the members of the Court study the transcript as to what transpired in the trial court and in the appellate courts along the way. Oral arguments are then heard by the attorney for the defendant, or appellant, and written briefs are studied. A vote is then held, and if there is a no majority the decision of the lower court is upheld. The practice followed is for the Chief Justice to assign one of the Justices who voted with the majority to prepare a written opinion. The Chief Justice, himself, takes his turn in this function. If the Chief Justice does not agree with the majority, then it falls on the Senior Associate Justice on the majority to assign the writing of the opinion. Any Justice who is in the minority has the right to submit a written opinion, or to remain silent. In some instances, a Justice on the majority may submit an individual opinion, concurring with the majority for differing reasons. Some of the most vigorous dissenting opinions may foreshadow a changing opinion if the matter is again considered.

Decisions of the United States Supreme Court are binding on the lower courts in both the state and federal systems. From time to time the Court overrides its own opinions. While the courts like to follow precedent, a change may be necessary to make the law consistent with the needs of a changing society.

Not all attorneys can appear before the United States Supreme Court. Those who are licensed as members of the local bar must file special applications with the Supreme Court, and another attorney who has already been admitted to practice before the Supreme Court must recommend the applicant.

After listening to the attorneys for both sides in a Supreme Court case, the Justices retire to their chambers to discuss it in secret. Witnesses are never called before the Supreme Court, since the decision is based solely on the evidence that was brought up in the record from the lower court. After the pros and cons of the case are discussed, the Chief Justice calls for a vote. The opinion in every case, both concurring and dissenting, is then read in a public session of the Court and is published in the United States Reports. United States Reports are abbreviated in legal citations as "US." A citation such as "439 US 537" would mean that a case was reported in Volume 439 of the United States Reports on page 537.

The Supreme Court will never render an advisory opinion—that is, the Court will not give an opinion about something that might happen in the future. The decision reached must involve a question that is squarely before the Court at the time. The Court will not give advice, and it will not act in a friendly, nonadversary situation. Likewise, the Court will not anticipate a constitutional question before it actually comes in issue before the lower courts. Also, the Court will not pass on the validity of a statute on the complaint of an individual who fails to show injury in the application for judicial review. Before a case may be heard by the full Court, it must be reviewed briefly by a Justice assigned to a geographical area of the United States. He must first be satisfied that a substantial constitutional question could be involved.

It should also be realized that a decision of the Supreme Court is not controlling for all time. An opinion of the Court must be considered the law of the land, but it can be overturned by a subsequent decision on the same point. As stated by Justice Felix Frankfurter in his book, *The Business of the Supreme Court*, ". . . great judiciary acts, unlike great poems, are not written for all time."

An opinion of the Supreme Court can, of course, be overriden by the adoption of a new constitutional amendment. This has been done, however, only four times in the history of the nation.

Virtually every law is likely to be repealed or changed someday. However, no individual has the right to decide that a particular law has no moral significance to him, and that he will not obey it. Likewise, a policeman or parole official must obey the law, whether or not he is in sympathy with that particular enactment. The lower courts are expected to uphold the law that has been decided by the appellate courts. Law and order cannot prevail unless the conformity is accepted by private citizens and public officials alike.

STRUCTURE OF STATE COURT SYSTEMS

Most of the states utilize court systems that are modeled after the federal structure. The intermediate court of appeals is positioned between the trial court and the court of last resort. Thus, states like

California and Illinois utilize a three-tiered system. A few other states, such as Kentucky and Kansas, have a two-level structure. In the latter system, appeals are made directly from the trial court to the court of last resort.

Texas has a three-tiered system to handle appeals in civil lawsuits but has only a two-tiered system to handle criminal cases. Under this setup, there are no appeals from the Texas Court of Criminal Appeals to the Texas Supreme Court.

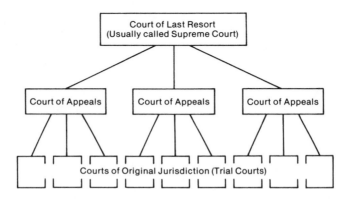

Figure 9–2   Example of a Typical Three-Tiered State Court System.

In the typical situation, an appeal goes from the state trial court to the appellate court that is next in line. In a two-tiered system this is the state supreme court or state court of last resort. In a three-tiered system, a convicted person can then ask the state supreme court, or court of last resort, to grant a hearing. There is no absolute right of appeal to the supreme court in most states. Usually, the state supreme court will hear the matter only if a significant legal question of public importance is involved.

After carrying an appeal through the state court system, an individual can request a hearing from the United States Supreme Court. A hearing will not be granted, however, unless the accused has first exhausted his appeals through the state court system. The United States Supreme Court Justices know that they do not have time to consider every frivolous appeal that may be made, and that most of these cases will be settled by the state courts. When an appeal is allowed by the United States Supreme Court, it must involve a matter which is a substantial problem of United States

Constitutional law. The problem must also be of sufficient gravity as to be of general interest.

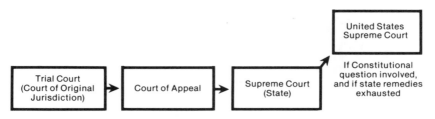

Figure 9–3   Appeal from Felony Conviction in Three-Tiered Court System. (Typical of California and Illinois Courts.)

Local Courts, or Courts of Limited Jurisdiction

To this point our examination of the courts has centered around the superior courts, or trial courts of general jurisdiction, and courts of appeal. All of the state court systems have so-called inferior courts, or courts of limited jurisdiction. These are the local courts, called justice courts, municipal courts, city courts, or magistrate's courts. They have authority to hear criminal cases that are considered minor in nature. Some states have small claims courts to handle civil lawsuits of a minor nature. Criminal actions in the inferior courts are usually limited to minor traffic matters, misdemeanors, or preliminary examinations of felony cases.

Appeals are seldom taken from the actions of inferior courts, usually because the time and money involved may not seem to be justified. When an appeal is taken from the ruling of a municipal court or justice court in California, it is heard by a three-judge appellate department of the superior court.

In most states, criminal jurisdiction is determined according to whether the charge is a misdemeanor or a felony. In civil cases the monetary value involved in the dispute determines jurisdiction. The state courts of original jurisdiction hold the power of review, or appeal, over courts of limited jurisdiction in almost all states.

ADMINISTRATION OF THE COURTS

Exercising the authority granted in the U.S. Constitution, Congress has established federal courts according to need. The administration of these courts, however, has remained under the control of the

Supreme Court. Some of this control is inherent in the power of the Court, and some control derives from legislation passed by Congress.
As stated by Justice Felix Frankfurter of the Supreme Court:

> In the exercise of its supervisory authority over the administration of criminal justice in the federal courts, this court has, from the very beginning of its history, formulated rules . . . to be applied in federal criminal prosecutions . . .[4]

In addition to regulating how federal trials shall be conducted from the standpoint of evidence, the Supreme Court has retained administrative control. In addition, in 1958 Congress authorized the Federal Judicial Conference, which was directed toward improvement of the administration of the federal court system. This group meets at least once a year and is composed of judges from the district courts, courts of appeal, and the Chief Justice of the United States Supreme Court.

The Administrative Office of the United States Courts, under a director appointed by the Supreme Court, is responsible for the supervision of court employees and the preparation and handling of a budget. Administrative Offices of the Courts have also been set up in several states to organize and administer judicial business.

COURT OFFICERS AND THEIR DUTIES

A judge is the chief administrative officer of a court. He is in charge of proceedings, and he makes decisions as to all questions of law or discretion. The judge may have a number of officials who assist him, depending on the nature and functions of the court.

A bailiff is a special kind of police officer whose duties are completely court-related. He preserves order in the courtroom, under the direction of the judge. He calls court into session and handles the security and confinement of prisoners. He may transport prisoners between the courtroom and the place of confinement.

The clerk of the court is a clerical or stenographic assistant to the judge. He prepares and maintains court records and serves as the custodian of fines and filing fees.

The court reporter is the stenographer who takes down a

4. McNabb v. United States, 318 US 332, 63 S Ct 608 (1943).

transcript of testimony, motions, and comments of witnesses and participants in a trial. It is this transcript that is reviewed by the appellate court when a matter comes up on appeal. Quite obviously, a court reporter must have unusual stenographic or recording skills to keep up with some of the animated exchanges that occur in the courtroom.

In some courts a recorder is a clerk who makes a record of documents, such as property deed records, that are subject to filing in the court records. In some other courts, a recorder is a type of magistrate.

A magistrate is an officer who has been given power to issue a warrant of arrest for a person charged with a criminal offense. This is a statutory designation in most states, such as California, where the following officials are magistrates (for the purpose of issuing warrants of arrest):

- Justices of the state supreme court
- Judges of the district courts of appeal
- Judges of the superior court
- Judges of the municipal courts
- Judges of the justice courts.

The sheriff is principal executive and administrative officer of a county. He works with the criminal and civil courts by serving subpoenas and processes, calling in jurors, executing judgments, and holding court sales. Perhaps just as important, he has the basic responsibility for preserving the peace and suppressing crime within his county.

The constable is an officer of a city. His duties are similar to those of the sheriff but his powers are less and his territorial jurisdiction is smaller. He has the responsibility of preserving the peace and executing the processes of the magistrate's courts and some other courts. He serves writs, attends the sessions of the lower courts, and has the charge of juries for these courts. He may have other legal duties, depending on the local and state law.

In the federal court system, the U.S. Marshal performs duties that are similar to the responsibilities of the sheriff in the state and county courts. Some states also have marshals, whose powers and duties correspond generally to those of the county sheriff or city marshal.

153

Independence of the Court System

The first judges in early England were personal representatives of the king and were answerable to the sovereign. In 1701, the English Act of Settlement was passed by the British Parliament to make certain that the English courts would be independent of the rest of the government. This came too late for some of the American colonists, however, as they were already living in the New World.

At any rate, the framers of the U.S. Constitution set up our Federal Government with the court system as a separate entity to balance the powers given to the executive and legislative branches. The courts in this country, both state and federal, have therefore never regarded themselves as answerable to any other part of the government. This independence is essential if decisions are to be rendered on an impartial basis.

It would be unrealistic to maintain that either the federal or state courts are free from political influences. Federal district judges, for example, are appointed by the President, with the consent of the United States Senate. Most nominations for a position of this kind come from political backers of the President, Senators, and Congressmen in the locality to be served by the judge. The individual appointed almost always has political ties to the administration.

There is an unwritten law that an appointment of this nature will not be approved by the Senate if the appointee is personally objectionable to one of the Senators from his state.

All individuals are subject to human frailties and pressures. The appointment of an individual to a job as a federal judge does not work a basic change in that person's character. The federal judiciary is basically independent, though, both from the standpoint of salary and from the point of view that the appointment is for life, pending good behavior. This independent position does insulate the man on the bench from most political pressures, even though no one is completely free from political influences. The results under the federal system have been of a very high order.

Judges on state courts have usually gone through a selective screening process, whether they were elected or appointed to their position on the bench. Usually, a candidate for a judgeship must receive the endorsement of the local bar association in order to be seriously considered. If the man has glaring disqualifications, these facts are frequently known to the press and aired to influential groups. There have been instances in which dishonest and corrupt individuals have reached judicial office. Considering the great number of positions filled at the state and local levels, though, the selecting process has worked remarkably well.

SELECTION, TENURE, AND REMOVAL OF STATE JUDGES

We have noted that federal judges are appointed by the President, with the consent of the U.S. Senate. From a practical standpoint, the appointment is for life, as only a few federal judges have ever been removed. (Four were removed in the first 200 years of our national life.)

Some state judges are elected and some are appointed. To get around the political control of judgeships, many states have worked out arrangements for screening and appointment processes that make use of bar association advisory committees and lay boards drawn from all geographical areas of the state. Various methods may be used to weed out the least desirable and poorly qualified candidates, with the screening board giving the governor a choice of two or three candidates who can be appointed.

Judges in lower judicial positions at the state level are usually chosen by election. Frequently, a prosecuting attorney or assistant prosecutor makes a name for himself as an energetic, conscientious prosecutor, and uses this reputation to be elected to a judgeship. Other successful candidates often have the backing of a good percentage of the local bar association.

Tenure of state judges is not so certain as that of their colleagues on the federal bench. However, a state judge who performs satisfactorily at his post can usually expect to remain in office. In addition, judges' terms are usually longer than those of other office holders. In California, for example, judges in the higher courts serve for twelve years and for six years in the lower judicial positions. The effect of this is that the community has a reasonable assurance of continuity and independence from these important officials.

All states have legal provisions to replace or suspend judges charged with a criminal violation. In addition, all states legally remove a judge from office when he is convicted on any crime of moral turpitude, in any court.

When the judge is a drunk, habitually immoral or notoriously unfit, there is considerable variance as to the removal action that may be undertaken. The law in some states follows the federal procedures of impeachment. In most instances, the impeachment process is very slow and cumbersome. Sometimes it seems to be nearly unworkable. At the same time, it prevents the removal of a worthy judge who will not bow to mob pressures.

California, along with some other jurisdictions, utilizes a commission on judicial qualifications to discipline or remove a judge who is unable or unwilling to perform his duties. The California commission is made up of five judges appointed by the California Supreme Court, two lawyers appointed by the state bar association, and two lay members appointed by the governor. This commission has an independent office and competent investigators, and promptly looks into complaints of judicial misconduct. This system seems to get effective action for legitimate complaints, while managing to remain free of partisan politics.

CONTEMPT OF COURT

Courts of justice have an inherent power to set their own rules and handle their own proceedings. Any act which is intended to embarrass, hinder, or obstruct a court in the administration of justice, or which is disrespectful of the court's authority or dignity, is defined as contempt of court.

In the words of Justice Felix Frankfurter of the United States Supreme Court: "What is indisputable is that from the foundation of the United States the constitutionality of the power to punish for contempt . . . has not been doubted.[5]

Two Kinds of Contempt

Contempts are generally divided into two classes of cases: (1) direct contempts, or those committed in the immediate presence or view of the judge, or so near as to interfere with court proceedings, and (2) indirect, or constructive contempts, or those actions occurring outside the court that defeat or hinder the administration of justice, or bring the court into disrespect. Usually, this class of contempt involves an order from the court, directing someone to do something.

Direct Contempt

An orderly, respectful attitude toward the court is consistent with the pursuit of justice. Practically all judges distinguish between a forthright, energetic defense of a client and an attorney or spec-

5. Green v. U.S., 356 US 165 (1958).

tator who insists on disrupting the court by directing verbal abuse at the court and its workings.

Typical cases of direct contempt would involve: parades outside the courtroom, with participants carrying signs stating that "The Judge is a Crooked Jerk" or "The Judge Is Unfair to Draft Resisters"; shouting at the prosecuting attorney and using obscene language; or spitting on a witness.

There is no legal requirement, but if the attack is verbal, most judges go to great lengths to warn the offender, holding him in contempt only after the offender persists in an objectionable course of conduct.

It seems that most cases of direct contempt involve lawyers who become emotionally involved in supporting their client. United States District Judge John J. Sirica, who presided over the Watergate trials, commented on this situation as follows:[6]

> A few lawyers cloud the issues, confuse the procedure and bait and badger the judge into committing error.
>
> When a judge loses control of his courtroom and permits lawyers to run the trial, that judge should hang up his robe permanently, for he is no longer able to perform his judicial duties.
>
> I don't think there is a judge who has sat on the bench who has not lost his patience or temper as a result of the action of some lawyer.
>
> ... many times as a trial lawyer, I was hard pressed to control my own temper due to anxiety or frustration, especially in an emotionally charged case ... And a few times I can remember making an in-court statement or addressing a judge in such a way that now, as a judge, I would not tolerate coming from a lawyer.

If the contemptuous act is a personal attack or verbal insult to the court, the judge may instantly cite and convict. But if the judge waits until the end of the trial to cite and convict the offending persons, then the accused is entitled to a hearing before another judge, with the trial judge disqualifying himself.

An individual accused of contempt has the right to a jury trial if the punishment meted out amounts to more than six months of imprisonment. The defendant in a case of this nature is being

6. Address to the American Bar Association Convention at Montreal, Canada, August 13, 1975.

punished without the benefit of an indictment, a jury trial, or the testimony of witnesses. In imposing a penalty, the judge has served as prosecutor, judge, and jury combined. On the other hand, the judge must be left with a free hand, so long as he runs his courtroom in an orderly, reasonable way.[7]

THE DEFENDANT'S RIGHT
TO A FAIR TRIAL

All Procedures During Trial
Must Reflect Basic Fairness

Almost everyone is familiar with the trial scenes in the old western dramas that appear on TV. The verdict in these fictional trials is rarely in doubt as irate frontiersmen take the law into their own hands. In the typical pattern, the jury's deliberations last for only a few minutes. Throughout the trial, the accused may be handcuffed from behind, with a rope already in place around his neck. Sometimes, even the judge takes part in the frameup against the accused.

This kind of drama faded with the passing of the old west. Even today, though, there are times when community feelings against the accused may run high, especially if the crime involves exceptional cruelty or brutality.

Private individuals, of course, have the right of free speech— they are free to express indignation at the criminal acts attributed to the accused. However, neither the judge, the prosecutor, nor the investigating police agency has this same right of expression or speech. During the trial, the judge cannot allow witnesses or private citizens to arouse the passions of the jury or witnesses who are attending the trial.

There are no specific words in the U.S. Constitution that specifically state that the accused must be given a fair trial. Legal standards set by the court, however, do require this.

Basic fairness and orderliness in criminal trials has been a part of English and American law since the time of the Magna Charta in 1215 A.D. The Fifth Amendment to the U.S. Constitution imposes a limitation on the Federal Government that says no person may be "deprived of life, liberty, or property, without due process of law; . . ."

---

7. Bloom v. Illinois, 391 U.S. 194 and Codispoti v. Pennsylvania, 418 U.S. 506, as well as Taylor v. Haynes, 418 U.S. 488.

A parallel clause is found in the Fourteenth Amendment, which became a part of the U.S. Constitution in 1868. This amendment prohibits state courts from using trial procedures that are basically unfair. In other words, no court may deprive an accused of those rights that are fundamental to an ordered scheme of liberty, or allow tactics that violate the ideas of impartiality in the civilized world.

The United States Supreme Court has used the Fifth Amendment to regulate the federal courts, and the due process clause of the Fourteenth Amendment as a means of imposing minimum standards of fairness on the state courts.

What Are Basic Requirements of a Fair Trial?

Due process of law entitles the defendant to an impartial trial in every respect. The trial cannot be influenced by outside conditions. What is meant here is that the court system alone, without any injection of outside mob feelings, must be used to determine whether there is guilt. The establishment of criminal responsibility, if any, must take place during the trial, based only on admissable proof presented at that time.

In the words of United States Supreme Court Justice Felix Frankfurter in *Irvin* v. *Dowd*: "One of the rightful boasts of Western Civilization is that the state has the burden of establishing guilt solely on the basis of evidence produced in court and under circumstances assuring an accused all the safeguards of a fair procedure."[8]

In the words of another court, a fair trial must be one "which hears and considers before it condemns, which proceeds [only] upon inquiry, and renders judgment only after hearing the evidence presented."[9]

A fair trial requires an orderly presentation to an impartial jury, and a judge whose neutrality is indifferent to every factor in the trial except that of the administration of justice.[10]

Stated another way, what is required in every criminal court is:

a fair and impartial jury and a learned and upright judge to instruct the jury and pass upon legal questions, and an atmos-

8. Irvin v. Dowd, 366 US 717, 81 S Ct 1639 (1961).
9. Johnson v. City of Wildwood, 184 A 616, 116 NJL 462.
10. State ex rel. Brown v. Dewell, 179 So 695, 131 Fla 566.

phere of calm in which witnesses can deliver their testimony without fear and intimidation, and in which attorneys can assert defendants' rights freely and fully, and in which truth may be received and given credence without fear of violence.[11]

There must be: ". . . an atmosphere of judicial calm; that while the judge may and should direct and control the proceedings, yet he may not extend his activities as far as to become in effect either an assisting prosecutor or a thirteenth juror."[12]

The merits of a case must never be prejudged. It would be highly improper for the judge to make a prejudicial statement during the course of the trial, such as telling the jury to "get on with the business of convicting the accused." This, of course, would be a clear-cut case of deprivation of due process, and the accused would be given a new trial on appeal.

Seldom is such a clearly prejudicial statement made by a judge. However, the defense attorney usually studies every word or expression of the judge, looking for something which shows a preconceived notion or opinion.

Bias, of course, will disqualify a judge, and will be used by an attorney to obtain a new trial for the defendant. "That which disqualifies the judge is a condition of mind, which sways his judgment and renders him unable to exercise his functions in a particular case."[13]

At other times there may be no specific exhibition or statement of prejudice by the judge. There may, nevertheless, be a lack of basic fairness in the proceedings. As said by Justice Tom Clark of the United States Supreme Court: ". . . one is deprived of due process of law when he is tried in an environment so permeated with hostility that judicial proceedings can be but a hollow formality."[14]

The case of *Moore* v. *Dempsey*[15] involved the prosecution of five Blacks for the murder of a white man, at a time when racial animosity was considerable. The United States Supreme Court indicated that feelings in the courtroom ran so strong that public passion had choked off the usual processes of justice. Witnesses were afraid to testify for the defense and attorneys were intimidated into not ask-

11. Floyd v. State, 148 So 226, 166 Miss 15.
12. Goldstein v. U.S., 63 F 2d 609. See also State v. Leland, 227 P 2d 785, 190 Or 598.
13. State ex rel. Mitchell v. Sage Stores Co., 143 P 2d 652, 157 Kan 622.
14. Rideau v. Louisiana, 373 US 723, 83 S Ct 1417 (1963).
15. Moore v. Dempsey, 261 US 86, 43 S Ct 265 (1923).

160

ing for a change of venue. It was apparent that a juror who seriously doubted guilt could not expect to continue to reside in that community. The whole trial process was swept along by public passion. In such a case the Supreme Court apparently had no trouble in concluding that it was too much like one of the old TV westerns—the defendants had been denied a fair trial under the due process clause of the Fourteenth Amendment.

The courts say that if the judge has any financial interest in the outcome of the trial, he cannot help but be prejudiced. A typical situation of this kind is that in which the judge or justice of the peace receives a money fee for each case in which he finds the accused guilty but receives nothing if the defendant is acquitted.[16]

Prejudicial Influence on the Trial Jury

There are other, less direct ways in which the trial may be unduly influenced against the accused. Not only must the judge remain impartial, but the officers and the attendants of the court must also refrain from words or actions that would influence the verdict. In one case, a court bailiff remarked in the presence of the jurors, "Oh, that wicked fellow, he is guilty!" On appeal, the conviction was reversed and a new trial granted, on the basis that the jury could have been influenced by the bailiff's remark.[17]

In another case, the jury was held for deliberation in the custody of two deputy sheriffs, who had earlier furnished damaging testimony against the accused during the course of the trial. The mere presence of the two deputies here was held to intimidate the jury, since the two officers were in close and continuous contact with jury members.[18]

The United States Supreme Court has repeatedly expressed the idea that "trial courts must take strong measures to ensure that the balance is never weighted against the accused."[19] At the very least, the defendant is entitled to a new trial if the way the first trial is run appears to be slanted against him.

One of the weaknesses of our system of American justice is that there is no way to ever retry the criminal if the trial court exhibits

16. Tumey v. Ohio, 273 US 510, 47 S Ct 437 (1926).
17. Parker v. Gladden, 385 US 363 (1966).
18. Turner v. Louisiana, 379 US 466, 85 S Ct 546 (1965).
19. Sheppard v. Maxwell, 348 US 333, 86 S Ct 1507 (1966).

prejudice in favor of the defendant and an acquittal results. An accused person may be tried once, and once only if acquitted. Practically all of the Supreme Court's supervision over trial court procedures is directed toward preservation of the rights of the individual defendant, with little or no attention given to situations where the trial is definitely slanted against the prosecution.

Defense Attorneys Sometimes Try to Get Police Officers to Exhibit Prejudice

There are times when some defense attorneys feel that they have no valid defense to present in behalf of their client. In a situation of this kind, some attorneys may try to cross-examine the investigating police officer in such a way that he will lose his temper and exhibit prejudice against the accused. The police officer must meet an attack of this kind by calmly showing the jury that he had nothing whatever against the accused, and that he was merely looking for the facts in his investigation.

It is almost impossible, of course, to completely eliminate emotional feelings from the criminal courtroom. The defendant almost always feels that he has a great deal at stake. Frequently, the police officers who were involved in the investigation of the crime have the feeling that their investigative techniques and skills are on trial. Here again, the individual officer must never let outside facts control his thinking. He must show that he was merely doing his job in an orderly, businesslike way, and that the accused was implicated by the facts that came out. If the investigator can take a detached, impersonal approach, his testimony will usually be very effective.

Press or TV Coverage That Creates a Prejudiced Setting for the Trial

Sometimes newspapers or TV reporters insist on giving a considerable amount of publicity to a criminal matter prior to trial. This may lead to serious differences between reporters and trial judges. The reporters claim that they should have the right to freely report all details about a crime and the resulting investigation, because of the First Amendment right of free speech. The courts and defense lawyers feel that the accused cannot be given a fair trial under the due process clause of the Fifth Amendment, if newspaper or TV publicity prejudices the thinking of the community against the accused. These lawyers fear that, consciously or not, the jury will be influenced to convict the accused.

The crusading newsman's view has often been that criminals and their dishonest friends will get off "scot-free" unless someone is allowed to inform the public about the illegal contacts these criminals may have with prosecutors, judges, or public officials.

On the other hand, a trial jury is expected to report for service with unbiased minds and to judge the case solely on the basis of the evidence presented in court. News accounts of a sensational, brutal crime may damage the case for the accused long before he has had an opportunity to clear himself. The basis of our system is to presume innocence, and at this stage, the accused is legally only a suspect who is being held for trial.

Whenever there is an especially horrible crime, there may be considerable pressure on the police in that area. There is a demand to find the criminal, and it is only natural for an arrest to attract attention. If an apprehension should be made, the police may infer that they are protecting the community and that the crime has been solved. Unusually heavy coverage by news sources of the crime itself and of the arrest may reduce the possibility for a fair trial.

Some observers feel that our country's legal system operates heavily in favor of the press. In England, for example, the newspapers and TV outlets cannot print any information about potential evidence until after a matter has been settled by the courts. The newspapers then have free rein to publish complete accounts of the trial and the evidence that was presented. The English view is that any improper tieup between criminals and their official contacts can be exposed after the trial as effectively as prior to trial.

Legal scholars who favor restriction of press stories argue that the law must not distinguish between the guilty and the innocent prior to trial. Therefore, the law must protect the guilty from accurate stories, to be sure that the innocent are protected from inaccurate stories.

Responsible newspapers, of course, will refrain from printing a sensational crime story if it appears that the disclosure may jeopardize someone's life. In almost all other situations, however, newsmen consider it their obligation to keep the public informed of criminal acts.

Reporters, of course, have excellent news sources of their own. Frequently, however, both state and federal officers feed information

163

to news sources, or guide reporters to sources of information. Some officers go even further—actually acting out the news or posing for the reporters.

In one case in a southern state, peace officers accommodated TV reporters by allowing them to record a twenty minute interview with a man who had just been arrested for a serious crime. The alleged voluntary confession of this suspect was recorded on film and exhibited three times in the next twenty-four hours on local TV broadcasts. The case was eventually reversed.[20]

In a somewhat similar case, police officials allowed a television reporter to press a microphone into the faces of two individuals who had just been arrested for robbing an old lady and killing her with a screwdriver. In this tense scene, the reporter asked the suspects what could possibly have caused them to do such a thing. One of the arrested individuals shot back an answer almost automatically, advising that the old lady had been stabbed before the suspects could stop to think. A reversal followed conviction here.[21]

In still another example, state police in the Midwest arrested an individual for armed robbery, held him up in front of TV cameras, and forced a money bag containing loot into his hands. Here again, the conviction was overturned.[22]

Most criminal courts never allow a news reporter to take moving pictures, television shots, or still photographs in the courtroom. That is why TV stations almost invariably show artist's sketches of individuals on trial. In *Estes* v. *Texas*,[23] the trial court did break with precedent and allowed the trial to be given TV coverage. The Supreme Court eventually reversed this conviction, solely because the trial had been televised. The Court pointed out: "From the moment the trial judge announces that a case will be televised it becomes a *cause célèbre* ... the televised jurors cannot help but feel the pressures of knowing that friends and neighbors have their eyes upon them."

The Court reasoned that the press could freely gather and report information from the courtroom, but that the television procedure distracted the judge, witnesses, jurors and Estes himself, to the extent that he did not receive a fair trial.

20. Rideau v. Louisiana, 373 US 723 , 83 S Ct 1417 (1963).
21. See Irwin v. Dowd, 366 US 717 (1961); Stroble v. California, 343 US 181 (1952).
22. See Turner v. Louisiana, 379 US 466 (1965); Sheppard v. Maxwell, 384 US 333 (1966).
23. Estes v. Texas, 381 US 532 (1965).

Perhaps the best way for the police to avoid a reversal in the appellate courts is for investigating and arresting officers to immediately take the accused to jail, without a press conference.

It is always desirable for peace officers to maintain friendly relations with newspaper reporters, but a news or TV man should never be allowed to delay the arresting officer, to have the officer pose the suspect for pictures, or to conduct an interview with the prisoner while en route to the jail. The police officer must remove anyone who impedes the arrest or the path to jail, without making enemies of the press. In some instances, obstruction of the arrest may be serious enough to warrant prosecution.

Almost every law enforcement agency has set policies as to the information that may be included in a press release following an arrest or an important investigation. If a newsman can obtain pictures at the scene of a crime, or of an arrest, he must be allowed to do so, as long as he does not interfere with the investigative process or the apprehension.

In general, peace officers can tell reporters the name of the accused, his reported age, and the nature of the charge, including details set forth in the warrant or the indictment. It is usually satisfactory to state when and where the suspect was arrested, and whether he was armed or resisted arrest at the time of the apprehension.

The police spokesman should never advise the press of any confessions made to investigators, or of any alibi that the accused claims. There should be no statements as to whether scientific tests or evidentiary evaluations appear to implicate the arrested man. The results of a police lineup should likewise not be revealed, and statements should never be issued to the effect that "he was identified by positive witnesses." Likewise, there should be no statements such as, "We have made an arrest and there is no doubt the crime is now solved."

Every police agency should, of course, strive to enlist citizen support by projecting a favorable public image. In maintaining this image, though, it is necessary to be firm, but fair. In taking his oath to uphold the law, an officer agrees to function under the operating rules of the law, as laid down by the courts. A police spokesman who unnecessarily releases information that eventually results in a reversal has done a disservice to his department and to the investigative efforts of his fellow officers. Likewise, he has failed to maintain an atmosphere conducive to a fair trial—a responsibility that is owed by the criminal justice system to every person accused of a crime.

The Courts

SUMMARY

The federal courts derive their authority from Article III of the U.S. Constitution, and the state courts owe their origin to provisions in the state constitutions or to specific statutes. There are variances in courts, however; they are graded from lower, or inferior, courts to higher, or superior, courts. The decisions of an inferior court may sometimes be changed by a superior court, or cases may be sent back to the lower court for a new trial. In the federal system, most criminal cases are tried in the United States District Court. If it appears that an injustice has been done, an appeal may be taken to a United States Court of Appeal, which is over a number of United States District Courts. From the United States Court of Appeal, a matter may be taken to the United States Supreme Court, if there is good cause.

In the states, the courts are much like the federal courts in the way they are graded from lower to higher, and in their methods of procedure. The lowest state courts are the municipal or justice of the peace courts in villages and rural communities. Some states call the next class of courts by the designation of superior courts, county courts, or district courts. Most states have a class of appellate courts above this superior-county-district class, with a state supreme court over all the state courts. If an injustice is done in the state courts, which involves a U.S. Constitutional right, then an appeal may be taken from the state supreme court to the United States Supreme Court. Generally, however, the United States Supreme Court will refuse to hear the matter until all the state remedies have been exhausted. Some states have only a two-tiered system for appeals in the court setup, while most have a three-tiered structure. The court of last resort in every jurisdiction handles the administration. All state and federal courts are independent of other branches of the government and cannot be controlled by the legislative or executive branches of the government.

In all courts the accused is entitled to a fair trial. From time to time there is some difference of opinion as to what a fair trial consists of. In general, however, the trial must be conducted in a calm, dispassionate atmosphere. The government, or prosecution, always has the burden of proving guilt, and innocence must be assumed until the contrary is proved. Guilt must be established solely on the basis of evidence produced in court, under circumstances assuring the accused a reasonable opportunity to disprove or explain away the evidence. Court officials and publicity media can never be allowed to build up an atmosphere of guilt that influences the jury or the judge.

QUESTIONS

1. Where do we find the legal authority to set up and operate court systems?

2. What are the basic differences between a trial court and an appellate court?

3. Is a jury used in both trial and appellate courts? Why?

4. What is a court of record? Why is there a need to preserve the record?

5. Does the federal court system utilize a three-tiered court structure? What about your state system?

6. How is a criminal case appealed from a state court to a federal court? Describe the process.

7. What types of matters are handled by the justice courts or magistrate's courts?

8. How are federal judges selected, and what is their term of office? What are the differences in state and federal procedures in this area?

9. How are judges removed from the federal or state bench?

10. Does the United States Supreme Court ever reverse itself on constitutional decisions? Why?

11. Is there any real benefit in having court decisions that preserve the stability of the law?

12. Is it more important to protect the general public from criminal acts, or to concentrate on protecting the legal rights of the accused? What is the basis for your statement?

13. List a number of the duties of the sheriff.

14. What does it mean to reverse a case? To reverse and remand?

The role of the grand jury as an important instrument of effective law enforcement necessarily includes an investigatory function with respect to determining whether a crime has been committed and who committed it.

Justice Byron White, United States Supreme Court, in *Branzburg* v. *Hayes,* 408 US 665 (1972)

chapter ten

GRAND JURY; TRIAL JURY; CORONER–MEDICAL EXAMINER

The purpose of this chapter is to describe the functions of the grand jury and the indictment process. Historical factors and contemporary issues will also be considered. This material provides details as to the functions and responsibilities of the trial jury, or petit jury as well as the activities and responsibilities of the coroner and state medical examiner.

THE ORIGIN AND FUNCTIONS
OF THE GRAND JURY

In early day England, the king's judges covered a large geographical area, travelling throughout the countryside to hold court. On arriving at a particular locality, the judge would call together a group of people from the neighborhood who would be likely to know the facts concerning any local crimes. The common people travelled very little, and almost everyone knew what their neighbors had been doing. The original grand jury, then, was a group called in by the

169

judge because they could be expected to have firsthand knowledge of the crimes that had occurred since the judge was last in that area.[1]

Eventually, the grand jury changed in makeup, becoming a group of persons summoned from all parts of the county, and acting as a body of inquiry to hear the evidence available concerning reported crimes. The basic function of the grand jury today is to consider whether prosecution should be initiated in those cases where grand jurors are satisfied a trial is warranted.[2]

The grand jury procedure works as a safeguard to accused persons, so that they are not arbitrarily hauled into court on the hunch or whim of some biased official. The grand jury members listen to complaints and accusations in criminal cases, thereafter voting either to prosecute or to withhold prosecution.

The members of the grand jury are first sworn in and instructed by the judge. In effect, the judge may tell the grand jurors that they are to act as the conscience of the community, voting to indict those individuals who should be brought to trial. The grand jury's consideration of alleged criminal violations is definitely not a criminal trial, since the only evidence that is usually presented is that which represents the prosecutive viewpoint. Then too, it should be noted that the prosecution is under no obligation to present the entire case against a suspect—only enough to convince the grand jury that there is good reason to believe the suspect committed a felony.

The grand jury is, in effect, an investigative body. All grand jury hearings are secret, except that some states permit the courts to order public sessions of the grand jury when the matter under consideration is one which affects the welfare of the general public, such as alleged corruption or dishonesty by public officials. There is good reason for keeping other grand jury hearings secret, since allegations may never be proved, and it would be unfair to permit publication of unsubstantiated charges. Usually, only the prosecuting attorney and necessary court officials are allowed to be in attendance at grand jury deliberations.

Procedures inside the grand jury room vary from jurisdiction to jurisdiction. The evidence presented is all under oath, but some informal procedures are allowed. Hearsay evidence is allowed in

1. Warren A. Seavey, Page Keeton, and Edward S. Thurston, *Cases on Torts*, (St. Paul: West Publishing Co., 1950), p. 2.
2. Rollin M. Perkins, *Criminal Law and Procedure*, 3d ed., (Brooklyn: The Foundation Press, 1966), p. 822.

federal grand jury deliberations, although some states require that regular court rules for the presentation of evidence be followed.

If a witness testifies falsely to the grand jury, the prosecuting attorney may realize what happened, since he will have access to outside facts to compare with the grand jury evidence. In a case of this kind, the grand jury evidence will be made public in a prosecution of the false witness for perjury.[3]

The accused individual has no right to appear before the grand jury to defend himself or to explain away an apparently criminal course of action. Sometimes the grand jury may want to call the accused individual so that he can explain disputed facts. The accused person has the right to refuse to testify before the grand jury. If he does answer questions, he cannot bring his attorney into the grand jury room, although he may be allowed to leave the jury room briefly to confer with his attorney.

If a grand jury refuses to vote an indictment, this does not mean that the accused was acquitted or exonerated of crime. A subsequent grand jury may hear the same or additional evidence and vote an indictment. This means, of course, that the matter will then be brought to trial. This is not regarded as double jeopardy by the courts.

In early day England, a trial jury consisted of twelve members, and was sometimes called a *petit*, or small, jury, in the language of the French Norman kings who had invaded England. A grand jury originally consisted of not less than twelve nor more than twenty-three men, and was therefore called a *grand*, or large, jury. Under our present system, when twelve members of the grand jury panel believe that the facts warrant prosecution, the vote is called a true bill of indictment, or simply an indictment.

In most jurisdictions, a grand jury still consists of not less than twelve nor more than twenty-three individuals, although in some jurisdictions the number has been changed by statute. In Oregon and Utah, for example, a grand jury may be composed of seven individuals; in South Dakota, not less than six nor more than eight; in Texas, twelve; in Idaho, sixteen; in Washington, twelve to seventeen; in North Dakota, sixteen to twenty-three; in California, nineteen, or twenty-three in heavily populated counties; and in New Mexico, twenty-one.

---

3. Paul B. Weston and Kenneth M. Wells, *The Administration of Justice*, 2d ed., (Englewood Cliffs: Prentice-Hall, Inc. 1973), p. 75.

GRAND JURY INDICTMENT REQUIRED
FOR FEDERAL FELONY PROSECUTIONS

By the time the colonists came to America, the grand jury had come to be recognized as a safeguard in the criminal justice system. The drafters of the U.S. Constitution therefore included a provision that "no person shall be held to answer for a capital, or otherwise infamous crime, unless on a presentment or indictment of a Grand Jury..."

This means that no one can be prosecuted for a felony in federal court unless that individual is first indicted. If a federal warrant is issued against an individual on the authority of the United States Attorney, the accused must wait until the next federal grand jury returns an indictment before trial can begin. If an indictment is not returned, then the matter is disposed of by automatic dismissal.

If a criminal is caught redhanded, or believes it is to his advantage to enter a speedy plea of guilty, he can waive the federal grand jury requirement. This, of course, is provided for in the federal rules of criminal procedure.

The right to a grand jury indictment, as set out in the U.S. Constitution, does not apply to felony prosecutions in the state courts. Procedures vary from state to state. The grand jury is of less importance in some jurisdictions, as felony prosecutions may be instituted in a number of states by an information filed by the prosecuting attorney. In still other states a grand jury indictment is required, with the accused not being permitted to waive a grand jury indictment.

After a true bill of indictment is returned by the grand jury, the accused is brought before a judge who is empowered to try felony cases. This arrest is based on a bench warrant issued by the judge who supervises the activities of the grand jury. The indictment is then read and explained to the accused, with the judge then giving the accused a chance to enter a plea to the indictment.

Contemporary Issues

In recent years, the grand jury system has come in for some criticism. In its historic role, the grand jury has been described as a "bulwark standing solidly between the ordinary citizen and an overzealous prosecutor."[4]

4. "Grand Jury Recommendations," *Los Angeles Times*, March 3, 1976, p. 10.

The argument here is that the members of the grand jury are almost totally reliant on the very public official whose potential excesses they are designed to check. Because they receive evidence only from the prosecutor, the jurors serve as little more than a rubber stamp for the recommendations of the district attorney. The argument continues that the accused has no right to appear unless called by the prosecution, and if called he is not allowed an attorney. In many instances the person under suspicion may not even know that the grand jury is making inquiries about his activities. This one-sided approach is undesirable, according to this argument, since the accused is being indicted although there may be considerable evidence in his favor to balance against the evidence indicating guilt.

This approach loses sight of the fact that the grand jury is made up of reasonable, intelligent individuals, who will indict only if there is enough evidence to indicate guilt. The grand jury was never intended to be a body set up to try the facts, or balance the evidence for and against guilt. The grand jury has always been designed to make certain that a person was not prosecuted unless there was sufficient evidence to cause belief of probable guilt.

If there is sufficient evidence to indicate guilt, then the public is entitled to see that the accused is tried. This is the basis on which the grand jury has always operated.

The historic view of the grand jury is that it has always worked as a screening process. If the accused is provided an attorney at the grand jury, is allowed to cross-examine witnesses, and is permitted to use all the procedures available at the time of trial he is, in effect, being given two opportunities to beat the criminal justice system.

Regardless of the arguments for and against the traditional grand jury system, legal scholars feel that the courts may order some changes in procedures. Some justices of the California Supreme Court have gone on record as believing that the prosecutor must inform the grand jury if the prosecutor is aware of evidence which may point to a prospective defendant's innocence. Whether this will become law following a court case that falls into this category has not been clarified.

THE TRIAL JURY AND ITS FUNCTIONS

Originally, only one kind of jury existed in England. It was made up of people in the neighborhood who knew almost everything that went on. At that time, people did not venture far, and few activities in the community remained secret for very long. In those days, the judge was the king's personal representative. He came into the community from outside and used the jury as a board of inquiry. He had the members swear under oath as to the common neighborhood opinion of the facts against the accused.

Somewhat later, people began to have less knowledge of all of the activities in their own village. The trial jury, then, developed as an offshoot of the original jury system, leaving the original as a jury of inquiry, or grand jury.[5]

The terms petit jury, trial jury, and jury all mean the same thing to us and are to be distinguished from the grand jury. For trial purposes, the jury is a distinctive feature of English and American law. European countries, other than England, who model their trial systems on the old Roman pattern, do not make use of a trial jury.

Selection of the trial jury is usually not considered a part of the trial proper. In most jurisdictions, criminal trials begin immediately after the trial jury is selected and sworn in.

As English law developed, it was specified that the jury must consist of twelve impartial men. In this country, most states set up a Commissioner of Jurors, with responsibility for preparing a list of persons eligible for jury service. This list is drawn from citizens who are residents of that county.

Certain persons are usually ineligible by law for jury duty. This category includes persons under eighteen years of age, nonresidents of the county, persons who do not fully understand the English language, and individuals who are not in full possession of their mental faculties.[6]

Other individuals are traditionally excused because they are somewhat indispensable to the community or because of the nature of their occupation. Those exempt include judges, attorneys, doctors and surgeons, dentists, firemen, teachers, peace officers of all kinds, and public officials. Persons who have been convicted of crime are excluded as undesirable.

Individuals are usually chosen from the jury lists for duty during an entire term, or session, of court. Laws generally exempt an individual from jury duty for more than one term of court in a given year. The clerk of the court usually selects jurors by lot, using a

5. Warren A. Seavey, Page Keeton, and Edward S. Thurston, *Cases on Torts,* (St. Paul: West Publishing Co., 1950), p. 2.
6. Rollin M. Perkins, *Criminal Law and Procedure,* 3d ed., (Brooklyn: The Foundation Press, 1966), pp. 909–11.

"jury wheel." The selected individuals then report to the clerk for duty.

This entire group is referred to as the jury panel. When the panel is filled, the trial judge usually informs the group as to their responsibilities. He then explains that some of the jurors will be chosen for duty in that particular case, and that some will be rejected or will be used in another trial.

Theoretically, at least, a trial jury is a cross section of the community in which the trial is to be held. The trial jury represents the average intelligence and attitudes of the area, and is considered to be as fair a group as can be chosen. It is the duty of the jury to receive the law from the judge, and to apply it to the facts as instructed by the court.

The United States Supreme Court has held that both state and federal courts must utilize fair procedures in selecting an impartial jury. A state law which specifically excludes any racial group from jury participation is clearly in violation of the U.S. Constitution. The usual complaint filed by a criminal defendant, however, is that the jury selection laws were improperly applied. In *Norris* v. *Alabama,*[7] a criminal conviction was reversed by the Supreme Court when it was proved that no Blacks had ever served on a jury in the area where the trial was conducted, although many Blacks were qualified to do so. A somewhat similar case also resulted in reversal by the United States Supreme Court because the procedure for drawing jurors was to put the names of eligible whites on white tickets and the names of eligible Blacks on yellow tickets.[8]

The accused who appeals does not necessarily have to be from the same racial or ethnic group that was discriminated against in selecting the jury. A convicted white man obtained a new trial by showing that Blacks had been systematically excluded from the jury used in the trial. The Supreme Court said that this was not proper jury selection.[9]

In the federal courts, the judge usually conducts questioning of the prospective jurors, and it is discretionary as to whether the judge will allow attorneys to ask questions or to submit questions to the judge. In state courts, attorneys for both sides are usually allowed to ask questions of the prospective jurors.[10] This examination of the

---

7. Norris v. Alabama, 294 US 587 (1935).
8. Avery v. Georgia, 345 US 559 (1953).
9. Peters v. Kiff, 407 US 493 (1972).
10. McKinney's Consolidated Laws of New York, Sec. 270.15.

jurors is called *voir dire,* and is usually begun by questions from the prosecuting attorney.

Jurors are usually asked whether they are acquainted with the defendant or any of the attorneys involved in the trial. The court may disallow questions by either side that are irrelevant to the examination, or that are repetitious. If a prospective juror indicates that he has a serious prejudice or bias that will prevent him from being a fair or impartial juror, then the judge may dismiss him from jury service or assign him to another trial. For instance, the prosecution may be against a defendant who is a prizefighter by profession. The prospective juror may claim that his father was killed by a prizefighter who deliberately picked a quarrel with him, and that he cannot remain unbiased in a judgment of any individual in this profession. Feeling that the prospective juror cannot decide fairly, the judge will discharge this prospective juror.

The judge may dismiss a prospective juror on his own initiative or at the request of either attorney in the case. What the courts mean by bias or prejudice is that the juror has a state of mind that will prevent him from deciding fairly. A juror dismissed in this fashion is said to be dismissed for cause. This does not mean that the juror has done anything wrong, but that he is obviously slanted toward one side or the other.

After jurors are dismissed for cause, an additional number may be dismissed by either attorney. This type of dismissal is called a "peremptory challenge," and is completely arbitrary. It is a method whereby either attorney can exclude an individual who seems to exude hostility toward that attorney's side, or is already against that attorney.

The number of prospective jurors who are excluded for peremptory challenges is usually set by statute, depending on the seriousness of the criminal charge involved. After all the challenges by both sides have been exhausted, the individuals who remain on the jury panel are eligible to serve.

If it appears at the outset that a criminal trial may be a long one, most states now have provisions for selecting alternate jurors. New York law provides:

> Immediately after the last trial juror is sworn, the court may in its discretion direct the selection of one or more, but not more than four additional jurors to be known as "alternate jurors." Alternate jurors must be drawn in the same manner, must have the same qualifications, must be subject to the same examination and challenges for cause and must take the same oath as

the regular jurors. After the jury has retired to deliberate, the court must direct the alternate jurors not to discuss the case and must further direct that they be kept separate and apart from the regular jurors.[11]

THE CORONER–MEDICAL EXAMINER

The coroner was an officer in early England. His duties have continued on the county level in modern American law. In some areas of the United States, the coroner may be called a medical examiner, while in other areas the medical examiner may be a separate officer who functions under the direction of the coroner.

The coroner and the medical examiner look into any death which occurs suddenly, or through violence. It is their job to determine if foul play was involved.

The medical examiner is usually required to be a licensed physician who is qualified as a specialist in pathology. Ideally, he should act as part medical doctor, part laboratory scientist, and part detective.

Authority—Jurisdiction
of the Coroner

The typical job performed by the coroner and/or medical examiner in most parts of the United States is spelled out in the California statutes on this subject:

It shall be the duty of the coroner to inquire into and determine the circumstances, manner, and cause of all violent, sudden or unusual deaths; unattended deaths; deaths wherein the deceased has not been attended by a physician in the 20 days before death; deaths related to or following known or suspected self-induced or criminal abortion; known or suspected homicide, suicide, or accidental poisoning; deaths known or suspected as resulting in whole or in part from or related to accident or injury either old or recent; deaths due to drowning, fire, hanging, gunshot, stabbing, cutting, exposure, starvation, alcoholism, drug addiction, strangulation, or aspiration; deaths in whole or in part occasioned by criminal means; deaths associated with a known or alleged rape or crime against nature;

11. McKinney's Consolidated Laws of New York, Section 270.30.

deaths in prison or while under sentence; deaths known or suspected as due to contagious disease and constituting a public hazard; deaths from occupational diseases or occupational hazards; deaths under such circumstances as to afford a reasonable ground to suspect that the death was caused by the criminal act of another, or any deaths reported by physician or other persons having knowledge of death for inquiry by coroner. . . .

In all cases in which a person has suddenly died under such circumstances as to afford a reasonable ground to suspect that his death has been occasioned by the act of another by criminal means the coroner is required to immediately upon receiving notification of the death report it both by telephone and written report to the chief of police, or other head of the police department of the city or city and county in which the death occurred, or to the sheriff of the county if the death occurred outside the incorporated limits of a city. The report shall state the name of the deceased person, if known, the location of the remains, and all other information received by the coroner relating to the death.

The coroner or his appointed deputy, on being informed of a death and finding it to fall into the classification of deaths requiring his inquiry, may immediately proceed to where the body lies, examine the body, make identification, make inquiry into the circumstances, manner, and means of death, and, as circumstances warrant, either order its removal for further investigation or disposition, or release the body to the next of kin . . .

For purposes of his inquiry the coroner may, in his discretion, take possession of the body, which shall include authority to exhume such body, order it removed to a convenient place, and make or cause to be made a post mortem examination or autopsy thereon . . .[12]

Functions and Processes
Used By the Coroner–Medical Examiner

As a part of the coroner's duties, he may furnish a set of fingerprints to the police or sheriff's bureau of criminal identification, so that the deceased may be positively identified by fingerprint comparison.

12. California Government Code, sections 27491-27491.4.

The coroner or medical examiner may analyze the organs of a deceased to determine whether death resulted from injuries, poisoning, or other violent means. Unless the remains are badly decomposed, the official can usually determine the cause of death. Even after a lapse of considerable time, the coroner or medical examiner can often contribute significant evidence.

After an examination of the body has been made, the usual procedure is for the coroner or medical examiner to call a special type of jury, which is known as a jury of inquest. The coroner presides, and the inquest jury (or coroner's jury as it is sometimes called) is placed under oath. This group then "inquires who the person was, and when, where, and by what means he came to his death, and the circumstances attending death . . . according to the evidence offered them or arising from the inspection of the body."

The jury of inquiry then makes a detailed written report that is usually filed with the county clerk, the prosecuting attorney, the police agency where the body was recovered, and any other interested police agency.

Under the law in early day England, a person could be prosecuted for murder or manslaughter, without indictment, if the report of the coroner's jury found that person responsible for the wrongful death. This procedure for doing away with the requirement of an indictment has not been uniformly followed in the United States. However, under the law in most states in this country, a finding of responsibility for wrongful death does authorize the coroner to order the arrest and commitment of the accused individual. In effect this procedure serves as the equivalent of examination and commitment by a magistrate, or the equivalent of a grand jury indictment.

In actual practice, the arrest power of the coroner is seldom used. Usually, the findings of the coroner's jury are placed on record, and the decision as to prosecution still rests with the prosecuting attorney.

The important feature is that the report of the coroner's jury brings the facts out into the open. If foul play did result in death, then it will no longer be possible to hide that fact. If, for any reason, the prosecutor is hesitant to prosecute, then the facts will come to the attention of the next grand jury for consideration of a criminal indictment.[13]

13. Thomas T. Noguchi, *Coroner's Laws,* (Los Angeles: County Board of Supervisors, 1974).

Authority To Inter

One of the coroner's other duties is to inter the remains of an unclaimed deceased or an individual who dies without sufficient money for a funeral. In most localities the coroner, under court supervision, can sell personal effects of an unclaimed individual or a pauper to pay these burial costs.

Generally, the coroner takes temporary custody of the property and effects of anyone who dies under questionable circumstances. It is usually a criminal misdemeanor to remove the body or any personal items until the police and the coroner have both had a chance to go over the scene and examine the evidence and circumstances of death.

SUMMARY

The grand jury procedure was set up as a safeguard to accused persons, so that they are not arbitrarily hauled into court on the hunch or whim of a biased prosecutive official or government investigator. Grand jury members listen to complaints and accusations in criminal cases, thereafter voting to either indict (cause prosecution) or to withhold prosecution. The grand jury is, in effect, an investigative or inquiring body. All grand juries are secret, unless the matter involves alleged corruption or dishonesty of public officials. Proceedings are informal, and the accused does not have the right to an attorney inside the jury chamber. In fact, the accused person does not even have a right to be heard. The make up of the grand jury consists of from six to twenty-three persons, varying from state to state. Under the U.S. Constitution, an individual cannot be prosecuted for a federal felony without being indicted by a federal grand jury.

A grand jury indictment is of less importance in some states, as a felony prosecution may be initiated in those jurisdictions by an information filed by the prosecuting attorney. In recent years, the grand jury system has been criticized because it does not give the accused the right to cross-examine witnesses and appear with his attorney. The grand jury was never intended to give these rights, as they are guaranteed at the time of trial. The grand jury is a safety valve that may keep the matter from ever coming to trial unless the facts so justify.

Trial jurors are usually chosen by lot from jury lists of citizens or voters. Persons in some occupational categories, such as policemen and firemen, are exempt from service. The Supreme Court has held that both state and federal trial juries cannot specifically exclude any specific racial group. Theoretically, at least, a jury is a cross section of the community. It is the duty of the jury to receive the law from the judge and to apply the law to the facts that are brought out at the time of the trial. Prospective jurors may be dismissed for prejudice, and each side can reject a predetermined number of jurors for no reason whatever.

The coroner's jury inquires into the causes of death in cases where there is doubt. Like the grand jury, a coroner's jury can decide to hold a person on suspicion of murder in connection with a wrongful death. The coroner also has authority to inter an unclaimed deceased.

QUESTIONS

1. Have the functions of the grand jury changed from its functions in early day England?

2. What are the basic differences between a grand jury and a trial jury?

3. Why is it said that a grand jury indictment works as a safeguard for the accused?

4. Are grand jury proceedings secret? When are they made public, if ever?

5. If a grand jury refuses to vote an indictment does this prevent the accused from ever being prosecuted for this alleged violation in the future?

6. How many people make up a grand jury? Does the number vary from state to state?

7. Must the vote of the grand jury be unanimous if an indictment is voted?

8. Does the U.S. Constitution require an indictment before an individual can be prosecuted for a felony? If so, does this apply to the state prosecutive systems?

9. Does the coroner or the police officer have authority to remove the victim of a murder or manslaughter?

10. What is the coroner's responsibility in notifying police officers of a death by foul play?

11. What is the basic objective of a coroner's jury or a coroner's inquest?

It is essential to the proper administration of criminal justice that dignity, order, and decorum be the hallmarks of all court proceedings in this country.

Justice Hugo L. Black, United
States Supreme Court in *Illinois* v.
Allen, 397 US 337 (1970)

chapter eleven

THE JUDICIAL PROCESS

The purpose of this chapter is to outline how persons are charged with a crime and how the court obtains jurisdiction or control over this individual for purposes of trial.

ACCUSATORY PLEADINGS: COMPLAINTS, INFORMATION, AND THE INDICTMENT

In the typical criminal case, an officer makes a report of what has happened. In his report, he lists the kind of violation that was reported, the damage or injury sustained by the victim, any available facts about the individual suspected of having committed the offense, and the amount of evidence that is available.

After the alleged crime has been investigated and documented sufficiently to point guilt at a specific suspect, the report is forwarded to the prosecuting attorney. The evidence is then evaluated to determine whether the suspect appears to be the person responsible for the violation.

When a decision is made to take prosecutive action, it is necessary to file an accusatory pleading, setting forth the specific violation that was supposedly committed.[1] Accusatory pleadings are of three kinds:

---

1. Wayne R. LaFavre, *Arrest: The Decision to Take a Suspect into Custody,* (Boston: Little, Brown & Co., 1965), p. 320.

1. A complaint;
2. A grand jury indictment; or
3. An information.

As defined in *Black's Law Dictionary*, "a complaint is a charge, preferred before a magistrate having jurisdiction, that a person named has committed a specific offense, with an offer to prove the fact, to the end that a prosecution may be instituted. . . . In some instances 'complaint' is interchangeable with 'information.'"

In most federal prosecutions, a complaint is used as the accusatory pleading. In some states, a complaint is the pleading used by the prosecuting attorney for offenses that are triable in the courts of inferior jurisdiction, while an information is used exclusively for matters triable in the superior courts or district courts. This is the situation in California.

An information differs from an indictment in that it is an action brought by a prosecutor or other designated official on his oath of office, rather than by a grand jury under a bill of indictment.

The filing of an information dispenses with the safeguards that are included in the grand jury system, but, in the opinion of legal critics, the use of an indictment as the accusatory pleading has some advantages. Unless there is a grand jury in session almost constantly, a matter will be brought to trial more rapidly by use of an information. For the good of the accused, as well as for the good of the community, it is desirable for a criminal accusation to be resolved as soon as fair procedures can be followed.

The filing of an information bypasses the grand jury safeguard inherent in convincing twelve grand jurors to vote for an indictment. In those jurisdictions where a grand jury is not used, however, the prosecutor must spell out a *prima facie* case to the satisfaction of the committing magistrate. By the term *prima facie,* the courts mean such evidence as will suffice until it is contradicted and overcome by other evidence. In contrast to the grand jury system, which does not allow the introduction of contrary evidence, the magistrate will allow the testimony of defense witnesses, and will permit the defense attorney to cross-examine the witnesses for the prosecution.

More than half the states now give the prosecutor the option of proceeding on an information or of seeking an indictment. Consequently, the prosecutor usually uses an information as the accusatory pleading. There may be times, however, when the prosecutor does not desire to initiate prosecution because of political implica-

184

tions or because he feels the facts indicate a borderline case. When this happens, the prosecutor may withhold the filing of an information, choosing instead to have it presented to a grand jury.[2]

The material that must be set out in an information includes the name of the person charged. This may be only an alias, if the real name of the accused is unknown, and the information may later be amended when the true name of the defendant is learned. The information must also include the place, the time, and the date when the offense was committed, as best it can be determined. It is not necessary to go into great detail but the information must set out enough facts so that the accused knows what he is supposed to have done and so that he has sufficient information to prepare and present his defense.

In most jurisdictions, misdemeanor prosecutions are started by the filing of an information, or by the filing of a complaint. The two processes are quite similar. A grand jury indictment is not needed in such cases.

JURISDICTION, VENUE, AND LIMITATIONS TO PROSECUTION

Jurisdiction or Authority of the Court

Criminal prosecutions are subject to some specific restrictions. One of these limitations is that of jurisdiction. The power of a nation or a sovereign to affect the rights of individuals, whether by legislation, by executive decree, or by the judgment of a court, is termed jurisdiction. Criminal jurisdiction is the inherent power to bring a case to trial. It is the authority, the capacity, or the right to act.[3]

Stated in other words, jurisdiction over the subject matter means authority over the class of cases to which this particular violation belongs. State courts have no power over federal offenses. For example, a state court cannot try an individual for a violation of the federal bank robbery statute but may prosecute under the same set of facts because of a state robbery violation. In this particular situation, both federal and state courts have jurisdiction.

2. Ronald L. Carlson, *Criminal Justice Procedure for Police*, (Cincinnati: The W. H. Anderson Co., 1970), pp. 41–43.
3. Rollin M. Perkins, *Criminal Law and Procedure*, 3d ed., (Brooklyn: The Foundation Press, 1966), pp. 653–694.

185

Jurisdiction over the Criminal Action ("*Situs* of the Crime")

It is necessary for the court to have territorial jurisdiction over the violation. This means, then, that the location of the crime must be within the space limits of the government unit having jurisdiction. As stated by one court, "It is a general principle of universal acceptance that one state or sovereignty cannot enforce the penal or criminal laws of another, or punish crimes or offenses committed in and against another state or government."

If a federal crime occurs anywhere within the United States, the federal territories, or on the high seas, the federal courts have jurisdiction over the *situs*. On the other hand, a Texas court would not have jurisdiction to try a criminal violation that took place in Michigan, even though there is a Texas law against this kind of violation.

One of the problems here is that it is sometimes very difficult to decide just where a crime did occur. The criminal's acts may have taken place in one state, while the harm caused by his acts occurred in a second state. The problem then is whether the person causing the harm can be punished in either state or in both.

If the crime occurred along the seacoast, it is to be noted that jurisdiction of state courts extends outward for three miles on any ocean bordering that state. If it is beyond the three-mile limit, the violation is a crime on the high seas, and is covered by federal law.

If there is a lake or river between two states, the courts usually hold that each state has jurisdiction to the center of the lake or the river. Most state courts go somewhat beyond this because of shifting currents in a river. They hold that a criminal offense committed anywhere on the river can be punished by the state court on either side. This, however, assumes that the act is illegal on both sides of the river. For example, fishing in the river may be legal in one state, but may be a criminal violation in the other. In a situation of this kind, a conviction could not be obtained unless it was definitely proved that the fishing was in the side of the stream adjoining the state that prohibits this activity.

If the crime occurs in an airplane or above the surface of the earth, the courts all agree that a state has jurisdiction over any crime committed in the air space above.

Some interesting problems may occur in the case of a running gun battle that crosses the state line. It is then up to the investigating police officer to determine where the activity occurred, as closely as possible.

The general rule, followed by all courts, is that the crime is considered to have been committed wherever the harm was inflicted. The reasoning of the courts on this matter is that the presence of the accused within this state is essential to make his act one which is done in the state. The presence need not be actual, however. It may be a "constructive" presence. The well-established theory of the law is that when one puts in force an agent for the commission of crime, he in legal contemplation accompanies this force to the point where the crime is actually committed.

In one case, the victim of an attack died in Texas as a result of a blow struck by the defendant in New Mexico. The New Mexico courts held that they had jurisdiction for a prosecution for murder or manslaughter.[4]

If a killer stood in one state and shot the victim in another state, the state in which the killer was located would not ordinarily have jurisdiction. Perhaps the only charge that could be filed in the first state would be that of illegally discharging a weapon at another person.

A number of exceptions to this rule have been brought about by state statutes. For example, Massachusetts has enacted a law declaring the place of death to be the *situs* for a murder prosecution. A number of other states have similar statutes.

In some types of crime, there may be a legal question as to where the offense was committed. This may, in turn give rise to jurisdictional disputes. For example, in the crime of false pretenses, the harm consists of wrongfully obtaining the property of another. Therefore, the jurisdiction lies in the place where the property was turned over by the victim, rather than at the site where the false claims or pretenses were made. In some cases, of course, the two locations may be the same.

In a criminal conspiracy the harm lies in the illegal agreement, even though the contemplated crime is planned for another location. Therefore, jurisdiction lies where the improper agreement was made. Some states take the approach that the crime of conspiracy does not come into being until an overt act is committed. Therefore, the location of the overt act is the place where there is jurisdiction.

Under modern American law, a thief can be convicted either in the state where he stole the property or in the state to which he has taken the stolen merchandise. This law has been brought into being by statute in most states.[5]

4. State v. Justus, 334 P 2d 1104, 65 NM 195 (1959).
5. California Penal Code, Section 497. See also 43 Ill 397.

Most states now have statutes providing that the state has jurisdiction over a crime committed in whole or in part in that state. In one case of this kind, the victim received a box of poisoned candy in Delaware that had been mailed in California. When the victim died, the person who mailed the candy was convicted of murder in California.[6]

Concurrent jurisdiction is sometimes established by statute. For example, an individual may be prosecuted in several states for the same activity, if the state statutes so provide.

FEDERAL JURISDICTION

The Federal Government has retained sovereignty, or control, over some federal lands, and a state court may have no jurisdiction there. If the *situs* involved is a federal military reservation, Indian reservation, or federal property, it may be necessary to research the title to the land and the history of that specific location. If the land was originally federal land and sovereignty was never given up to the state by written document, then the state courts never obtained any jurisdiction. For example, if it is land bought by the U.S. Government for a Post Office that was previously under state jurisdiction, then the jurisdiction remains with the state. The Federal Government does not automatically acquire jurisdiction over the *situs* to land, unless there is a special enactment of the state legislature, granting jurisdiction to the Federal Government.

Unless the jurisdiction was ceded by the state, the state court would have jurisdiction over the theft of a lady's purse in the lobby of the U.S. Post Office. By federal statutes, however, the Federal Government would have jurisdiction over a violation of federal postal laws at this location. If the postal violation was a simple theft, the state would also have jurisdiction, under state theft statutes.

Concurrent Federal and State Jurisdiction

The activities of a criminal may often constitute violations of both federal and state law. A kidnapping or a theft of government property would be examples of this type of offense. In the latter instance, the violation may be a theft violation in state court and may be a theft of government property in the federal courts. In most of these instances, two separate crimes are committed. The activities of

6. California Penal Code, Sections 27 and 778a, and 132 Cal 231.

the accused include all of the elements or requirements of a specific federal law and a specific state law. As a result, two separate prosecutions are possible. In most situations, this is not regarded as double jeopardy or former jeopardy, which would prevent prosecution in both locations.

If an individual is indicted in two or more locations, the matter will normally be tried in the court first obtaining jurisdiction over the person of the accused by arrest. In no case does the accused have the right to select the location where he will be tried first. Where two or more courts have concurrent jurisdiction of the same offense, it is established law that the court first acquiring jurisdiction of the prosecution retains it to the end.

Which Court in the State System Handles a Prosecution?

Once it has been decided which government unit (federal or state) has jurisdiction to handle a particular case, there must be a determination as to which court will handle the matter. Usually, state statutes specify which court in the location of the crime has authority to try and to punish the accused for the violation involved. In legal language, the court in which the prosecution is brought must be competent according to its own standards. Most states specify by statute the particular court in which felony charges can be tried and in which misdemeanor cases will be heard. In California, for example, a felony will be tried only in the California Superior Court, while a misdemeanor will be tried only in the municipal or justice courts.

As a generalization, the usual criminal case will be tried in the court of general jurisdiction, unless some other court has been specified for this purpose. The name of this court of general jurisdiction will vary from state to state. In some locations this tribunal is designated as the district court, the superior court, or the circuit court. In some cities of large size, the newspapers may report that a trial will be held in the criminal court, which is a common designation for a district or division of the district court, superior court or circuit court to which criminal cases are assigned.

Jurisdiction Over the Person

It is necessary to bring the accused before the court in order to try him. This is called obtaining jurisdiction over the person. Absentee trials are never permitted—that is, the accused must be brought before the court at the time the trial starts. If he escapes while the trial is in progress, most courts allow the trial to continue. This is based on the idea that the accused could have had his day in court but that he chose to run away. This is essentially different from a civil trial, where a default judgment may be awarded in a civil court against an individual who refuses to come in and defend himself.

Interstate Extradition or Interstate Rendition

In substance, Article IV of the U.S. Constitution specifies that a fugitive who is located in another state shall be surrendered on demand of the executive of the state from which he fled. Title 18, United States Code, Section 3182, provides additional details as to how this procedure shall be carried out. Whether the fugitive is guilty or innocent is of no consequence in this procedure and the state where the fugitive is located has no right to look into this matter.

It is interesting to note that any type of crime, whether felony or misdemeanor, is extraditable. It is also worth noting that a wanted individual can be extradited for an act that is not a violation in the state where he has sought refuge. There are some decisions to the contrary in this situation, however. Most courts hold that the legality of the wanted individual's arrest is not material to obtaining jurisdiction over his person. For example, a wanted individual may be kidnapped by a bail bondsman who stands to lose a large sum of money if the accused does not appear on the day set for trial. Once the accused has been brought back to the demanding state, he may be tried for one violation, although he was extradited for another alleged crime.[7]

The Statute of Limitations

Some criminal matters can be prosecuted only within a specific period of time. The question here is just how long the state will hold a criminal act against an individual. From a practical standpoint, witnesses may die or lose their remembrance of criminal events. By statute in all states, there are now limitations on most prosecutions, except for the most serious crimes. This is also true in federal courts.

The view taken by the courts is that the operation of the statute

---

7. William A. Rutter, *Criminal Procedure,* 5th ed., (Gardena, California: Gilbert Law Summaries, 1973), p. 128.

of limitations is more than a defense to a criminal complaint. Instead, it terminates the jurisdiction of the court and therefore does away with the possibility of prosecution or punishment.

The general rule followed by the courts is that the statute of limitations begins to run when the crime is completed. This is true, even though the crime may be one that has been concealed and not disclosed until much later. Some statutes, however, provide that the statute of limitations does not begin to run until the crime is first discovered. The general rule is that the filing of an information or indictment, or the issuance of an arrest warrant will stop the running of the statute.

Some crimes are considered so serious, however, that there is no statute of limitation to bar prosecution. Pertinent sections of the California Penal Code, for example, are as follows:

California Penal Code

§ 799.   [No limitation for murder, embezzlement of public moneys or falsification of public records: When prosecution may be commenced.] There is no limitation of time within which a prosecution for murder, the embezzlement of public moneys, and the falsification of public records must be commenced. Prosecution for murder may be commenced at any time after the death of the person killed, and for the embezzlement of public money or the falsification of public records, at any time after the discovery of the crime.

§ 800.   [Limitations for other felonies: Three years: Six years.] An indictment for any other felony than murder, the embezzlement of public money, the acceptance of a bribe by a public official or a public employee, or the falsification of public records, must be found, and information filed, or case certified to the superior court, within three years after its commission. An indictment for the acceptance of a bribe by a public official or a public employee, a felony, must be found, and the information filed, or case certified to the superior court, within six years after its commission.

§ 801.   [Misdemeanors: One-year limitation.] An indictment for any misdemeanor must be found or an information or complaint filed within one year after its commission.

§ 802.   [Limitation where defendant out of State when or after offense was committed: Time of absence from State

191

excluded.] If, when or after the offense is committed, the defendant is out of the State, an indictment may be found, a complaint or an information filed or a case certified to the superior court, in any case originally triable in the superior court, or a complaint may be filed, in any case originally triable in any other court, within the term limited by law; and no time during which the defendant is not within this State, is a part of any limitation of the time for commencing a criminal action.

§ 803. Indictment found, when presented and filed. An indictment is found, within the meaning of this chapter, when it is presented by the grand jury in open court, and there received and filed.

There are some circumstances under which the running of the statute of limitations is suspended. The legal language for this occurence is that the "Statute is tolled." A general rule here is that if the accused becomes a fugitive and stays out of the jurisdiction of the state, the statute will not operate as long as he is outside of the jurisdiction. By statute in some states, the statute of limitations is suspended while any other indictment is pending for the same offense.

Ex Post Facto Clause

An individual can be punished for acts only if those acts constituted a criminal offense at the time they were committed. This is a type of limitation on criminal prosecution known legally as an *ex post facto* law. This type of law is prohibited by the U.S. Constitution and by state constitutions in practically all states. If an act is legal when done, it cannot become criminal by a subsequent enactment of a legislature. In addition, the legislature cannot increase the penalty for an act done in the past. Any increase in punishment can apply only to acts committed in the future.[8]

VENUE

It is usually preferable to hold a criminal trial in the same locality where the crime occurred. Witnesses are easier to locate and interview. The accused is generally from that area himself, and a nearby

8. U.S. Constitution, Article I, Section 9, provides that "no state shall . . . pass any . . . Ex Post Facto law . . . ."

trial spares him the hardship of having to go to court in a remote area.

The Sixth Amendment to the U.S. Constitution grants the accused the right to trial in "the State and federal district wherein the crime shall have been committed."

Generally, state statutes also specify that the accused is to be tried in the county where the crime took place. Jurisdiction usually refers to the authority or power to try a criminal case—venue refers to the locality where the trial will be held.

As far back as the criminal law can be traced in England, the accused always had the right to a change of venue if it appeared that an impartial trial could not be had in the proper county. Most states grant this right by constitutional provision, by statutory enactment, or by decisions that follow the old common law. Where it appears that there is a strong probability that bias exists throughout the community, the defendant should not be compelled to go to trial before a jury whose members, or some of them, are influenced by adverse sentiments.[9]

The burden of requesting a change of venue usually rests with the accused, and this request must be made prior to the time that the case goes on trial. The usual procedure is to file sworn statements with the court, setting out the unfavorable publicity and other facts that show a wide prejudice against the defendant.

Whether a change of venue will be granted lies within the discretion of the trial judge. Appellate courts usually will not question this decision unless there is a showing that the judge abused his discretion.

In several recent cases, however, the appellate courts have indicated that a strong showing of actual prejudice need not be proved by extensive evidence and that the traditional approach is no longer adequate. These cases seem to mark a trend toward granting a change of venue on any serious claim of prejudice.[10]

Other cases have held that the need for an impartial jury is a basic ingredient in the due process requirement of the Fourteenth Amendment of the U.S. Constitution. *Rideau* v. *Louisiana, Irvin* v. *Dowd,* and *Sheppard* v. *Maxwell* all held that intensive inflammatory publicity or public prejudice would be sufficient for a reversal of the

9. People v. Sandgren, 75 NYS 2d 753. See statutes in McKinney's Consolidated Laws of New York, Sec. 230.20 and California Penal Code, Section 777.
10. Maine v. Superior Court, 68 Cal 2d 375 (1968); Fain v. Superior Court, 2 Cal 3rd 46 (1970).

conviction. It is therefore incumbent on the court to grant any reasonable request for a change of venue, as well as to suppress prejudicial publicity insofar as possible.[11]

If there is any question as to whether the accused can obtain a fair trial, the California Supreme Court has pointed out that a change of venue should be granted:[12]

> A motion for change of venue or continuance shall be granted whenever it is determined that because of the dissemination of potentially prejudicial material, there is a reasonable likelihood that in the absence of such relief a fair trial cannot be had. A showing of actual prejudice shall not be required.

COURT APPEARANCES AND PROCEEDINGS

After an indictment, a complaint, or an information has been filed, a warrant is issued for the arrest of the person charged.

Arraignment and Preliminary Hearing

Once an arrest has been made, the officer has a duty to immediately bring the accused person before a magistrate to answer the charge. This part of the criminal justice procedure is called the arraignment. During the arraignment, the magistrate explains the situation to the prisoner, and lets him know where he stands.

Civilized people have always had a fear of being thrown into jail without knowing why, or without realizing what can be done about it. In addition, unless there is some system for automatically bringing every arrested person before court authorities, there is always the possibility that a jailer might lose track of a prisoner and he could be confined indefinitely.

What Happens at the Arraignment

At the arraignment, the prisoner is called upon by name and the charge is read to him. If there is any question of his ability to understand, the magistrate will explain the charge to him.

11. Irvin v. Dowd, 366 US 717 (1961); Rideau v. Louisiana, 373 US 723, (1963); Sheppard v. Maxwell, 384 US 333 (1966).
12. Fain v. Superior Court, 2 Cal 3d 46 (1970).

The magistrate then informs the accused of his right to an attorney, pointing out that an attorney will be furnished to him if he is unable to obtain a lawyer himself. It is also explained to the accused that he has a reasonable time to obtain a lawyer, and that he can wait to confer with this lawyer before further procedures. If the charge is a felony, the accused is not required to enter a plea at this time. Rather, the magistrate advises that he can wait for the attorney and that a preliminary hearing will be set for him, unless he wants to dispense with the hearing and proceed directly to trial. Some courts allow the accused to plead guilty at this stage, but some will not permit this unless an attorney is present. Regardless of the accused's wishes, the sentencing seldom takes place at this time, as the judge usually wants to know something more of the accused's background, family life, prior criminal record, and motivation.

The Arraignment Must Be Prompt

Both state and federal statutes require that the arrested person must be taken promptly before a magistrate or judicial officer. If a federal magistrate (United States Commissioner) is not readily available, the federal prisoner must be taken before the nearest available state magistrate for arraignment. The wording of the state statutes as to prompt arraignment may differ, but the intent of the various statutes is the same.[13]

In the federal courts, the McNabb and Mallory cases[14] resulted in the rule that a confession taken from a federal prisoner while being held unnecessarily before arraignment would be excluded at the time of trial. This procedure did nòt arise out of a constitutional right, but because the United States Supreme Court feared that officers could put off an arraignment indefinitely, hoping to get the accused to confess.

In 1968, the Federal Omnibus Crime Control and Safe Streets Act was passed by Congress,[15] providing that confessions made voluntarily within six hours of arrest are admissible in the federal courts, even though the accused had not yet been taken before a magistrate.

---

13. "... The person arrested shall, without unnecessary delay, be taken before the nearest or most accessible magistrate ..." See Kentucky Rules of Criminal Procedure, S. 3.02; "Defendants shall be forthwith carried before the most convenient magistrate." See Arkansas Statutes, S. 43–601.

14. McNabb v. U.S., 318 US 332 (1943) and Mallory v. U.S., 354 US 449 (1957).

15. Title 18 United States Code, Section 3501.

Under this act, the confessions made voluntarily by the accused will be admitted at the trial. But if the delay in arraignment exceeds six hours, the burden is on the arresting officer to show that the additional time was used up in long distance or transportation delays in bringing the prisoner before a magistrate.

Since the prompt arraignment rule was not considered a constitutional right, the federal courts have never made it binding on state officers. Some state courts have rejected this principle, but statutes do require prompt arraignment in many jurisdictions. It is also worth noting that a delay in arraignment is one of the circumstances considered by the jury in ascertaining whether a confession was voluntarily given to investigating officers.

All courts agree that the arresting officer can book the prisoner, obtain fingerprints, and go through the regular identification procedure prior to arraignment. If it appears that a quick investigation will result in clearing the arrested person, most courts will allow this additional delay. Some other courts have held that a delay in arraignment is proper while an eyewitness identification is being conducted, or until a lineup can be arranged.

The courts are inclined to look closely at any delay in arraignment. Prompt arraignment seems to be the only way to avoid certain legal problems.

THE PLEA

When the accused is arraigned, he is instructed to enter a plea in answer to the charge that has been filed against him. This plea is made orally, in open court, and is entered in the written record prepared by the court reporter. If the accused is undecided, most states have statutory requirements that he must be given a reasonable time in which to decide how he wants to plead.

The accused is said to stand mute when he refuses to give any plea at all or gives a nonresponsive answer when questioned by the judge as to how he pleads. In early day England, if the accused was so stubborn that he would not enter a plea, the practice was to have the prisoner crushed or starved until he decided to give a definite answer. Courts in the United States have never allowed this kind of procedure. American judges automatically enter a plea of not guilty if the accused stands mute. Also, if the accused seems to have serious doubts, the judge will instruct the clerk to record the plea as not guilty.

196

All courts allow the defendant to enter a plea of not guilty or guilty for most crimes. If the charge is an unusually serious one, such as murder, some states have statutes that do not permit the acceptance of a guilty plea.

In addition, the federal courts and a number of state courts allow the accused to plead *nolo contendere*. This is an old Latin legal phrase that means, "I will not contest it." This has the same legal effect as a plea of guilty, insofar as the criminal charge is concerned. In many instances, the accused may be faced with a civil lawsuit in addition to the criminal charge. The victim of the crime may seek monetary compensation from the defendant in the civil court action. A plea of guilty to a criminal charge will be admitted as proof of wrongdoing in a civil lawsuit, as a matter of course.

On the other hand, a plea of *nolo contendere* will dispose of the criminal charge but cannot be taken by the court as proof of wrongdoing by the accused in a civil suit growing out of the same incident. In effect, then, a plea of *nolo contendere* reaches the same result as a guilty plea in the criminal trial, while requiring the victim to prove a case if he wants to collect civil damages.

By pleading *nolo contendere,* former Vice-President Spiro Agnew admitted the facts charged against him for the criminal prosecution, but said in effect that the admissions were not to be used against him elsewhere.

Some states make provision for other pleas to be filed, under circumstances that apply to some particular cases. California, for example, utilizes a plea of not guilty by reason of insanity. In some states, this is automatically included in a plea of not guilty, with the accused's attorney being able to assert the insanity claim as the trial unfolds.

In addition, some jurisdictions require the filing of a special plea if the accused wants to claim an alibi, or wants to base his defense on the fact that a prosecution would constitute double jeopardy. In most states, however, a plea of not guilty puts every material issue in doubt, and allows the defendant to raise the defense of lack of jurisdiction, the running of the statute of limitations, entrapment, insanity, or any other claim that should exonerate the accused.

When a plea of guilty is entered, it must be completely clear that the defendant understands and accepts the consequences of the plea. In the federal courts, the trial judge is not required to accept a guilty plea. There are times when he may feel that justice will best be served by declining to accept a guilty plea. In any event, the federal judge is required to question the defendant personally, to be assured that the accused knows what he is doing and realizes the consequences. This questioning must take place even though the defendant appears in court with his attorney. In addition, federal judges also usually require some evidence of guilt other than the defendant's admission.

The rules for the acceptance of guilty pleas in the state courts vary widely from jurisdiction to jurisdiction. The differences involve how far the judge must go in questioning the defendant personally and whether there must be some outside evidence available to support or corroborate the guilty plea.[16]

If a judge later believes that a guilty plea was not completely voluntary, or was made when the defendant did not understand the nature of his act, most courts allow the plea to be withdrawn prior to sentencing. The federal courts have held that failure to allow a withdrawal of a guilty plea under such circumstances constitutes a denial of due process. This only holds true, however, in a situation where the accused has not yet been convicted and sentenced. After sentencing, few courts are lenient in allowing a defendant to set aside his guilty plea on the claim that he did not understand it. After all, the accused has been through the whole trial procedure, where the judge has usually explained the consequences, and there must be a showing that the explanation was unclear before consideration is given to a request to change the plea at this stage.

On a few occasions, the courts have allowed a guilty plea to be set aside after judgment because the defendant's attorney seriously misled him as to the punishment that he could expect. It is almost impossible to determine whether the defendant is lying in his claim that he was misled, and most courts are justifiably reluctant to set aside a guilty plea under such a claim. In perhaps the majority of states, a guilty plea can be set aside after conviction only if it can be shown that the defendant entered into it in reliance on an unkept promise from the trial judge or the prosecuting attorney.[17]

As a practical matter, a high percentage of guilty pleas are entered after the attorney for the defendant works out some kind of a deal, or arrangement, with the prosecution. In the typical situation,

16. See Williams v. New York, 337 US 241 (1949), in which the United States Supreme Court held that the defendant had no constitutional right to an adversary proceeding as result of persons supplying adverse information to the sentencing judge.
17. Monrad G. Paulsen, *The Problem of Sentencing*, (Chicago: American Law Institute, 1962).

the defendant agrees to plead guilty in exchange for a promise that the prosecutor will recommend a light sentence, or will move to dismiss some other outstanding criminal charges, or will allow the defendant to plead guilty to an attempt or to another charge that carries a lesser penalty.

This plea bargaining process, as it is called, has been recognized as a legitimate procedure by the United States Supreme Court. Nationwide, approximately 90 percent of serious crimes were cleared by plea bargaining in 1975. This is justified by prosecutors on the basis that a sure conviction will be obtained, and that the state will benefit from savings in costs, trial time, and efficiency. Proponents of the system also point out that the courts might be seriously clogged if all criminal cases were prosecuted.

Problems Associated with Plea Bargaining

Opponents of the plea bargaining system feel that it is a perversion of justice. They point out that it is wrong for society to make concessions to those who have violated the law. If there is simply not enough evidence to convince a jury, then the basic operation of our criminal justice system provides that the accused should not be convicted.[18]

Plea bargaining was almost unknown until the 1930's. Prior to that time, pleas of guilty had been actively discouraged by the English and American courts. Legal scholars almost unanimously contended that the adversary type of contest in the trial court was the surest test of justice.

Those who are in favor of plea bargaining argue that the process enables the prosecutor to obtain a conviction in a shaky case that might not stand up on trial. Others point out, however, that plea bargaining is sometimes the easy way out for the lazy or conniving prosecutor. It is also noted that the process is sometimes the tool of the politically oriented prosecutor, who is afraid to damage his conviction record by taking the case to trial.

Frequently, there may be real basis for the claim that through plea bargaining the prosecution permits a hardened criminal to get off too lightly, with resulting damage to the criminal justice system.

18. V. A. Leonard has pointed out that plea bargaining ". . . has become quite fashionable in recent years for the reason that it reduces the cost of judicial administration; in addition, it is less demanding on the talents of the prosecution." See V. A. Leonard, *The Police The Judiciary and The Criminal,* 2d ed., (Springfield, Ill.: Charles C. Thomas Publishers, 1975), p. 229.

As stated by United States Supreme Court Justice Felix Frankfurter in a public address, ". . . justice must satisfy the appearance of justice."

The objections to the plea bargaining system have been ably stated by California State Attorney General Evelle J. Younger:

> There may be cases in which the circumstances justify "charge bargaining"—in which the prosecutor agrees after conferring with the defendant or his lawyer to reduce the charge, and the defendant agrees to plead guilty to the reduced charge.
>
> But "sentence bargaining" is another matter. In sentence bargaining, the defense and prosecution agree on what would be an appropriate sentence in the event of a guilty plea; the plea is made, conditioned on a sentence no heavier than the one agreed upon. The judge must then decide whether to accept the plea with the limitation on his sentencing discretion, or reject it and force the case to trial.
>
> Bargaining has no place in the sentencing phase of our system of justice. And yet, a 1970 California law gives statutory approval to all types of sentence bargains. . . .
>
> Before 1970, plea bargaining had a doubtful legitimacy as a result of the U.S. Supreme Court's ruling that threats or promises could make a plea of guilty involuntary and thus invalid.
>
> But two 1970 cases—*Brady* v. *United States* before the U.S. Supreme Court, and *People* v. *West* before the California Supreme Court—resolved doubts about the constitutionality of plea bargaining. Both rulings justified plea bargaining partly by noting its mutual benefits: the defendant gets a lighter sentence, and the state saves the cost of the trial.
>
> But what neither decision answered is how either of these "benefits" furthers the purpose of our criminal justice system—to discourage crime. Avoiding costly trials, and adjusting punishments, are not ends in themselves, but only a means to an end—the protection of our citizens. These means should be adjusted to achieve maximum citizen protection consistent with the constitutional rights of the accused, not to achieve a benefit to individual defendants or to officials in the justice system.
>
> Other justifications for plea bargaining also have weaknesses:
>
> *A guilty plea shows that the defendant is contrite and in a frame*

of mind to be rehabilitated. But is this true? Contrition is the product of conscience, and if the defendant's plea results from bargaining, it may only reflect maneuvering to escape his dilemma.

Plea bargaining, by avoiding mandatory sentences for serious charges, sometimes permits the judge the flexibility to tailor the sentence or probation to the individual. But a judge's approval of bargains which circumvent the law is not the solution to a sentencing system that needs overhaul. Instead, judicial criticism of sentencing requirements should be directed to the legislature.

If plea bargaining were invalidated, guilty pleas would dry up and the courts would be inundated with trials. We do know that there was only a modest increase in guilty pleas when sentence bargaining became more widespread after it was authorized by law in 1970.[19]

Other prosecutors have stated that abolition of plea bargaining could increase the trial loads of the courts. They maintain, however, that this would be temporary, as many defendants would get the message in a short time, plead guilty, and throw themselves on the mercy of the court.

THE PRELIMINARY HEARING

At the time of the arraignment, the committing magistrate schedules a preliminary hearing for the accused. The legal meaning of a preliminary hearing is exactly the same as for a preliminary examination. Occasionally, the committing magistrate may allow the preliminary hearing to be held as a continuation or extension of the arraignment, but this is unusual, as the accused usually needs time to obtain an attorney and talk over his defense.

The basic objective of the preliminary hearing is to determine whether there are reasonable grounds for believing that a crime was committed by the accused. Like the arraignment, the preliminary hearing is held before a magistrate. (The United States Commissioner is the magistrate in federal cases.) The magistrate listens to the evidence and then asks himself, "Is there reasonable probability to feel that a crime has been committed and that the accused person

19. Evelle J. Younger, "Change Plea Bargaining Law," *Los Angeles Times,* Part X, p. 1, December 14, 1975.

was responsible for it?" In different words, "Would an average person out on the street think that the defendant committed the violation he is charged with, based on the evidence brought forward at this hearing?" The test here is probability, not a conviction beyond a reasonable doubt. The latter is required in a jury trial.

If the magistrate does not conclude that there is reasonable belief of guilt, then he will order the accused released and the charge against him dismissed. On the other hand, if the proof indicates the likelihood of guilt, then the accused will be bound over for trial.

In the language of one court describing a preliminary hearing:

> It is [not] . . . a trial for the determination of accused's guilt or innocence, but simply a course of procedure whereby a possible abuse of power may be prevented, and accused discharged or held to answer, as the facts warrant.[20]

In examining the role that the magistrate plays in such hearings, it should be noted that most magistrates also have authority to try minor violations. It is important to distinguish between a trial in which the magistrate has jurisdiction, and a preliminary hearing held by the magistrate, which neither determines guilt nor innocence but merely ascertains whether there is enough evidence of guilt to hold the accused for a court trial.

In the federal system of criminal procedure, the basic purpose of the preliminary hearing is to ascertain whether there is reasonable evidence of guilt, but the hearing is also conducted to determine whether the accused should be required to post bail, released on his own recognizance, or held in custody. As a practical matter in federal cases, the determination as to whether the accused will eventually go to trial is made by the grand jury, regardless of the outcome of the preliminary hearing.

In some states, such as New York, there must be a finding of cause at the preliminary hearing before grand jury consideration will be given to the case.[21] Still some other jurisdictions use the preliminary examination to ascertain whether the defendant should be bound over for trial. In effect, the states that use this procedure bypass the grand jury.[22]

20. State v. Langford, 293 US 436.
21. McKinney's Code of Criminal Procedure, Section 180.70.
22. California is in this class. See California Penal Code, Section 872.

In most states the accused does not need to go through a preliminary hearing unless he chooses. He can waive the right to a preliminary hearing and reach the trial stage without delay.

Why There Is More Attention to Preliminary Hearing in Some States

There seems to be a pattern in some states in which the defense attorney appears to fight "tooth and nail" through the preliminary hearing, thereafter entering a guilty plea on a plea bargaining arrangement with the prosecutor. This, of course, is in a situation in which the accused is bound over in the preliminary hearing. In the federal courts and in those states that require a grand jury indictment before trial for a felony, the crux of the battle seems to center around the trial, rather than around the preliminary hearing.

Some defense attorneys take the approach that the preliminary hearing furnishes them an opportunity to learn what evidence the prosecutor has, and to "freeze" the testimony of government witnesses. Court decisions in recent years have also expanded the defendant's right to discovery. According to this legal idea, the accused is allowed to ask for any evidence in the possession of the prosecution which would serve to excuse or mitigate the accused's conduct. In other words, this is a technique for uncovering what evidence the prosecution may present. The defense may then be better able to judge how to counter this evidence.

Discovery

Under the federal court rules on discovery, the defendant and his attorney are allowed to inspect confessions or statements that the defendant made to investigating officers or to the grand jury. This is allowed, especially where the defendant claims that he cannot remember exactly what he said to the investigating officers, and in instances where considerable time has elapsed since the statements were made. This often works to the disadvantage of the prosecutor. Even if the defendant cannot remember what he said to the investigating officers, he has nothing to fear if he repeats the truth. If he is not guilty, he can certainly remember the truth and cannot be hurt by sticking with it. On the other hand, if he is guilty and is attempting to cover up that fact, the accused must know exactly what he said to the investigating officers, to make certain that he is consistent in all his claims.

203

The federal rules also allow the accused to have copies of confessions or signed statements that are available to the prosecution, along with medical reports and laboratory examinations. For example, a ballistics report from the FBI laboratory as to a bullet examination would be provided to the defense attorney.

In addition, the defendant and his attorney would be entitled to examine books, physical evidence such as a knife used in the crime, records, and other materials that would be essential to the defense. In federal cases, the accused does not have a right to examine other physical evidence that was not examined, to obtain the names and addresses of individuals who may be called as expert witnesses, or to receive copies of the witness' signed statements.

Under the so-called Jencks Rule, however, after a government witness takes the stand, the defendant is allowed to inspect any statements or confessions made by the witness to government investigators or attorneys. The theory is that this may force government witnesses to be completely accurate. This examination may also aid the defendant's attorney in cross-examination of the witnesses.[23] Names and addresses of all government witnesses need not be provided to the defense, unless the charge is a capital offense.

One of the basic principles of discovery in the federal courts was enunciated by the United States Supreme Court in *Brady* v. *Maryland*.[24] The Court said in this case:

> Suppression of [any] evidence favorable to the accused, on a discovery request, violates due process of law, where the evidence is material either to guilt or to punishment, and irrespective of the good faith or bad faith of the prosecution.

The state laws and procedures pertaining to discovery are confused. In California, for example, the courts have held that the defendant must make some showing that the requested evidence would help his case. However, he does not necessarily need to use the requested evidence at the trial. California law requires the prosecution to furnish, upon the accused's request prior to trial, the identity of eyewitnesses who are alleged to have seen the crime, along with their addresses and copies of their statements to the police. As any experienced investigator knows, this opens up the way for retaliation in the form of criminal assaults against witnesses, and even murder.

23. Jencks v. U.S., 355 US 657; 18 U.S. Code, Section 3500.
24. Brady v. Maryland, 373 US 83 (1963).

Most courts allow the defense to inspect real evidence before the case comes to trial. This includes such items as a knife, fingerprints, or a scarf dropped at the scene of the crime, along with the written reports of experts who have made scientific examinations of these items.

The theory of the courts in allowing discovery is that substantial justice may not be done unless the jury is aware of the facts both for and against conviction. Unless the defense is allowed the discovery process, goes the argument, there is a possibility that evidence to excuse the defendant may never come to light. The federal courts, and most state courts, hold that the prosecution is just as entitled to the right of discovery as is the defense. As a practical matter, there is seldom any information of help to the government that can be obtained by discovery. Generally, however, if the accused intends to base his defense on the opinions of medical or scientific experts, the government can obtain the written reports that have been furnished to the defense by means of the discovery procedure.

The courts have not completely settled a number of situations that are related to discovery techniques and procedures. Some of the Justices of the United States Supreme Court have indicated that they are in favor of more liberalized rules pertaining to discovery, to assist the defense. Many prosecutors are convinced that the justice system can suffer considerably by disclosing to the defendant the names, addresses, and expected testimony of all government witnesses. Actual cases show that prosecution witnesses may be coerced or pressured if the accused or his friends can identify and locate witnesses. The accused already knows details about what his course of conduct has been in the past. If he also knows the details of the prosecution's case, he may be in a better position to fabricate a false alibi, or to induce a witness to commit perjury.

All witnesses, of course, have an obligation to testify as to what they know. It is questionable, though, whether the courts have the right to put a witness through an extended period of fear prior to the time of trial.

Freezing the Testimony of the Government Witness

Another reason why some defense attorneys spend as much time as possible in the preliminary hearing is to fix, or freeze, the testimony of government witnesses. Several months may elapse between the time of a preliminary hearing and the actual trial of the case. The government's presentation may be seriously damaged if an investigating officer is not able to testify consistently on the two occasions. It is not unusual for the defense attorney to attempt to develop differences. With this in mind, he may cross-examine an investigating officer in great detail. At times, the defense attorney may realize that he is not likely to bring out evidence that is favorable to his client. In the end, though, it may be useful to his client if witnesses become confused or are unable to remember their prior testimony. The investigating officer should obtain a transcript of his own testimony before the magistrate at the preliminary hearing, and should review this with the prosecuting attorney. This may be especially important if there is any question as to the testimony that will be expected of the officer at the time of trial. Confusion in the testimony of prosecution witnesses, however honest, generally inclines the jury toward acquittal.

Pretrial Hearings

The defense attorney may request the judge to conduct hearings prior to the time of trial, usually for one of three problems:

1. He may ask for the suppression of some of the physical evidence against the accused. What this means is that the evidence may be thrown out entirely.

2. He may ask for the suppression of a confession or a signed statement given to a government investigator by the accused.

3. He may endeavor to learn what evidence the prosecution has through the discovery procedure. How this discovery process works has been discussed previously.

These requests by the defendant's attorney are usually submitted to the court in the form of written motions. In a narcotics prosecution, for example, the accused may claim to his attorney that state officers violated his rights in searching him and taking narcotics from his person. If the trial judge feels that there could be any reasonable basis for the defendant's claim, the judge will hold a conference with both the prosecuting attorney and the defense attorney, prior to the time of trial. During this hearing the judge will make a ruling as to whether the evidence in dispute will be suppressed or will be entered as evidence for jury consideration at the time of trial. Of course, the defendant can appeal an adverse ruling that may be handed down by the judge.

Pretrial hearings of this kind are not actually considered a part of the criminal trial, but investigating police officers may be required to attend and testify under oath before the judge in chambers. This, of course, is not open to the general public.

In a typical hearing of this kind, the accused may claim that officers had no right to search him, and that a gun, narcotics, or stolen property found during this search should therefore be suppressed. This, of course, is under the legal theory that any evidence obtained under an illegal search is improper. (This is known as the Fruit of the Poison Tree Doctrine.)

When a hearing of this kind is scheduled, the judge may ask questions and inquire in detail as to how the search was conducted and under what circumstances an accused individual may have given a signed confession. In a hearing of this kind, the burden is usually on the party that challenges the legality of the evidence.

There is one exception to this rule, however. If the government representative conducted a search without a warrant, but claims that consent was given for the search, then the government has the burden of proving by clear and convincing evidence that the consent was given voluntarily, without pressure or coercion. In a matter of this kind, the judge will rule after hearing a detailed account from the officers and the accused. If there is a dispute as to the facts, the judge will allow the evidence to be admitted and he will leave it to the jury to decide whether the version of the accused or the police officer will be believed.

Other Pretrial Motions

By filing other motions prior to the time of trial, the defense attorney may be able to abruptly terminate the prosecution's case, or may be able to better prepare his defense. For instance, if the defendant feels that he was not furnished enough facts about the crime he is supposed to have committed, then the defense attorney may file a motion for a bill of particulars. If the judge agrees that the alleged crime was not sufficiently spelled out, it may be necessary for the prosecutor to file additional information, setting out more facts to enable the defense to know the specific details of the alleged crime.

If the defendant feels that he will not get a fair trial because of local prejudice, he may file a motion for a change of venue. This may result in the trial being moved to another location.

If the defense attorney believes that an indictment did not sufficiently allege a criminal violation, or was not obtained in accordance with required legal procedures, the defense may file a motion to quash the indictment. If the judge agrees that the indictment inadequately charged a specific crime, the defendant's motion will be upheld and the defendant will be released. In a situation where some details have been left out of the prosecution's paperwork, an amendment may be made and the prosecution may then continue.

SUMMARY

Criminal prosecutions are begun by the filing of one of three kinds of accusatory pleadings: (1) by a complaint, (2) by an information, or (3) by the return of a grand jury indictment. Sometimes the term "complaint" is used interchangeably with "information." In most federal prosecutions a complaint is used, followed by the return of an indictment if the case involves a felony. In some states, a complaint is the kind of pleading that is used for offenses triable in the inferior courts, while an information is used for cases triable in the superior courts or district courts (felony cases). An information or a complaint is an action brought by an investigating officer and the prosecutor. An indictment is returned by a vote of the grand jury. In a good number of states a grand jury indictment is not a necessary prerequisite for prosecution. In those jurisdictions where a grand jury is not used, the prosecutor must spell out a *prima facie* case to the satisfaction of the committing magistrate.

Before anyone can be tried for a crime, the court must have jurisdiction over the offense. In short, the offense must have been committed within the sphere of coverage of that court. The courts of one state cannot enforce the laws of another state. Generally, all courts say that the crime was committed where the harm was inflicted. When an individual puts in force an agency for the commission of crime, the law traces through to the place where this force becomes harmful to the victim. Some exceptions are made by statute. Federal courts have jurisdiction over federal crimes in all states, federal territories, and on the high seas. In some instances both state and federal courts have jurisdiction to try a crime. Statutes of limitations prevent the prosecution of most crimes, unless prosecution is undertaken within a specified number of years or unless the accused person has fled from the jurisdiction of the court. Venue refers to the locality where an alleged crime took place. Generally, under American law, the accused has the right to be tried in the locality where the offense occurred. The accused can obtain a change of venue if the public has become aroused or inflamed to such an extent that a fair trial appears unlikely. After the accused has been arrested, an arraignment must take place promptly. At the arraignment the accused is allowed to enter a plea to the charge. If the accused is undecided, the judge enters a plea of not guilty and forces the prosecutor to prove a violation. At the time of the arraignment, the magistrate schedules a preliminary hearing for the accused. At the preliminary hearing the prosecution must present enough evidence to convince the magistrate that there are reasonable grounds for believing that the crime was committed by the accused. If the magistrate is not convinced, then the accused is released.

QUESTIONS

1. What are the basic differences between an indictment and an information? Who files an information?

2. When an information is filed, does the accused have any protection against prosecution by a biased or incompetent prosecutor?

3. What is meant by the jurisdiction of a court?

4. Can one state or jurisdiction enforce the penal laws of another state? If so, under what circumstances?

5. Which state has jurisdiction over a crime committed on a river or lake between two states? Is that what is meant by a crime on the high seas? Explain.

6. Does state court authority on the ocean extend for one and one-half miles, three miles, or twelve miles?

7. Do the courts usually say that the test as to jurisdiction is where the harmful force was set in motion, or where the harm was inflicted on the victim?

8. If a rifleman in Texas deliberately shot across the state line and killed his enemy in New Mexico, could he be prosecuted in Texas for a criminal assault? For murder in New Mexico? For both possibilities?

9. Do some states now have statutes allowing prosecution for crimes committed only in part within that state?

10. What is concurrent jurisdiction? Give an example of concurrent state and federal jurisdiction.

11. If a crime is prosecuted in federal court, and later in state court, is this regarded as double jeopardy?

12. What is the basic purpose of a preliminary hearing?

13. Does a preliminary examination take the place of a preliminary hearing in some states?

14. How much proof must be presented against the accused in a preliminary hearing—must the case be proved beyond a reasonable doubt? By the weight of the evidence? By proof of reasonable probability or likelihood?

15. Are there some states that require both a preliminary hearing and a grand jury indictment in felony cases?

16. What is meant by the legal technique called discovery?

17. What kind of facts must be disclosed by the prosecution under the discovery rule?

18. Is the prosecution entitled to obtain information under the theory of discovery, or is it a one-way street?

19. Explain how the defense attorney uses a preliminary hearing to freeze the testimony of the prosecution witnesses.

20. List three of the most common situations in which the defense attorney may file a motion requesting a pretrial hearing.

21. What is the result for purposes of the trial if the judge rules to suppress a particular item of evidence?

From the very beginning, our state and national constitutions and laws have laid great emphasis on procedural and substantive safeguards designed to assure fair trials before impartial tribunals . . .

Justice Hugo L. Black,
United States Supreme Court
in *Gideon* v. *Wainright*,
372 US 335 (1963)

chapter twelve

THE JUDICIAL PROCESS CONTINUED—THE TRIAL AND ITS AFTERMATH

The purpose of this chapter is to describe the steps taken in the conduct of a criminal trial. This material outlines how the trial progresses, with basic descriptive material on the major technical aspects—how evidence is presented, how the trial unfolds, and how a verdict of guilt or innocence is reached. Then the sentencing process is considered, as well as when probation may be granted, and the problems of double jeopardy.

The Accused Must Be Competent to Stand Trial

It has always been the law in all parts of the United States that an accused individual cannot be tried, sentenced, or punished unless he is sane. The courts point out that the accused must be able to understand the nature of the legal action that he is facing. Then too, the courts insist that the defendant must be able to consult with his lawyer to assist in the preparation of his case. The mere fact that the accused refuses to work with any lawyer would not, in itself, be conclusive proof of incompetency.

The question of the accused's mental ability to stand trial may be raised by the judge, the defense attorney, or the prosecutor. The law always presumes that the defendant is capable of standing trial, until there is a showing to the contrary. In most states a jury is brought in to decide the issue, but in other jurisdictions, the judge will have the accused given a mental examination by psychiatrists or other experts appointed by the court.

If it should be found that the accused is incapable of standing trial, the usual procedure is to commit him to a mental institution until he is mentally able to be tried. Commitment to the mental institution in no way prohibits future prosecution or serves as a way of disposing of the criminal charge.

However, the accused may not be held indefinitely to await trial. After a reasonable time has elapsed, the state must either put the accused on trial or seek a permanent commitment to an asylum.

THE TRIAL

In most jurisdictions the pattern of a criminal trial is as follows:

1.   The information or indictment filed against the accused is read to the jury by the court clerk. The plea entered by the accused is then given.

2.   The prosecuting attorney makes an opening statement. In most courts the defendant's attorney may also make an opening statement, if he so chooses. In the prosecution's statement, the attorney for the government will outline the specific evidence he intends to introduce, how the specific bits of evidence will tie together, and the conclusions that may be drawn from the evidence. In other words, he presents a blueprint of the prosecution's case.

     The defense attorney may deliberately refrain from making an opening statement. This is because the defense is not obliged to prove anything, and the jury may unknowingly expect the defense to back up any statements that are made.

3.   The prosecuting attorney calls witnesses who testify and present evidence to prove the government's contentions. This is sometimes called the government's case in chief, or the state's case in chief.

     The evidence presented here may take many forms. It may include oral testimony of individuals who saw or heard what happened; physical or demonstrative evidence, such as exhibits or weapons; or testimony by expert witnesses as to their professional opinion.

4. Sometimes a case ends at this stage, without ever being submitted to the jury for a decision. The trial judge may, at his own discretion, take the case from the jury when it is obvious that the government did not present evidence sufficient to sustain a conviction, even if the evidence was believed in its entirety. The judge may do this, either on the motion of the defense attorney or on his own initiative. It is pointless to go through a jury deliberation if the proof was lacking. This is called a directed verdict, and is a type of acquittal. The defendant is immediately released from custody when the judge directs a verdict in his favor.

5. If the prosecution's evidence spells out a case, the accused's lawyer may then open the defense. Some courts allow the defendant to reserve his opening statement until this part of the trial. The defense, of course, is not required to put on any witnesses. The defense lawyer may decline to call witnesses of questionable reliability, since they may be tripped up easily.

6. After the proof is presented, both sides in the adversary contest have an opportunity to rebut that proof. In originally presenting evidence, the attorney who calls the witness begins by asking questions to draw the witness out. This is called "direct examination," or "the examination in chief." After the prosecution has completed questions, the witness is turned over to the defense attorney for "cross-examination." Most courts limit cross-examination of all witnesses to those matters discussed by the witness during his direct examination. Some other courts follow the so-called Massachusetts rule, which allows cross-examination on anything the witness knows that is relevant to the case.

After the cross-examination is finished, the prosecution has the right to rehabilitate the witness by asking for additional clarification of matters on the same subject. This is called "redirect examination." The defense witnesses may also be cross-examined in a similar manner and may be asked for additional clarification by the defense attorney on redirect examination. The witness may give reasons for his actions or statements, in order to explain unfavorable inferences from matters brought out on cross-examination or direct examination.

7.   When the evidence has all been presented, the prosecuting attorney has the right to argue the case to the jury. At this point, he reviews the evidence presented that was favorable to the government's case and makes comments as to the inferences that may reasonably be drawn from the evidence. The defense attorney then argues his case to the jury. The prosecution then has the right to be heard a second time to explain erroneous conceptions that may be presented by the defense.

8.   The judge will then give the charge to the jury, explaining the jury's duty and obligations in the case. If requested by either side, the judge may include charges (legal explanations) that relate to any points of law involved in the case. In the federal courts and in a number of state courts, the judge has complete authority to comment on the evidence and the weight that may be given to it. He may also comment on inferences to be drawn from the evidence. In most courts, the judge will read and give certain written instructions to the jury. These set forth the legal principles or guidelines which should be used by the jury in applying the facts of the case. The judge also supplies the jury with written forms for possible verdicts, such as "guilty," "not guilty," etc. The jury is then taken into the jury room where intruders are not allowed. The jury is given an adequate opportunity to weigh the evidence and make a decision. If there is doubt as to the legal significance of a particular piece of evidence, the jury may request additional instructions from the judge.

Before a verdict of guilty can be rendered by the jury, every element of the crime charged must be proved beyond a reasonable doubt. The courts define reasonable doubt along the following lines:

> It is not a mere possible doubt; because everything relating to human affairs, and depending on moral evidence, is open to some possible or imaginary doubt. It is that state of the case which, after the entire comparison and consideration of all the evidence, leaves the minds of jurors in the condition that they cannot say they feel an abiding conviction, to a moral certainty, of the truth of the charge.

In a criminal trial, the basic prosecutive technique is to place witnesses on the stand and have them testify on direct examination. Thereafter, of course, these witnesses may be questioned by the defense attorney on cross-examination. There are some ways in which hearsay evidence or opinion may show up as evidence before the jury. The great bulk of all evidence, however, is through testimony of a witness as to what this individual saw, heard, or perceived through the physical senses (observation, hearing, smell, touch, or taste).

In general, the prosecutor asks the witness to state what he observed, heard, etc. at a particular place on a particular day. After these answers are furnished, the prosecutor is then entitled to ask additional questions that fill out the details in the answers previously given by the witness.

WITNESSES

Many kinds of evidence may be presented during the course of a criminal trial. This evidence is whatever "is capable of being weighed in the scales of reason and compared and estimated with other matter of a probative sort." Evidence may be a physical object or instrument used to commit the crime, such as a gun, a knife or a club. It may also be some object that creates some inference of guilt. In addition, it may consist of verbal testimony from an individual on the witness stand who observed or heard what took place.

The courts, of course, consistently say that every accused is presumed innocent until proven guilty. In addition, the courts inform the jury that every witness is presumed to speak the truth. If the unexplained testimony of one witness contradicts that of another, it is quite apparent that one of the witnesses is either mistaken or untruthful. Here, the courts say that the presumption that every witness is truthful may be overcome by the manner in which the witness testifies, by the nature of his or her testimony, by evidence affecting his or her character, interest or motives, or by contradicting evidence.

The jury is not required to find in favor of the side that presents the most witnesses, nor those that testify in a forceful, overbearing manner. The court does expect the jury to evaluate all the facts, the physical evidence, if any, and to side with those witnesses who seem believable under all the attendant circumstances. The jury should evaluate the witnesses, considering their reputation in the community, their ethics in business, and reputation for fair dealings with neighbors and acquaintances.

A witness has not committed a crime if he honestly testifies to facts that are not true. It is possible for anyone to be mistaken. But the courts insist on the truth and can never overlook perjury. The judge may instruct the prosecutor in open court to file perjury charges against a witness who appears to deliberately disregard the truth.

Impeachment of a Witness

In its most commonly used meaning, impeachment is a procedure for the removal from office of a public official for misconduct in office. Impeachment of a witness has a different legal meaning. In a criminal or civil trial, impeachment is the procedure for offering proof to show that a witness who has testified is not worthy of belief. This is not a technique for physically removing a false witness, it is a way of convincing the jury that the witness is either mistaken or dishonest.

Basically, a witness can be impeached in two ways:

1. By having other witnesses present evidence that shows or tends to show that the first witness has testified to an untruth. A variation of this type of impeachment is to show that previous statements by the witness were inconsistent with the witness' present testimony.

2. By exposing the fact that the witness has a bias, a motive for testifying in a particular way, or by showing that the witness has a poor reputation for truth and veracity. This is an indirect method that demonstrates to the jury that this particular witness may not be worthy of belief.

Impeachment, then, is a means of discrediting a witness so that other witnesses or other evidence will be believed. In impeachment, both the prosecutor and the defense attorneys are limited as to what they can ask the witness on cross-examination. State and federal statutes set out procedures for impeachment. For example, in California a state statute allows the impeachment of a witness by the party against whom he was called because of contradictory evidence, or by showing a bad general reputation for truth and veracity. Under this California law, evidence of particular wrongful acts committed by the witness cannot be used to impeach, unless proof of a felony conviction can be shown. This must, however, be a felony conviction for which a pardon was never granted, along with a certificate of rehabilitation.[1]

1. See Harris v. U.S., 401 US 222 and California Evidence Code, Sections 780–91.

It is a universal rule of law that the defendant cannot be forced to take the witness stand. If the accused voluntarily takes the stand in his or her own behalf, then the witness may be questioned about prior felony convictions, and may be impeached by presenting evidence of one or more convictions of a felony.

In most jurisdictions the judge can comment on the evidence, as well as the weight to be given to a particular bit of testimony. This is not allowed in some states, however. If the judge is permitted to comment, it can be expected that he will emphatically draw attention to testimony that is doubtful.

Through all this it must be kept in mind that it is the trial jury's job to weigh the evidence, to balance the testimony, and to decide who is telling the truth. There are times when honest witnesses may testify to exact opposites. The system depends on the good judgment of the jury and the ability of the jury members to sift out evidence that is false or mistaken.

The Privilege Against Self-Incrimination

It is a basic principle of English and American law that the ordinary witness cannot refuse to testify. An individual will be held in contempt for declining to take the witness stand. But no person can be required to testify to facts that may incriminate him. The Fifth Amendment to the U.S. Constitution provides: "No person . . . shall be compelled in any criminal case to be a witness against himself."

This privilege is recognized in the constitutions of forty-eight of the fifty states. The two remaining states, New Jersey and Iowa, achieve the same result in different ways. New Jersey allows the privilege by statute. The Iowa courts read the privilege into the due process clause of the Iowa Constitution. The effect of the prohibition is that a prosecutor or police official may never use either moral or physical means to force an individual to give testimony that may result in his conviction.

The courts have held that this privilege protects not only the defendant, but a witness as well. In addition, the privilege may be claimed in any kind of administrative hearing, in investigative inquiries before a legislative body, at a coroner's inquest, or before any court.

It is also to be noted that a witness in a federal court cannot be compelled to give testimony which could later be used in a state criminal prosecution. Likewise, forced state testimony cannot be used in a federal court proceeding.

219

A defendant is not required to put on any witnesses whatever. Or, the defendant may put on other witnesses and not take the stand himself. The prosecution can never call the defendant to the stand, so as to force him to claim his privilege against self-incrimination in the open courtroom. In addition, a prosecutor is not allowed to make any comment to the jury to the effect that the defendant must be guilty, since he refused to take the stand as a witness during his own trial. This is the law in both federal and state courts.

Some states have tried to get around this restriction by passing a statute that specifically permitted the prosecutor to comment on the defendant's refusal to come forward as a witness. A California law to this effect was held unconstitutional.[2] The reasoning of the United States Supreme Court in this case is that every defendant enjoys this right and it would be penalizing the defendant to force him to speak out to claim it.

There is a difference of opinion in the court decisions as to whether the trial judge is under a duty to tell the jury that the accused need not testify. Some defendants feel that this focuses unnecessary attention on the failure to testify.

Granting Immunity to a Witness

Federal laws and statutes in a number of states allow the prosecuting attorney to grant immunity from criminal prosecution to a witness. Once this immunity has been granted, a witness must testify or be held in contempt of court. Since the purpose of the immunity statutes is to obtain testimony for the prosecution, it has been uniformly held that the witness has complete immunity. In other words, the witness cannot be required to testify for the purpose of having the prosecution develop other testimony which may then be used against him in a subsequent prosecution.

Implied Consent Statutes

A number of states utilize so-called implied consent statutes. These laws provide that an individual who accepts a license from a state, such as a driver's license, has implicitly agreed to submit to an alcohol test in return for the privilege to drive. The claim has been made that this device allows the state to force an individual to give testimony against himself in order to retain his driver's license against

---

2. Griffin v. California, 380 US 609, 85 S Ct 1229 (1965).

a possible revocation. These laws have been upheld in the state courts, however.

Does Privilege Against Self-Incrimination Apply to Furnishing Evidence?

Legal authorities are in agreement that the privilege against self-incrimination centers around the right not to be forced to communicate information. But the accused can be forced to submit to a reasonable examination of his person or his clothing.

The United States Supreme Court has consistently upheld authorities in the taking of fingerprints, photos, measurements and blood samples. It is important to note, however, that this taking of physical objects or evidence applies only when the suspect is in lawful custody.[3] (This means that the suspect has to have been arrested on a valid warrant or on probable cause.)

Police and prosecuting authorities do not have the right to take an individual into custody for the sole purpose of obtaining specimens for comparison. In *Davis* v. *Mississippi*,[4] police authorities rounded up a number of individuals on the street in a "dragnet" operation. Fingerprints were then taken from all of these individuals, although there was nothing to connect them with a rape case. A comparison of the fingerprints of these suspects resulted in a positive identification of a fingerprint left at the scene of the rape. The suspect was then prosecuted and convicted. It was conceded that the fingerprint was taken during an illegal arrest, and the United States Supreme Court therefore overturned the conviction.

Of course, police officials can take blood samples, hair specimens, handwriting samples, or other items for comparison by inducing the suspect to sign a consent form. Approved by all courts everywhere, a consent form is merely a written permission allowing investigating authorities to take and use samples from the suspect. No particular wording is needed for a consent form, provided the consent form makes it clear that the specimens have been voluntarily given and can be used for comparison with known evidence or specimens associated with the criminal. The consent form should include the date and the place, with a description of the kind of specimens to be furnished, the name of the individual furnishing these materials, and a statement that the specimens were given

3. Schmerber v. California, 384 US 757, 86 S Ct 1826 (1966).
4. Davis v. Mississippi, 394 US 721, 89 S Ct 1394 (1969).

221

voluntarily. Some police departments and investigative agencies furnish consent forms, with blanks that may be filled in, to investigative officers who are likely to come in contact with physical evidence or individuals suspected of a criminal violation.

It is important for the consent form to reflect that the specimens were voluntarily given by the suspect. Preferably, the form should be signed by witnesses who hear the suspect state that the samples were voluntarily given. It may also be advisable to have a consent statement of this kind prepared by the prosecuting attorney.

It is also recommended that urine samples, blood samples, and other specimens from the suspect's body be taken by a nurse or physician, under approved medical conditions. It is not completely settled as to how far the courts will go in allowing an investigator to obtain samples of this kind, but the statements made by the courts consistently imply that no more force should be used than is absolutely necessary, and nothing should be done that could jeopardize the suspect's health or well-being.[5]

The courts also agree that handwriting specimens may be taken from a suspect for comparison with known handwriting of the criminal. This is not prohibited by the privilege against self-incrimination. However, if the specimens are not already in existence, and the suspect refuses, there is no way that he can be forced to provide them.[6]

The courts indicate that the investigator or police officer must act reasonably when obtaining specimens for courtroom use. Activity that suggests brutality will probably prevent the samples from being used as evidence in court.

Police Lineups As a Form of Self-Incrimination

Police officials frequently use a lineup procedure for the identification of criminals by those who were eyewitnesses to a crime. In the typical situation, the suspect and five or six other individuals of the same approximate age, size, and racial appearance are viewed in a lineup. These persons should also be dressed in similar or like fashion. The object of the lineup, of course, is to determine whether a witness can pick out the suspect from others with the same general appearance and features.

5. Schmerber v. California, 384 US 757 (1966).
6. Gilbert v. California, 388 US 263 (1967).

Unless considerable care is given to the handling of the lineup, the defense attorney may claim that the procedure was unfair. If the trial judge can be convinced of this, then the identification by witnesses will not be allowed as evidence during the trial. Police must be careful to not let one witness be present when another is viewing the lineup. Otherwise, the charge can be made that one witness influenced the other. If one person in the lineup is asked questions, requested to walk about, or engage in any other activity, then all individuals in the lineup should be taken through the same routine.

Nothing should be done, intentionally or otherwise, that could be regarded as suggestive or as pointing unusual attention toward a specific person in the line. Some police departments take detailed movies of the whole procedure, so that a charge of unfairness cannot be sustained.

There are three possible constitutional law problems that may be involved in forcing a suspect into a police lineup. These are:

1. Whether the suspect is being forced to provide evidence against himself, in a kind of self-incrimination;

2. Whether this is the kind of procedure in which the accused has a right to an attorney; and

3. Whether this lineup procedure is so suggestive to the witness as to be unfair, and to therefore be contrary to due process of law.

All criminal courts in the United States allow visual identifications to be made in open court during the course of the trial. The defendant's lawyer is present and is free to cross-examine the witness as to how the identification was made. Also, all courts are in agreement that the defendant has no right to deliberately surround himself with individuals who are similar in appearance (look-alikes), for the purpose of confusing courtroom witnesses.

In judging the fairness of police lineup techniques, the United States Supreme Court has said the trial court should consider whether alternative methods could have been used, and whether the approach that was actually taken seems basically unfair. In *Stovall* v. *Denno*,[7] a suspect was located near the scene of the crime and taken immediately to a hospital where the assault victim was in critical condition. No formal lineup procedure was held. The suspect was the only Black in the room when the identification was made by the

7. Stovall v. Denno, 388 US 93 (1967).

victim. No attempt had been made by the police to locate Black individuals of similar size and age to be used in a lineup. In reviewing this case on appeal, the United States Supreme Court said that these facts, in themselves, did not make the identification basically unfair. The Court pointed out that only a short time had elapsed when the suspect was located and taken to the hospital so the identification was apt to be accurate. The Court also took notice of the victim's condition, pointing out that the victim was seriously injured and that there was a possibility he could die before a regular lineup could be prepared. In addition, a procedure of this kind permits the suspect to be released immediately, if he is not the wanted individual.

In a California case, the victim reported to police that the crime had been committed by a male of Mexican descent who had a black eye. A suspect was located and placed in a police lineup of persons of Mexican descent who were of approximately the same age and size. The suspect, however, was the only one in the lineup with a black eye. On appeal, the California courts allowed the identification to stand. They made this decision on the basis that the lineup would have been unreasonably delayed by attempting to find a number of other individuals of similar age, size, and racial descent who had black eyes.[8]

In *United States* v. *Wade*,[9] the United States Supreme Court held that a police lineup conducted after the accused has been formally charged with a crime is a "critical stage of the proceedings," at which the accused has the right to have an attorney present. This decision took place in 1967. Five years later, however, in *Kirby* v. *Illinois*,[10] the United States Supreme Court decided that an individual does not have a right to an attorney at a police lineup until after that person has been formally charged with a crime.

In addition, the Wade case had been repudiated and overturned by the federal statute called the Omnibus Crime Control and Safe Streets Act of 1968, which provided that eyewitness identification of an accused was not made inadmissible by the fact that an attorney for the accused was not present at the time of the lineup.[11]

In a lineup, the courts have no objection to forcing the suspect to allow witnesses to observe the suspect's person, to require the suspect to speak, to wear a type of clothing worn by the criminal,

8. Martinez v. State, 274 Cal App 2d 487.
9. U. S. v. Wade, 388 US 218 (1967).
10. Kirby v. Illinois, 404 US 1055 (1972).
11. Omnibus Crime Control and Safe Streets Act of 1968, Title 15 United States Code, Section 3502.

and to walk in a manner known to have been used by the criminal. To require the suspect, alone, to wear a distinctive type of clothing that was worn by the criminal would be so suggestive as to be unfair.[12]

The courts agree that there are some occasions when a suspect can be viewed individually by the victim or another witness, without having to be placed in a lineup of individuals of the same general size, build, race, and other physical characteristics. These instances are:

1. When the suspect is still at the scene of the crime when located;

2. When the victim may be close to death and there is reasonable doubt as to whether there may be enough time for a lineup;

3. When the suspect insists he is innocent and requests to be taken immediately to confront the victim or other witness; or

4. When the victim is personally acquainted with the suspect, and has advised that this is the person who committed the crime.[13]

The Expert Witness

An expert witness is an individual called to testify by either side because of unusual technical, scientific, or medical ability. In the definition of one court, professional witnesses are: "Persons who are professionally acquainted with some science or are skilled in some art or trade, or who have experience or knowledge in relation to matters which are not generally known to the people."[14]

The courts, of course, cannot afford to waste time, so they generally allow only those witnesses to testify who have personal knowledge of the crime. The expert witness does not testify as one who saw or heard what happened. He testifies as to his scientific opinion regarding conclusions that can be drawn from the evidence presented by regular witnesses.[15]

12. See Simmons v. U.S., 390 US 377 (1968).
13. See Corpus Juris Secundum, Eyewitness Identification.
14. Miller v. State, 131 P 717, 9 Okl Cr 255.
15. Ronald L. Carlson, *Criminal Justice Procedure for Police*, (Cincinnati: The W. H. Anderson Co., 1970), p. 75.

Before anyone is allowed to testify as an expert witness, the attorney desiring this testimony must convince the trial judge that this individual really does have unusual knowledge or ability, and that it is pertinent to the case being tried. In some instances, the unusual skill or knowledge that qualifies the expert may be acquired from practical experience. In any event, the trial judge has the sole authority to decide whether the witness is a real expert and whether his testimony would throw any real light on the guilt or innocence of the accused. The judge is expected to allow expert testimony that will help the jury arrive at the truth, but the defendant has no right to demand that expert witnesses be heard.

Frequently, the expert may be a laboratory technician from the police scientific laboratory, the state bureau, or the FBI laboratory. The expert is expected to be unbiased, although his or her salary may be paid by the state or federal government. Any expert witness who is not paid by a governmental agency is usually paid a fee. Since the expert's unusual knowledge is for hire, the side that calls the expert to the stand undoubtedly expects favorable testimony.

Even highly qualified expert witnesses may not be in agreement after examining a piece of physical evidence, although specialists in the physical sciences will usually reach similar conclusions. Medical experts or psychiatrists will frequently testify to opposite conclusions as to the mental condition or sanity of a defendant in a criminal trial. These varying conclusions may represent honest differences of opinion, or may reflect the inexactness of some branches of science.

As to a typical case, an expert witness who is a specialist in blood chemistry may be called to testify as to suspected blood stains in a murder case. In the same trial, a ballistics specialist may testify as to whether a bullet found in the body of the victim matches up with samples fired from the defendant's gun. A third expert who is a soil chemist may testify as to whether particles on the accused's shoes match soil particles found at the scene of the crime.

MOTIONS

A motion is an application, either written or verbal, for a ruling or review by the judge on a particular aspect of a criminal procedure. It requests the judge to give a decision as to whether a specific action should be struck down or allowed to stand. A motion can be made at any stage of the prosecutive action as it becomes applicable. An appeal, however, is not appropriate until after the verdict and judgment of a criminal case have been handed down by the judge.

Any motion that is made must be timely. When improper testimony is being offered by a witness, an immediate objection should be made. If the judge goes ahead and allows the improper testimony over the objection, then this incident will subsequently serve as the basis for an appeal after the trial has been disposed of by the trial judge. Except for a motion to dismiss in the interest of justice, a motion must be timely, or the right to make it will be lost.

A motion to set aside judgment, or a motion to dismiss in the interest of justice, is a request for the court to throw out the prosecution as improper on its merits. A judgment rendered against an individual convicted of a crime beyond the statute of limitations would be one example of an improper prosecution.

There are a number of motions that may be made, usually by the defense attorney, as developments unfold during the course of the trial. Specific motions could include: motion to exclude evidence in a pretrial hearing; motion to quash a search warrant (a search warrant claimed to be illegal); motion to set aside an information or indictment (as being improperly returned); motion for a severance (to obtain a trial separate from other defendants in the same case); motion to suppress (the exclusion of illegally obtained evidence); motion for pretrial discovery; motion for change of venue (because of massive prejudice or community hostility at the location where the trial is to take place); motion for a directed verdict, or a motion requesting advice to acquit (requests for an instruction to the jury to acquit because a case was not proved beyond reasonable doubt), or in the latter instance (advice from the judge to acquit, which is not binding on the jury); motion for a new trial (which may be based on the discovery of new evidence). In the last situation named, all courts require newly discovered evidence to be very substantial, with a strong possibility that earlier discovery and introduction of this evidence would have altered the outcome of the trial.

Trying Two Defendants Jointly

In most instances, the prosecuting attorney may file only one complaint or indictment against two or more defendants who supposedly commited the same criminal act. Legally, this is called "joinder."

Generally, the trial judge has the discretion to hear the case either jointly or separately in the federal courts and practically all other jurisdictions. In deciding on this, the judge usually balances the efficiency of individual trials against the costs that may be involved.

If the attorney for one defendant can convince the judge that his client will be prejudiced by a joint trial, then the judge will order that the defendants be prosecuted separately. Legally, this is called a severance. If each individual refuses to admit the crime and throws the fault on the other, this does not automatically entitle either to a severance. If one defendant confesses, the other accused persons may be able to obtain a severance. The confession of one individual is admissable against him only. Under the rules of criminal evidence, this confession is "hearsay" in regard to other defendants and is therefore not admissable against them.

For a long time, the federal courts allowed the confession of one defendant, and the judge then instructed the jury that it was not to be considered against any other defendants. In *Bruton* v. *United States*,[16] the Supreme Court indicated that this procedure could be expected to color the thinking of the jury toward other defendants. Therefore, a severance must be granted unless the confession can be made in such a way that it does not make references to other defendants either directly or by inference.

Trying the Accused on Multiple Charges

The courts frequently combine prosecutions for multiple violations into a single prosecutive action. They do this in order to save time and money in witness fees, court costs, and administrative duplication.

Ordinarily, separate counts may be filed by the prosecutor, but the violations may be decided in a single trial if they were the outgrowth of a continuous course of action. If the violations were widely separated in time, with different witnesses, then they will usually be handled as separate trials.

If either the accused or the prosecution can present a reasonable argument to show prejudice, the judge has authority to grant a severance. Perhaps the most common situation of this kind involves a series of crimes in which one was very inflammatory, and likely to arouse the feelings of the jury. The accused may be able to convince the judge that bringing another criminal charge to the attention of the jury would unduly prejudice the jury against him. If the judge agrees, he will order separate trials.

16. Bruton v. U.S., 391 US 123 (1968).

DOUBLE JEOPARDY

Criminal trials would never come to an end if the issues in dispute could be raised time after time until a jury was found that would convict. Ancient Greek and Roman law followed the principle that an accused person could not be prosecuted more than once for the same offense. This principle was incorporated into the English common law and was codified by Blackstone, the famous English law scholar.

The Fifth Amendment to the U.S. Constitution specifies that "no person shall be . . . subject, for the same offense, to be twice put in jeopardy." This means, of course, having to run the risk of conviction a second time. This is somewhat different from the old common law principle that the accused should not be prosecuted again for the same offense after he had once been convicted or acquitted.

The U.S. Constitutional provision goes beyond the common law concept, which could possibly allow the case to be withdrawn from the jury after trial began in the expectation of finding another jury which might be more likely to convict. The court restriction is against second jeopardy, whether or not the prosecution progressed to a verdict. This court principle is called "double jeopardy," "former jeopardy," or "twice in jeopardy."

This prohibition is grounded on the two ideas of fair play and expediency for the courts. After all, a system of justice must respect the findings of its own courts, and it would not be proper to subject an individual to endless prosecutions regardless of the nature of the crime.[17] In addition, the courts would have an impossible work load if no verdict was ever final.

For many years it was unsettled as to whether the prohibition of the U.S. Constitution applied to state prosecutions as well as those in federal court. In *Benton* v. *Maryland*,[18] the United States Supreme Court ruled that double jeopardy is a fundamental right that applies to both federal and state trial.

17. As stated by the Supreme Court of the United States in Green v. United States, 355 US 184 (1957), ". . . the state with all its resources and power should not be allowed to make repeated attempts to convict an individual for an alleged offense, thereby subjecting him to embarrasment, expense and ordeal and compelling him to live in a continuing state of anxiety and insecurity."
  See Rollin M. Perkins, *Criminal Law and Procedure,* 3d ed., (Brooklyn: The Foundation Press, 1966), pp. 725–29.
18. Benton v. Maryland, 395 US 784, 89 S Ct 149 (1969). Palko v. Connecticut, 302 US 319 (1937) and Mahon v. Justice, 127 US 700 (1888).

When Double Jeopardy Applies

Generally, the courts say that the accused has been placed in jeopardy when a competent jury is sworn in to hear the case, or when the first witness takes the oath in a trial without a jury. When either of these conditions is met, the defendant cannot be prosecuted again, and it is not necessary for the trial to go on to an acquittal or a conviction.

It should be pointed out, however, that a mistrial usually permits a second trial, since the courts say this is not double jeopardy. A mistrial is a false start that may cause the trial to begin all over again with a new jury. To avoid a dismissal for double jeopardy, however, the mistrial must not be the fault of the prosecution.

For example, if the judge dies during the trial or the defendant becomes so ill that he cannot stand to continue, a resulting mistrial will not prevent a retrial of the defendant. Also, if the jury is never able to agree on a verdict (hung jury), a second prosecution does not justify a claim of double jeopardy. However, if the prosecution has caused the mistrial, a claim of double jeopardy would be sustained if a second prosecution was begun.

If the accused is convicted and subsequently wins a new trial on appeal because of an error during the original prosecution, it is not regarded as double jeopardy. The courts say the accused waives his double jeopardy right when he appeals.[19] A mistrial resulting from the prosecutor's failure to call a necessary witness would be an instance of this kind.[20]

In case of an appeal, the defendant cannot be charged with a more serious crime if granted a new trial. The courts usually say that the defendant was considered to have been cleared of all more serious charges.[21]

What Is the Same Offense?

There is considerable disagreement among the courts as to when the defendant is being tried for "the same offense."

1.   The principle usually accepted by the courts is as follows: if an individual commits two separate crimes in one act, a conviction

19. U.S. v. Tateo, 377 U.S. 463 (1964).
20. Downum v. U.S. 734 (1963).
21. Price v. Georgia, 398 U.S. 323 (1970).

for one crime will not prevent prosecution for the other. For example, in one case an archer deliberately shot an arrow at his estranged ex-wife, but missed the target and killed a passerby. The archer could be convicted of the attempted murder of his wife as well as the murder of the passerby. A plea of former jeopardy would not be allowed.[22]

2. A smaller number of courts, however, follow a somewhat different approach. The decisions on this matter say that double jeopardy will apply if the two injuries resulted from the same act and the same intent. Double jeopardy would not be involved in the case of the archer shooting at his estranged ex-wife unless the archer intended to kill the passerby with the same arrow.

3. Still other courts in this situation look to the evidence that would be necessary to obtain a conviction under the second prosecution to see whether exactly the same evidence would have sustained a conviction under the first prosecution. When the evidence is identical, these courts hold that the defendant is being prosecuted a second time for the same crime.

4. A small number of courts hold that only one crime has been committed if the claimed violations arose out of the same transaction.

Appeals by the Prosecution

There are only three states in which the prosecution has the right to appeal the result of a criminal trial. In other jurisdictions the constitutional provision against double jeopardy has been interpreted to prevent the prosecution from appealing if the accused is acquitted.

There seems to be a trend, however, toward granting the right of appeal to the prosecution in some holdings of a pretrial nature. In Illinois, for example, criminal code provisions allow the state to appeal an unfavorable ruling suppressing evidence that is claimed to have been illegally obtained by the government, or to appeal a court order dismissing the charge against the accused.

It is the judge's duty to make certain that the jury is properly instructed. For this purpose, most courts have a manual of approved

22. Cicucci v. Illinois, 356 U.S. 571 (1948).

jury instructions that have been tested by appeals in prior cases. It is up to the judge to let each juror know that he is free to vote according to his own conscience, but that he must make every reasonable effort to arrive at a decision with other members of the jury.

Some federal courts allow a jury to go home at night, returning to continue deliberations on the following day. Other federal courts do not follow this practice, however. There is also a difference of opinion in state courts as to whether the jury must be locked up for the night. In most states, this is left to the discretion of the trial judge.

A jury will be discharged if a verdict of guilt or innocence cannot be reached after a reasonable period of deliberation. Here again, the judge has discretion as to what is reasonable. When there is no agreement, and the jury is discharged, it is called a "hung jury."

After discharge, the prosecution can start the trial over again with a new jury. Failure of jurors to agree does not constitute double jeopardy. In fact, a case that continues to result in a hung jury can be tried any number of times. It is very unusual, however, for a case to be tried more than twice. After the evidence has been considered by a second jury, without a conviction, the prosecutor usually has serious doubts as to the merits of his case. At times, the judge may also step in, advising the prosecution off the record that the government has had two opportunities to convict, and that further prosecution may be considered harassment, or may place an unreasonable burden on the defendant.

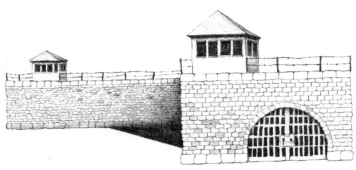

THE SENTENCING PROCESS

A jury trial terminates when a unanimous verdict of acquittal or guilty is reached, and the jury foreman reports this fact to the judge. In most jurisdictions, the jurors are then polled (questioned) by the judge or a court clerk, to verify their vote. If there is disagreement, the jury is sent back to the jury room for further deliberations. If there is hesitation or doubt, the trial judge will not accept the findings.

If the jury returns a verdict of acquittal, the judge must accept it. If the judge forms the impression that the jury may have misinterpreted the law, however, the judge can send the jury back for further consideration, after again informing the jury as to the law which governs this particular case.

In most situations the jury can find the accused guilty of a less serious crime than the violation with which he was charged. In violations where it is pertinent, the jury can find whether or not the accused used a dangerous weapon. Similarly, the jury has the authority to decide the existence of a prior conviction, if the accused is charged with being a habitual criminal.

If the accused waived his right to a jury trial, the judge hearing the case announces his findings in substantially the same way that they would be handled in a jury trial.

After a verdict of guilty is announced by the jury, the judge will usually order the defendant committed to jail, although he may be continued on bail if he is not considered a serious danger to the community.

Sentencing is always done by the judge, but in a number of states, the jury is permitted to set the sentence or to recommend punishment for certain kinds of violations. The federal law requires that the defendant shall be sentenced without a reasonable delay. State laws frequently specify a specific period in which sentence must be imposed. The courts allow this period to be extended, however, if the judge finds good cause.

On the day set for sentencing, the judge orders the defendant brought back into court, if he has been held in jail. If the defendant was allowed to remain on bail, then he is expected to come in voluntarily or a "bench warrant" will be issued for his arrest. When the defendant is brought before the court, he must appear with his attorney unless the court is one of those that will allow him to waive this right. If there is any question, however, the judge will insist that his attorney be present or will appoint an attorney for him.

At this time, most courts allow the defendant to exercise the right of "allocution," which is the right to make a verbal statement as to why the court should be lenient with him or as to why he should not be sentenced at all. There is no set rule on this matter, but most judges will allow the defendant a reasonable amount of time in which to express his feelings and to give reasons why he thinks he deserves consideration.

Immediately thereafter, the judge pronounces sentence. The judge must then notify the defendant of his rights to appeal in federal court.

Between the date of conviction and the time of sentencing, the judge and members of his staff have conducted an investigation into the background of the defendant. Usually, this job is assigned to the court's probation officer, who prepares a detailed, written report.

In some states the sentencing judge has discretionary authority to authorize a physical and mental examination for the convicted individual. In New York State for example the code provides:

> . . . In the case of a felony or a Class A misdemeanor, or in any case a person under the age of 21 is convicted of a crime, the court may order that the defendant undergo a thorough physical or mental examination in a designated facility and may further order that the defendant remain in such facility for such purpose for a period not exceeding 30 days.[23]

Under the New York statutes, a judge may not sentence a defendant convicted of a serious offense until the judge has received a fingerprint report from the New York State Identification and Intelligence system or a police department report with respect to the defendant's prior arrest record.[24] This, of course, enables the judge to decide whether the convicted person could likely benefit from probation, or whether he may be a dangerous menace to society.

In most states where presentence investigations are required, a copy of the presentence report, a copy of any presentence memorandum filed by the defendant, and a copy of any medical, psychiatric, or social agency report submitted to the court or to the probation department in connection with the question of sentence must be delivered to the person in charge of the correctional facility to which the defendant is committed. This must be done at the time the defendant is delivered to the facility.[25]

In setting a sentence, the trial judge will usually take into account the kind of crime and the seriousness of the offense. He will also consider whether the crime was an individual act, or whether it

23. McKinney's Consolidated Laws of New York, Section 390.30.
24. McKinney's Consolidated Laws of New York, Section 390.10.
25. McKinney's Consolidated Laws of New York, Section 390.60.

was part of a whole series of offenses. The judge is also interested in the defendant's prior criminal record, his age, and family connections. He will usually consider whether the defendant pleaded guilty or was convicted after a long, costly trial, even though there was an abundance of convincing evidence of guilt. The judge also usually considers whether the accused will be a menace to society and whether individuals in his family may be able to influence him to take his conviction to heart and lead a proper life. Some trial judges feel that a lighter sentence may be justified for an individual who pleads guilty, since the guilty plea indicates a readiness to accept responsibility for his acts and is an indication that the defendant is seeking rehabilitation.

A number of options may be available to the judge who pronounces sentence. He may grant probation, especially if the conviction was the first serious confrontation with the law that the defendant had experienced. Usually, probation will not be granted if the convicted individual is a menace to public safety or if it is obvious that he will not seek help or have remorse for his actions.

Usually, probation is not allowed if the offense is an extremely serious one. In considering probation, the judge may desire to know whether the defendant can hold a job and support his family, since a prison sentence may force the family to go on welfare. In addition, the court may consider whether the defendant may be able to make some restitution to the victim, or the victim's family, if he is allowed to work. The judge weighs the facts here and will not grant probation unless he believes that society will benefit more from supervised relief than from imprisonment.

In some states, the judge may sentence the defendant to a specific term of years in a penal institution. If the convict is a young man, the judge may specify that the sentence is to be served in a reformatory. If the defendant has been convicted of two or more crimes, or is already serving a sentence for another conviction, it is necessary for the judge to decide whether the present sentence is to run concurrently (at the same time) or consecutively (one after the other with the prior sentences). This decision is within the discretion of the trial judge, although in some instances a consecutive sentence may be stretched so far into the future that the defendant cannot expect to live long enough to serve it.

Under the federal court system, the district judge may set a specific term of years, or may authorize federal correctional officials to do so. In some states, the judge sentences the defendant to an indeterminate sentence. Under a system of this kind, the terms may

235

vary. In some states, the judge specifies the minimum and the maximum terms to be served by the defendant. For example, he may sentence the defendant to a term of not less than five nor more than fifteen years for armed robbery. In still other states, the sentence may not specify a minimum period, but will set out a maximum sentence. Under this system, some prisoners may serve the entire maximum sentence.

The Indeterminate Sentence

Under so-called indeterminate sentence laws, the judge sets both a minimum term and a maximum term for the sentence that must be served. This difference could span a considerable range of years. The time served for assault with a deadly weapon, for example, could vary from six months to life, depending on evaluations as to the progress being made by the prisoner toward reform. The length of time served would eventually be set by an adult authority or parole board, after hearings with the prisoner and prison officials.

Regarded as a bold and liberal experiment by correctional authorities in the 1920's and 1930's, the indeterminate sentence concept was adopted into law in the states of California and Washington. In late 1976, however, California switched back to a system in which the sentencing judge initially determines the length of the sentence.

The indeterminate sentence system originated with the idea that prisons are similar to hospitals, and that some inmates will be rehabilitated more quickly than others. The indeterminate sentence is supposed to assure the early release of persons ready to leave prison. On the other hand, some convicts can function well in a controlled setting such as a penitentiary, but are not stable enough to function well in the outside world.

Part of the rationale behind indeterminate sentencing laws was that the question of release should be taken out of the hands of the sentencing judge, who might either be unduly harsh or unduly lenient, and who might be affected by politics. The contention was also made that the members of the state adult authority should be experts in penology and human behavior, and should therefore be able to more intelligently determine when the convict is ready for release or parole.[26]

---

26. See Daniel Glasser, *The Effectiveness of a Prison and Parole System,* (Indianapolis: The Bobbs-Merrill Co., Inc., 1964), which has a discussion of practical measures to use in reforming criminals.

While the indeterminate sentencing system seems good in theory, many correctional authorities have questioned the results obtained. In some instances, an individual may be kept in prison year after year for a minor violation. In other cases, the convict can receive the equivalent of a life sentence, with no certainty that he will ever be released, although the crime was not of the type intended to be punished by a lengthy incarceration. Convicts frequently complain that this system causes them to lose hope.

Disparity in Sentencing for Similar Offenses

There are undoubtedly disparities in sentences given to individuals convicted on identical charges. Some of this variation is owing to the different backgrounds and philosophies of the individual judges who decide the sentences. Some students of the criminal justice system feel that it would be more equitable for sentences to be worked out by a panel of judges. There seems to be good reason to favor this approach.

Often, however, the judge is aware of many factors that never come to the attention of the newspapers or the public. One holdup man, for example, may have gone out of his way to hurt the victim after the robbery. Another individual convicted for the same crime may have merely taken the loot and departed. The judge may have gained the impression that the convicted man had no remorse whatever, while the other individual may have begun self-rehabilitation before the trial was completed. Instances of this kind may, of course, be nothing more than good acting on the part of the accused individual and there undoubtedly may be times when a judge can be taken in by such behavior. Most judges, however, have the worldly experience to evaluate situations of this kind.

There may never be a perfect system for eliminating disparities between sentences. The possibility of sentencing by a panel of judges may, however, offer opportunity for improvement.

An unusual approach to sentencing was enacted into law in California in 1976 (Statutes of 1976, Chapter 1139). Under this law, fixed sentences are applied to all crimes, except those that carry the death penalty or a life term. The new California sentencing system is designed to reduce disparities in sentences handed out by judges.

Unless probation is granted, the judge must choose from among three alternative terms of imprisonment specified by the law. There are four classes of sentences, depending on the seriousness of the crime. One class of sentence specifies terms of three, four, or five years for crimes such as sale of heroin or burglary involving safe-

237

cracking. When a prisoner comes up for sentencing for a crime in this class, the judge must choose the middle term of four years, unless the prosecution or defense can persuade the judge in a hearing that the sentence should be raised to five years or lowered to three years. The judge is required to choose the middle term, unless aggravating or mitigating facts can be shown.

Unequal Punishment Because Of The Defendant's Financial Condition

In 1970, the United States Supreme Court accepted the argument that greater punishment could not be imposed on a poor man than a rich man, because of the poor man's inability to pay a fine. Prior to the case of *Williams* v. *Illinois*[27] it had been very common for justices in the inferior courts or municipal courts to sentence a drunk to a sentence such as "$25.00 or twenty-five days." For many years, the drunk without funds had been forced to stay in jail because he could not meet the fine. In *Williams* v. *Illinois*, the claim was made that a penniless defendant should not be forced to go to jail because of his lack of money. It was felt this was unfair treatment because of his economic condition. In the Williams case and the Tate case,[28] the Supreme Court accepted the idea that the defendant must be given a reasonable opportunity to pay a fine that is within his economic means. Only if he deliberately refuses to pay an amount that he is able to pay, can he then be imprisoned.

Cruel and Unusual Punishments are not Allowed

The Eighth Amendment to the U.S. Constitution prohibits "cruel and inhuman punishment." The United States Supreme Court held that this prohibition applies to the individual states through the due process clause of the Fourteenth Amendment.

There have been few cases involving this constitutional provision and they have been divided into two groups. One class of cases takes the approach that an individual may not be subjected to any treatment that is barbaric, cruel, or degrading. In other words, a court can sentence a man but can never strip him of his basic dignity. If a convicted individual was sentenced to be chained to a post and spat upon by other inmates, the sentence would undoubtedly be struck down. Any form of physical torture would likewise be prohibited.

27. Williams v. Illinois, 399 US 235 (1970).
28. Tate v. Short, 401 US 395 (1971).

Burning at the stake would be forbidden as a form of execution for the same reason.

The second class of cases involves sentences which have been set aside because the appellate court believed that the sentence was disproportionate to such an extent that it shocked the moral sense of the community. In other words, there must be a reasonable correlation between the sentence and the criminal act. In one instance of this kind, the convicted individual was sentenced to twelve years in irons at hard labor. This sentence resulted from a conviction for falsifying public records. The United States Supreme Court considered this sentence excessive, and the sentence was set aside.[29]

CRIMINAL REPEATERS (RECIDIVISTS)

Some individuals will admit that they would continue indefinitely in a life of crime, except for the fact that imprisonment is simply too trying a mental experience. Other convicted persons do not seem to

29. Weems v. U.S., 217 US 349 (1910).

be so disturbed by the process. (In con talk, "some do hard time, and some do not.")

In an effort to force criminals to conform to the rules of society, a number of states have passed so-called "habitual criminal statutes." Some of these laws increase the punishment for repeated involvement in any kind of felonies, while other statutes make the penalty more severe for two or more convictions for the same specific crime. Some enactments of this type make a criminal repeater ineligible for parole.

A repeater (recidivist) may be charged both with having committed a specific crime and with being an habitual violator. These are separate felonies, and the accused may be sentenced on both charges.

The procedure usually followed is to require separate pleas from the accused. Since evidence of a prior conviction cannot be presented to the jury hearing the current charge, the habitual criminal charge must be held until after a verdict is reached by the jury on the specific violation. The court will then allow the prior conviction to be raised in connection with the allegation of repeated violations. Some states utilize two separate juries to hear the two matters involved. Other jurisdictions utilize only one jury, allowing evidence of the prior conviction to be presented only after a verdict has been reached on the specific violation.[30]

Sexual Psychopath Laws

Some states have statutes that permit the trial judge to determine whether a convicted person is a mentally disoriented sex offender. After conviction in California, for example, a hearing may be held to determine whether the convicted person is a sexual psychopath. If such is found to be the case, the convicted individual may be committed for treatment to a state hospital, where he is held "until no longer a danger to the health and safety of others."[31]

While sexual psychopath laws were undoubtedly well-intended, there is a question as to whether these laws operate as planned. The criticism is sometimes made that laws of this kind permit judges to

---

30. See Spencer v. Texas, 385 US 554 (1966) and Burgett v. Texas, 389 US 109 (1967). In most jurisdictions, allegations concerning prior convictions cannot be read to the jury trying the charge of the first offense. See California Penal Code, Section 1025.

31. California Welfare and Institutional Code, Sec. 5501.

sentence minor deviates for indefinite periods to mental hospitals that lack capability to assist the convict. Some students of constitutional law are of the opinion that in singling out individuals of this kind, the justice system must afford treatment or give up the idea of segregation.[32]

Juvenile Convictions—Youthful Offender Procedures

An enlightened system of justice treats all violators as equally as possible. One exception is that American courts are understandably reluctant to handle juveniles in the same way as adult criminals. In one sense, this is an admission that adult offenders are not as likely to be reformed as younger violators.

Every offender should, of course, realize that he must face the consequences of his acts. However, the juvenile has often had only limited experience to draw from. He may be more naive in the ways of the world, and easily persuaded toward crime by older companions.

A criminal record may leave a blight on the convicted person's reputation for years, even though he lives an exemplary life thereafter. This is one of the unwritten penalties exacted by society. To avoid this stigma for a single conviction, most states have passed youth offender laws or juvenile delinquency statutes.

The courts of these states usually have two procedures: one for ascertaining whether the juvenile is guilty, and the second to provide special handling to the juvenile if he is not discharged. These youthful offender laws are uniform in purpose, but they vary considerably in application.

Some states destroy the fingerprints and booking record of the juvenile first offender, provided the individual is able to avoid arrest thereafter for a set period of time. Other states have differing procedures that eventually allow the first offender to resume his life with a clean record.

Under most of these statutes, the youthful offender process is not, accurately speaking, a criminal prosecution. It is a quasilegal action. According to this reasoning, a youthful offender adjudication is not a judgment of conviction for a crime or any other offense.

Most state statutes leave it to the discretion of the juvenile

---

32. See McNeil v. Director, 407 US 245 (1972).

judge at the outset to decide whether an individual below a certain age should be treated as an adult or as a juvenile for court purposes. In some instances it is mandatory that the offender be treated as a juvenile. In some instances the decision is based on whether the judge feels that the accused could benefit from the care and treatment afforded by the juvenile courts.

Under most procedures followed, the youthful offender is given a hearing that corresponds to the trial of an adult, although the procedure may be quite informal in tone. Nevertheless, the juvenile will not be held unless evidence is produced to prove guilt beyond a reasonable doubt. The juvenile is entitled to an attorney, and he must be afforded his rights, just as though he was an adult. The only exception is that he is not entitled to a jury trial.[33]

If the juvenile is found to have been responsible for a criminal act, a second procedure is used in most states. This involves a consideration of evidence in determining how the juvenile should be handled. If the prospect for rehabilitation seems encouraging, he may be placed on probation and returned to home care and court supervision, if the home environment seems to be reasonable. Insofar as possible, the juvenile will not be placed in a regular prison, where it is feared he may make contact with hardened convicts.

The New York state courts reach the same end result, although they utilize a different approach. In New York, a juvenile is put on trial in the same manner as any other individual, and a youthful offender adjudication is postponed until a criminal conviction has resulted. This conviction may be based either on a plea of guilty or on a jury finding. After a presentence investigation, the court declares its findings on the youthful offender. In some instances the youthful offender classification is mandatory. In other cases it is optional and is left up to the judge. His decision usually depends on the age of the youth, the nature of the offense, and the youth's prior record. Even though this system postpones an adjudication until after conviction, the judge begins record sealing and privacy actions at the outset of the trial, if it appears that the accused may be eligible for youthful offender status. If it is determined that the accused is a youthful offender, the New York judge vacates the conviction and continues with the record sealed.[34]

In California, all violators under the age of twenty-one fall under the jurisdiction of the juvenile court. If the judge feels that

33. McKiever v. Pennsylvania, 403 US 528 (1971).
34. McKinney's Consolidated Laws of New York, Section 720.20.

the youth is already too hardened to benefit by being handled as a juvenile, the judge has the option of ordering a regular criminal trial, if the youth is sixteen or over and is accused of a felony, or if the youth is eighteen or over and is accused of a misdemeanor.

If the matter is retained in juvenile court by the California judge, he has three options:

1. To dismiss the matter if adequate proof is not forthcoming;

2. To place the youth on probation for up to six months; or

3. To declare the youth to be a ward of the juvenile court. Usually, this results in a commitment to the California Youth Authority. A minor who completes this commitment will be released on his twenty-first birthday or on the expiration of two years, whichever occurs last. In addition, the criminal charges will be dismissed.[35]

SUMMARY

The accused must be competent to stand trial—that is, the defendant must be sane, able to understand the nature of the charges, and able to participate in the defense. In the trial, the prosecutor introduces the evidence to show guilt. This usually consists of the testimony of eyewitnesses—persons who heard or saw what happened. Physical evidence is also introduced. The defense is then allowed to rebut this evidence, and to cross-examine the witnesses. Defense witnesses can also be presented and cross-examined by the prosecutor. The accused can never be forced to testify or furnish evidence. The defendant is not required to put on any evidence or call any witnesses, and cannot be required to take the witness stand or be cross-examined without voluntarily testifying in his or her own defense. If a witness is not being prosecuted, however, immunity from criminal prosecution can be granted by the prosecutor and the witness can be jailed for contempt if he refuses to testify. Blood samples, urine samples and other specimens can be taken from the suspect's body if a lawful arrest of the suspect has been made. Handwriting specimens can also be required by the court for comparison with samples of evidence. Two defendants may not be tried jointly if the judge is convinced that the rights of either accused may

35. California Welfare and Institutions Code, Sec. 602 to Sec. 1179.

be prejudiced by the joint trial. In addition, an accused may not be twice subjected to the possibility of punishment for the same offense.

If the jury returns a verdict of acquittal, the judge must accept it and free the accused, unless it seems clear that the jury misinterpreted the law. If the accused waives the right to a jury trial, the judge hearing the case announces findings in substantially the same way that they would be handled in a jury trial. Sentencing is always done by the judge, but in a number of states the jury is permitted to set the sentence or recommend the sentence to the judge. The defendant and the defendant's attorney appear before the judge at the time of sentencing, and the defendant is allowed to make a verbal statement asking for mercy or for a light sentence. In most states sentencing takes place only after an investigation of the convicted individual's background by the court probation officer. In setting the sentence, the judge usually takes into account the seriousness of the violation, the defendant's prior criminal record, age, family connections, personal attitudes, and whether the subject is a fit person for probation. Cruel or unusual punishments will be struck down or altered by the appellate courts. Under the indeterminate sentence system, the judge does not sentence to a specific term. Instead, the sentence specifies a minimum term and a maximum term. The sentence actually served is determined by the state adult authority or state parole board, based on the prisoner's record, attitudes, and hopes for success in the outside world. In 1976, California changed from an indeterminate sentence system. The sentencing judge now sets the length of time to be served at the time sentence is passed.

QUESTIONS

1. What material is presented by the prosecuting attorney in his opening statement at the time of trial?
2. What is meant by "direct examination," or "examination in chief."?
3. In cross-examination, may the witness be asked questions that do not pertain to the material discussed on direct examination? Why?
4. If the jury does not agree on a verdict, may the case be retried? If so, how many times?
5. In general, what is meant by the privilege against self-incrimination?

6. Is the defendant required to put on a specific number of witnesses in connection with his defense? Why?

7. What are the basic requirements for a legal police lineup?

8. Does an accused have a right to an attorney in a police lineup?

9. Under what conditions may police take urine, blood, or handwriting samples from a suspect?

10. What is meant by a fair trial? Outline some of the conditions that must be present in a fair trial.

11. May court attendants or bailiffs urge the jury to convict the accused? Why?

12. Can the jury find the accused guilty of a less serious crime than that violation with which he was charged?

13. What is the defendant's right of allocution?

14. Do most courts conduct a background investigation before sentencing? Explain your answer.

15. What are some of the factors that a judge will usually consider in sentencing the convicted individual?

16. What is an indeterminate sentence? What are the objections to it?

17. What remedies have been proposed to correct the disparities in sentencing?

18. Have the courts had anything to say about the argument that greater punishment could not be imposed on a poor man than a rich man, because of the poor man's inability to pay a fine?

19. Is an excessive sentence considered cruel and unusual punishment?

20. What is a habitual criminal statute? Is it constitutional?

21. What is meant by a sexual psychopath law?

22. What are the arguments for juvenile delinquency laws that try juveniles separately, or handle them separately from adult offenders?

Effective treatment in an institution involves much more than safe custody, improving health, developing educational and vocational skills, and stimulating wholesome leisure-time interests. There must be a climate favorable to the growth and change of personality.

Manual of Correctional Standards, 6th ed., (College Park, Md.: American Correctional Association). 1946, p. 577.

chapter thirteen

CORRECTIONAL CONCEPTS AND PROBLEMS

The purpose of this chapter is to examine those objectives that society seeks to achieve through corrections. There are many problems in this area that closely affect society and the criminal justice system.

THE ROLE OF PREVENTION

We have pointed out earlier that the basic purpose of the criminal justice system is to eliminate, or at least to reduce, crime and delinquency. Obviously, it is to the benefit of society as a whole to remove those conditions that spawn crime. The factors that contribute to the making of delinquents and criminals are many and complex. The sooner preventive techniques can be applied in instances of this kind, the more likelihood there is for success. Many of the causal factors that incline individuals toward crime arise from destructive early human relationships, especially those relating to the home. Therefore, it seems vital for society to strengthen relationships in the family, in the schools, and in other institutions that shape the lives of our young people. Many of these factors carry over into correctional concepts.

Public Attention

Almost invariably, the public interest in a criminal case centers around the arrest and trial of the offender. After the sentence is imposed, newspapers and television reporters turn to other interests. It is apparent, however, that at this stage of the proceedings the real work of the criminal justice system has hardly begun. The court conviction focuses attention on the defendant as an individual needing special attention to persuade that person to live within the law.

Up to the time of sentencing, we could say that the system has served the general public. The system must now concentrate on the specific individuals, seeking to return the convict to a useful place in society. This, in turn, will indirectly benefit the general public.

The basic organization of the criminal law was designed to set up a system of penalties and threats to discourage potential offenders. It is the fear of these sanctions that has a deterring effect on most persons. When an individual goes ahead and disregards these sanctions, however, the prosecutive system must come into play, followed by sentencing.

What is Society Looking For in the Sentencing Process?

When a verdict of guilty is returned, the trial judge completes the trial procedure by imposing sentence. In broad terms, the judge may take into consideration the seriousness of the social damage involved in the offense, and the way in which the crime was committed. At the same time, the sentence should also reflect society's hope and expectations for rehabilitation.

A number of present day authorities on correctional procedures believe that sentencing should involve a combination of three basic concepts:

1. The use of noninstitutional treatment for those offenders who can benefit from such handling;

2. The need for incarceration for really dangerous criminals; and

3. Institutional handling and treatment for those in between the requirements of probation and prolonged imprisonment.[1]

1. *Manual of Correctional Standards,* 3d ed., (College Park, Md.: American Correctional Association, 1966), pp. xx, xxi, 34.

Most criminologists are in agreement that society can accomplish nothing by a vindictive, or punishment theory of sentencing.[2] For thousands of years the governments and rulers of many lands followed the old concept of "an eye for an eye, and a tooth for a tooth." Even today, there are still some countries where a thief will have his hand chopped off with a sword immediately after conviction. Undoubtedly, penalties of this kind will have a sobering effect on some persons who may be tempted to violate the law. However, a system of this kind is not in keeping with our ideas of humane, civilized treatment.

The wording of our criminal laws is usually designed to punish the individual offender by imposing a penalty corresponding to the gravity of the offense committed. Thus, in one sense, most of our statutes are worded in terms that are punitive, rather than reformative in character. At the same time, the constitutions of many of our state governments contain a statement to the effect that "the enforcement of the criminal laws of this State shall be based on reformation, and not upon vindictive justice."

As a civilized society, we can never consider a return to a vindictive system, with sentencing for punishment's sake. On the other hand, we can never have an effective system of justice if law enforcement officers do not immediately bring violations to the attention of the prosecutors, if prosecutors do not bring criminals to answer for crimes they actually committed, and if the courts allow technical obstructions that hamper conviction after the accused has had fair treatment and the agreement of reasonable jurors as to his guilt.

Many officials who have had close contact with violators and criminals agree on the following concepts regarding punishment. Most criminals are not deterred appreciably by the possibilities of long sentences or serious punishment, so long as they feel these consequences are problematical, or somewhere in the indefinite future. The criminal is deterred by the likelihood of arrest almost immediately after the offense is perpetrated, and by the prospect of prompt prosecution for the crime he actually committed. This seems to be true, even though the criminal feels the judge will be completely fair to him. It is the certainty of apprehension and punishment, rather than the harshness of the sentence that reinforces the sanctions of the criminal justice system.

Of course, authorities on penology do not completely dismiss the concept of punishment. Almost any convict will tell you that a

2. Ibid, pp. 3–39.

prison sentence is punishment in itself, regardless of the fair and humane standards that may be followed by the prison administration. It is not possible to make confinement so pleasant that the inmates will not regard a penitentiary sentence as punishment. Prison officials know it is neither justifiable nor necessary to add to the punishment that automatically accompanies separation from family and friends, loss of liberty, the hours of uncertainty, and the loss of reputation that follows a prison term.

It is apparent that imprisonment furnishes society some protection from criminals, merely by confining violators for long periods, up to life imprisonment. But since the vast majority of prisoners eventually return to society, it is obvious that imprisonment has limited value in this regard.[3]

The Judge Needs Specific Information for Sentencing

As a class, judges have considerable experience, education, and exposure to the problems of the world. Few judges, however, have the time to personally delve into the background, family and economic problems, capabilities, and potentials of the individual standing before the bar to be sentenced.

In the staffing alignment usually followed in this country, the probation service makes inquiries on behalf of the judge. As the court's investigative arm, the probation officer determines whether the subject has had previous problems with the law, as well as

3. For background reading on corrections, deterrence, and reformation, see the following:

Charles L. Newman, *Sourcebook on Probation, Parole and Pardons*, Second Edition, Springfield, Ill.: Charles C. Thomas Publishers, 1964

Walter M. Moberly, *The Ethics of Punishment*, Hamden, Conn.: Archon Books, 1968

Manual of Correctional Standards, Issued by the American Correctional Association, College Park, Md.: Second Edition, 1959

Harry E. Barnes and Negley K. Teeters, *New Horizons In Criminology*, Englewood Cliffs: Prentice-Hall, Third Edition, 1959

Paul W. Keve, *The Probation Officer Investigates*, (Minneapolis: University of Minnesota Press), 1960

Richard A. McGee, "The Administration of Justice," Crime and Delinquency, July, 1959, pp. 225–39.

Henry M. Hart, Jr., "The Aims of the Criminal Law," Law and Contemporary Problems, 23, # 3 Summer, 1958, pp. 404–10.

determining his attitudes toward the current difficulty. The probation officer delves into the subject's social adjustments, family relationships, and the causal connections that led up to the commission of the crime. In addition, inquiry is made into the subject's economic problems, employment record, and work adjustments.

Based on the facts developed, as well as on experience and judgment, the probation officer will make a recommendation to the judge as to the best disposition of the case. The judge can be expected to follow the recommendation in a good percentage of cases. While he has confidence in the parole officer, however, the judge may not always agree with the recommendation. As a former lawyer, the judge may have access to personal information through the lawyers involved in the case. In addition, the judge has usually had the opportunity to observe the accused during the trial, and has been able to assess the defendant's attitudes. At times, too, the judge may feel that institutionalization is in order, although probation has been recommended.

Probation in Lieu of Imprisonment

In certain types of cases in all jurisdictions, the trial judge is authorized by statute to grant probation to a convicted individual. This means that instead of sentencing the individual to the penitentiary, the court allows this person to remain at liberty, but upon certain conditions that may be set by law and by the judge. In the most serious types of crimes, such as murder, the statutes usually do not allow a convicted person to be given probation.

For a good number of persons, the shock of arrest, trial, and the imminent actuality of punishment is enough to awaken responsibility in the individual for personal actions. If it is clear that this condition has been reached, the judge will usually grant probation. This, of course, may not meet the demands of those in the community who cry out for punishment, but it may satisfy the objectives of society.

In granting probation, most judges set certain basic criteria that must be satisfied at the minimum. This does not mean, however, that the judge will automatically grant probation.

Sentencing is an awesome responsibility. No one is ever completely infallible as a judge of human nature. This includes judges as well as probation officers. Then too, there may be times when the convicted individual has an honest intent to live within the letter of the law, but may not be able to resist criminal opportunities when faced with new pressures and circumstances.

If a judge makes a mistake in allowing the convicted individual to continue at liberty, he may subject innocent people in the community to the possibility of serious harm. On the other hand, if the judge errs in ordering a prison sentence, the prisoner's added exposure to criminal influences in the prison could eventually harm society more than if probation had been granted. Probation must remain a judgmental decision, and the public must retain confidence in our judges. From time to time, however, instances come to light in which a young criminal hoodlum has been continued on probation through four or five separate convictions, progressing from minor crime, to armed robbery, to murder. Many individuals in the general public are convinced that if the criminal did not learn from an experience on probation, then he should be sent to prison for a subsequent crime.

It is a humane desire to use liberal standards in granting probation. It is society, though, that must bear the cost of undeserved concessions in this regard.

In the final analysis, no criminal can be improved except from within. The most important idea in probation is not control of the probationer who answers to supervision, but rather to encourage the probationer to understand himself and to gain strength in making independent decisions concerning his own behavior. The responsibility assumed by the offender will be decisive, regardless of the regularity or high quality of the supervision that is afforded.

A satisfactory program for probation usually includes the following four ideas:

1.   The program must consider the background, capabilities, limitations, and problems of the probationer;

2.   Since improvement must come from within, the program must be designed to make the probationer a participant in the activities that are designed to help him;

3.   The conditions of probation should be clearly set out, and the consequences of violating these provisions should be made known. It should be emphasized to the convict that the community is providing a second chance to the probationer, and that the community cannot be expected to overlook a disregard for this opportunity; and

4.   The basic idea of supervision is to enable the offender to

understand personal, individual problems, so the probationer can make decisions to successfully deal with them.[4]

If Probation Is Not Granted— Institutional Differences

If the judge does not feel that the convict is a good risk for probation, then the convicted person will be sentenced to a penal institution. In some jurisdictions, the judge has discretion as to where the sentence should be served. In other jurisdictions this is determined following classification procedures by the board of pardons and paroles or the adult authority.

It has long been recognized that relatively inexperienced criminals are influenced toward criminal careers by continued exposure to hardened convicts. Therefore, correctional officials seek to segregate offenders as much as possible. Young offenders who are likely candidates for reform are confined in minimum security prisons. Case-hardened professional criminals, and those regarded as troublemakers or escape risks are usually segregated in maximum security institutions. It is important that the convicted individual be classified as to whether contact with confirmed criminal repeaters will likely prove harmful to him.

Practically all penologists agree that first offenders and some other violators do not usually need to be confined behind solid stone walls, inside steel cells. If classification procedures are effective, many prisoners can benefit by assignment to prison farm work camps, minimum security facilities, or to outside work projects. In institutionalization of this kind, supervisory foremen or guards may serve in place of the heavily armed guards that may be needed in conventional prisons.[5]

In the first place, the inmate who is admitted to a minimum security institution receives a psychological boost, since it is obvious that this person could be confined in the main prison. Then too, the prisoner in minimum security is not normally exposed to the enforced idleness that may create unfavorable attitudes toward rehabilitation. In minimum security the prisoner may retain some sense of accomplishment in performing assigned tasks. Usually, it

---

4. *Manual of Correctional Standards*, 3d ed., (College Park, Md.: American Correctional Association, 1966), p. 21 and Chapter 6, pp. 98–113.
5. Ronald L. Carlson, *Criminal Justice Procedure for Police*, (Cincinnati: The W. H. Anderson Co., 1970), p. 120.

enables the prisoner to remain in better physical condition, and to maintain better personal relationships with the staff and other inmates than would be likely inside a conventional prison. It may also help in getting the prisoner accustomed to work on a regular basis.

There are some other benefits in operating minimum security facilities. Work camps may be set up far more economically than a regular prison facility, and camps may be increased or decreased, according to need. The problems associated with overcrowded prisons may be relieved by the use of minimum security installations or work camps, and the cost to the taxpayer is less. In making decisions for the rehabilitation of prisoners, taxpayer cost is important but it should not be allowed to prevent prisoner rehabilitation.

On the other hand, it is obviously easier to escape from a minimum security institution. However, if prisoners understand that they may be apprehended quickly and will always be prosecuted for escape, instances of this kind may be kept to a minimum.

Giving the Prisoner
Something to Look Forward To

If the prisoner has little hope for the future, many penologists believe that he is far more likely to be involved in crime inside the prison walls, in riots, and in persisting in serious crime when released.

Some of this feeling of hopelessness may be dispelled if the prisoner can be convinced that he is still a person of worth, in spite of his mistakes. Any prisoner who has ever done serious time is aware that he can never reenter the outside world at exactly the same level as before. The problem is to convince the inmate that there are new values that are worth his attention. Education and job training are two of the most important programs that should be held out to prisoners.

Education

Various studies indicate that between ten and thirty percent of prison inmates in the United States are fundamental illiterates. The high of thirty percent is reached in institutes with a large percentage of Black and foreign-born or non-English speaking inmates. This means that these inmates test at the third grade level or below on standardized reading achievement tests.[6]

6. Ibid., pp. 483–90.

The effect of this deficiency is that such a prisoner can scarcely dare to hope for a good job. He is not able to read or understand the instructions that may be a required part of the job, if he should be lucky enough to obtain a job.

If an individual can be taught to have some pride in the job that he does, then there is hope that he will obtain and retain employment, rather than drift back into a life of crime. Vocational or technical education in every prison may therefore represent funds that are well spent.

In larger institutions, a considerable number of prisoners are interested in obtaining high school equivalency diplomas, while a number of others are seeking courses at the college level. Some institutions undoubtedly hold convicts who have the ability and educational requirements to teach, if this possibility can be pursued within security restrictions.

To assist in rehabilitation, taxpayers should consider prison educational programs with three objectives in mind:

1.   To give every inmate an opportunity to obtain at least a vocational education, so that he will be able to obtain a job;

2.   To offer courses for academic betterment, so that the prisoner with a vocation can improve his economic opportunities. In short, this means that the prisoner will eventually improve his vocational position.

3.   To offer courses that will provide cultural betterment, and broaden the inmate's horizons, thereby giving him more interests in free society, while at the same time enabling him to better adjust to his circumstances in prison.[7]

Work Factors in Prison

Penologists agree that idleness may be one of the most serious problems in a penal institution. Yet, most state prisons are little more than "idle houses." Even in states with large tax rolls, only a small percentage of the inmates may be utilized in industrial jobs.

There has long been an idea in this country that prisoners are unable or unwilling to work, and that a prison work detail represents harsh discipline. Because of the lack of jobs in the outside world during the depression, Congress passed a federal law prohibiting the interstate transportation of prison-made goods. The idea here was

7. Ibid., p. 483.

that goods could be made cheaply in prison, and that such merchandise would unfairly compete with regularly manufactured articles, thereby leading to unemployment.

During World War II, however, prison inmates voluntarily worked in prison to help the war production of this country. This was very helpful to the war effort, as many American workers were in the armed forces.

It is also worth noting that many prisoners feel that it is far easier to "do time" if they are allowed to occupy themselves with work. Mental attitudes may be improved, since prisoners gain a ·sense of accomplishment from this activity. Also, while prison pay scales are very low, the inmate may be able to accumulate a little money from his work. Furthermore, high and profitable production records have been established in prison locations where work is available. Of course, the prison "rock pile" may be of questionable value, since nothing of real value is produced.

If work can be provided in prison, most penologists believe that the inmate should be paid a decent sum of money for his work, and that the bulk of this money should be accumulated or given to his dependents. It is not contended that convict pay scales should approach the pay of union laborers on the outside, but neither should the pay consist of a few pennies a day. Paying the prisoner a decent wage could work to the benefit of the taxpayer by taking some dependents off the relief rolls, or by giving the discharged individual a nest egg that would help to put him on his feet at the time of his release.

To reiterate, suitable employment for a paroled or discharged inmate is essential for rehabilitation; it allows the individual to regain some of his lost standing in society. Therefore, the prisoner without basic education should be given enough educational skills to allow him to be successful on the job. This does not mean that prisons should be converted into large factories. However, there may be good reason for spending taxpayers' money for job training for convicts.

Parole

A prison sentence for a specified number of years does not always mean that the convicted individual will be confined in the penitentiary for that length of time. By statute he may be released earlier on parole, after serving a specified part of the sentence.

An individual given an indeterminate sentence, such as five to ten years for armed robbery, may be eligible for parole after serving the five year minimum, minus time off for good behavior. (Methods for calculating good behavior vary from state to state.)

In some states, a person sentenced for a fixed number of years may be eligible for parole after serving one-third of the sentence. If sentenced for life, some states allow the convict to be considered for parole after serving terms varying from seven to twenty years.

Parole is the procedure through which prisoners are selected for release and the service through which they are furnished guidance, control, and assistance in serving the last part of their sentence within the free community. The terms of parole are consistently set out by statute. For instance, under federal law a prisoner is eligible for consideration after serving one-third of the prescribed sentence for a federal felony conviction. This does not necessarily mean that the prisoner will be released on parole at that time, but it does guarantee that his record and his efforts toward rehabilitation will be reviewed by the federal parole board after completion of one-third of the sentence, and at regular intervals thereafter. In these hearings, the board seeks to find out whether the inmate can control his behavior and will value his freedom enough to remain within the law. Authorities in the correctional field agree that a few inmates do not need supervision or guidance upon release from prison, but that for a time the great majority can benefit from some form of supervision.[8]

Society has a real interest in the release of prisoners, since these individuals have been committed for definite terms by the criminal justice system, and release on parole sometimes seems to fly in the face of the sentence that was meted out. The police department in any large city can usually list case after case in which a paroled convict was involved in murder, armed robbery, or rape almost immediately after release. It is therefore important that the parole system include both a careful selection process for those to be released, as well as a workable system for supervision after the selection is made.

Individuals in the general public are frequently skeptical of probation and parole. These persons sometimes assert that both probation and parole are based on compassion for the offender. They point out that in the real world, reward and punishment are the facts of life. Society has long operated on the idea that every person is responsible for his or her own acts. Under our system of

8. Ibid, p. 98.

justice, fear of punishment alone prevents the bulk of people from violating the law. Probation and parole seem to be somewhat at variance with these ideas, and some individuals sense a disturbing inconsistency here. It should be remembered, though, that rehabilitation is as important to society as it is to the criminal.

Some correctional officials believe that probation and parole should be available to the individual offender, since he may otherwise become a worse menace to the wellbeing of society. There are sanctions that are tied in to probation and parole, and if used constructively, the offender may be able to control his activities in the future.

The systems used to approve prisoners for parole are frequently subject to criticism. Penal institutions are filled with individuals who behave well in the controlled atmosphere of a prison, yet revert to savagery as soon as they are set free. As a prison-wise convict in a California prison put it, "Inmates who are up for parole humble themselves before the parole board or adult authority, grovel in their past sins and praise the prison system for rehabilitating them for a return to live on the streets." Experienced corrections officials are supposed to be able to spot these individuals.

At times, the parole board or adult authority may be pressured by state officials or penal authorities to relieve crowded conditions inside the state prisons by granting additional paroles. This, of course, is wrong. Parole should be granted only on an individual basis, and then only when the inmate has progressed to the point that he can make his own way, with reasonable guidance. It is a serious mistake to place the community in jeopardy by premature release of a potentially dangerous individual.

In October 1975, the state of Georgia began the release of approximately 7,000 inmates from the prison system. The stated purpose of these releases was to make room in the prisons for new offenders. This action was taken on a decision by the Georgia Board of Pardons and Paroles, a five-man body appointed by the governor.

Under the decision made by this Board of Pardons and Paroles, the inmates released early were not supposed to include those convicted of violent crimes. A Georgia Department of Corrections official conceded, however, that the program had been placed into effect so swiftly that no one was certain whether violent criminals were reaching the street. This official explained that the practice of plea bargaining had complicated the issues, since an armed robber may have pleaded guilty to a lesser offense and would be released before authorities had time to look into the background of specific cases.

Many thinking officials complained bitterly about this release procedure. Some stated that it was unfair both to the public and the convict "to just dump the inmate out in the street, with little chance of finding a job." A number of knowledgeable officials pointed out that those without employable skills would likely engage in serious crimes within a very short time.

Where to fix blame in a situation of this kind may be open to debate. The state board of corrections or other responsible body must plan budgets to house prisoners. The governor has the responsibility to plan for prisoner needs, and he must bear at least part of the blame if he does not obtain appropriations from the state legislature. The legislature, too, may be at fault. The public must insist on a reasonable amount of appropriations.

If the press accepts responsibility for bringing issues before the public, then there is an urgent need for the facts to be reported and brought into focus. Many observers also feel that a situation of this kind reflects serious deficiencies in the board of pardons and paroles and the state department of corrections.

We can argue endlessly as to the conditions that cause crime.[9] In recent years, the claim has frequently been made that the criminal offender is somehow not responsible for his or her acts. People who

9. Ibid., p. 351. This manual points out that "the factors which contribute to the making of delinquents and criminals are many and complex."

make this claim argue that society has placed some at a disadvantage and that society alone must accept the blame for what the violator has done.

Most responsible penologists feel that there is no truth whatever in this assertion. By extending this theory from class to class, criminal responsibility could be fixed on only the most wealthy and talented individuals. It is true that, in terms of economic and social opportunities, individuals are not born equal. Absolute equality may never be reached in any human society. Therefore the law demands that the individual accept responsibility for his own actions.

There has never been a time in history when food, clothing, and shelter were as easily obtainable as they are today. Inequalities persist; however, society must recognize that many institutions are inadequate and that improvements should be made. Society should continue to extend support to rehabilitation programs, but crime should not be excused or blamed on forces beyond the control of the individual. When enough members of society adopt the attitude that criminal acts can never be rationalized or condoned, crime will decline substantially.

Many private citizens feel that they have no responsibility for the administration of justice. These individuals explain that crime is a job for the police, for the courts, and for prison officials and correctional authorities. This, of course, is simply not true. Throughout history, societal standards insisted on by the citizenry have had an important influence on the control of crime.

A convict's rage against imprisonment may mix explosively with warped philosophies of justification. It is not unusual for a hardened convict to convince himself that he is not guilty. All the while he knows that he was caught in a case in which the facts were undisputed. What he is trying to say is that the system is unfair in continuing to confine him, so he rationalizes that he was not guilty in the first place.

Importance of the Parole Officer

The parole officer who supervises and assists the inmate also figures prominently in the success of the system. This official must be understanding, yet able to command respect; sympathetic, but firm. It is also important to limit the number of parolees that are to be handled by one parole officer. Supervision can never be adequate if the parole officer's work load is too great. While this load may vary from time to time, the parole officer must have sufficient time to gain reasonable knowledge of individual potentials and problems and to be available in time of need.

It is also advisable for parole conditions to be fixed by the paroling authority or board. These conditions should serve as guides to the inmate in adjusting to the outside world. Conditions should not be placed on the parolee's conduct unless the board intends to insist on compliance. Conditions of parole should not be unenforceable, needlessly restrictive, or inappropriate for the parolee's specific problems. Some authorities on correctional methods feel that some of the restrictions should be gradually removed as the parolee demonstrates that he is able to adjust to his own situation.

Typical conditions of parole are presented in the following list:

CONDITIONS OF RELEASE

1. RELEASE: Upon release from the_____Rehabilitation Center you are to go directly to the program approved by the Parole and Community Services Division and shall report to your Supervising Agent or other person designated by the Parole and Community Services Division.

2. RESIDENCE: Only with the approval of your Supervising Agent may you change your residence or leave the county of your residence.

3. WORK: It is necessary for you to maintain gainful employment. Any change of employment must be reported to, and approved by, your Supervising Agent.

4. REPORTS: You are to submit a written monthly report of your activities unless directed otherwise by your Supervising Agent. This report is due at the Agent's office not later than the fifth day of the following month and shall be true, correct, and complete in all respects.

5. ALCOHOLIC BEVERAGES: The unwise use of alcoholic beverages and liquors causes more failures on release than all other reasons combined. You shall not use alcoholic beverages or liquors to excess.

6. NARCOTICS: You may not possess, use or traffic, in any narcotic, marijuana or dangerous drugs in violation of the law. By reason of your commitment to the _____ Rehabilitation Center, you are required by Welfare and Institutions Code, to participate in anti-narcotic testing. You shall participate in such program and agree to conform to the in-

structions of your Supervising Agent regarding your participation therein.

7.   WEAPONS: You shall not own, possess, use, sell, nor
have under your control any deadly weapons or firearms.

8.   ASSOCIATES: You must avoid association with former
residents of the _____ Rehabilitation Center, former
inmates of penal institutions or other narcotic addicts unless
specifically approved by your Supervising Agent, and you must
avoid association with individuals of bad reputation.

9.   MOTOR VEHICLES: Before operating any motor vehicle you must have written permission from your Supervising
Agent, and you must possess a valid operator's license.

10.   CO-OPERATION and ATTITUDE: At all times your
co-operation with your Supervising Agent, and your good behavior and attitude must justify the opportunity granted to you
by this release.

11.   LAWS and CONDUCT: You are to obey all municipal,
county, state and federal laws, ordinances, and orders, and you
are to conduct yourself as a good citizen.

12.   CASH ASSISTANCE: In time of actual need, as determined by your Supervising Agent, you may be loaned cash
assistance for living expenses. You may be loaned such assistance in the form of meal and hotel tickets. You hereby
agree to repay this assistance; and this agreement and the obligation remains even though you should be returned to the
_____ Rehabilitation Center.

13.   SANITATION: You are not to provide blood for trans-
fusion purposes because of the danger of transmitting disease
thereby.

14.   SEARCH: You shall submit to a search of your person,
your residence and any property under your control upon request by your agent, any agent of the Department of Corrections or law enforcement officer.

SPECIAL CONDITIONS: _____

For individuals in prison, the outside world seems increasingly
more desirable, and the institution more confining. But reentering
society usually poses a number of problems. It is not surprising,
then, that many prisoners report experiencing a period of disillu-
sionment a short time after release.

FEDERAL CORRECTIONAL SYSTEM

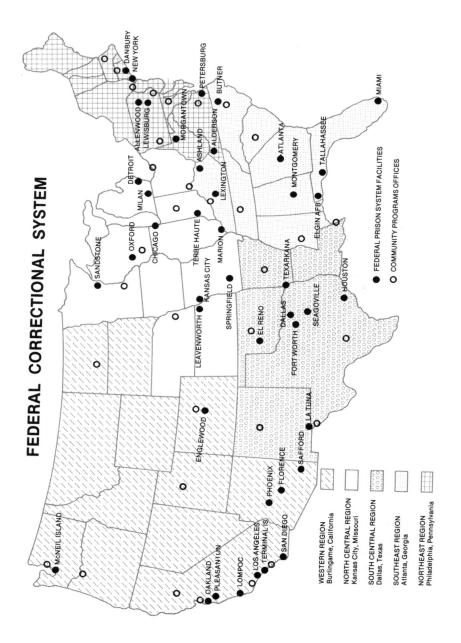

● FEDERAL PRISON SYSTEM FACILITIES
○ COMMUNITY PROGRAMS OFFICES

DANBURY
NEW YORK
PETERSBURG
BUTNER
MORGANTOWN
ALLENWOOD
LEWISBURG
ASHLAND
ALDERSON
ATLANTA
TALLAHASSEE
MONTGOMERY
MIAMI
DETROIT
MILAN
OXFORD
SANDSTONE
CHICAGO
TERRE HAUTE
MARION
LEXINGTON
ELGIN AFB
KANSAS CITY
LEAVENWORTH
SPRINGFIELD
EL RENO
DALLAS
TEXARKANA
SEAGOVILLE
HOUSTON
FORT WORTH
ENGLEWOOD
LA TUNA
SAFFORD
PHOENIX
FLORENCE
McNEIL ISLAND
LOS ANGELES
TERMINAL IS.
SAN DIEGO
OAKLAND
PLEASANTON
LOMPOC

WESTERN REGION
Burlingame, California

NORTH CENTRAL REGION
Kansas City, Missouri

SOUTH CENTRAL REGION
Dallas, Texas

SOUTHEAST REGION
Atlanta, Georgia

NORTHEAST REGION
Philadelphia, Pennsylvania

After a short time on the street, the convict has discovered that most of his friendships terminated with his arrest and eventual conviction. Most of these friendships were forged in crime, anyway, and parole requirements forbid associations with known criminals. The result is that the releasee must make completely new friends.

There are a number of other pressures outside of prison that the inmate is not accustomed to facing. In the typical pattern, the convict's wife managed to live on a combination of welfare and hope while her husband was in prison. Family problems and frustrations that lay dormant may now come to the surface.

Unless the prisoner has the promise of a new job, he may go for weeks without money in his pockets. Aware of this condition, old acquaintances may repeatedly tempt the convict with offers of pushing heroin or participating in the numbers racket. Convicts rarely possess those unusual skills that make them prime job candidates, and their prison record automatically eliminates many from consideration. As frustrations pile up, it is more and more difficult to resist the offers to go back into criminal pursuits.

Most correctional authorities agree that few convicts have a predetermined plan to go back into crime. However, they do not plan on the unexpected frustrations and pressures. When the convict has no job and few prospects, he may look for the easy way out. His old acquaintances and friends are usually not motivated toward reform.

REVOCATION OF PAROLE OR PROBATION

It may be damaging to a prisoner to continue to hold him in prison after he is ready to assume his place in free society. Parole is, of course, the procedure by which prisoners are selected for release and given guidance in their adjustment to the outside world. In the past, many courts and administrative officials have taken the approach that parole or probation included conditions that were granted to a convicted individual, rather than a right enjoyed by that person. Many judges still speak of parole or probation as an act of grace or clemency. The United States Supreme Court has made it clear, however, that neither probation nor parole can be revoked on a mere whim or unsupported charge. Some individuals have claimed that they were returned to prison merely because a probation or parole officer had a personal dislike for them. At the same time, the Supreme Court has taken the position that the constitutional safeguards provided to an individual on probation or parole need not be followed as rigidly as for an individual who had not been previously tried and convicted.

Parole

In *Morrisey* v. *Brewer*,[10] the United States Supreme Court ruled that a parolee arrested for a claimed violation of his parole is entitled to two separate hearings. The first of these must be conducted by an impartial hearing officer. This hearing officer cannot be the same parole officer who authorized or caused the parolee's arrest. The purpose of this hearing is to reach a decision as to whether there are reasonable grounds to indicate that the parolee is in violation. This conclusion may be reached if there is cause to believe either: (1) that he has violated the conditions laid down for his parole, or (2) that he has committed a new criminal violation.

In the first hearing, the defendant is entitled to the following safeguards:

1. There must be a written notice as to the purpose of the hearing, as well as a statement setting out the alleged breach of parole;

2. The parolee has the right to appear and be given reasonable time to present arguments or evidence, and to be heard in his own defense. During this hearing, he should be permitted to ask reasonable questions of persons who claim that he is in violation; and

3. After the hearing officer has considered the evidence, he must make a statement as to whether he feels probable cause exists for revocation, along with listing the facts that caused him to arrive at this conclusion.

If the hearing officer rules against the parolee, the latter may be placed in jail to await a second hearing, which is conducted by the parole board. This second hearing must be held within a reasonable time, taking into consideration the evidence, the schedule of the parole board, the need to locate witnesses, and other varying condi-

10. Morrisey v. Brewer, 408 US 471 (1972).

tions. At this second hearing, the following basic rights must be extended to the parolee:[11]

1. He must be given a written notice of the alleged violation;

2. He must be furnished with a summary or outline of the evidence against him;

3. He must be afforded a reasonable chance to be heard in person, and to present his own witnesses and evidence;

4. He must be allowed to question and cross-examine those who present evidence against him. He will not, of course, be given unlimited time, and control of the hearing must remain with the parole board. The right to cross-examine may not be extended to confidential informants, provided the hearing officer is satisfied that there may be good cause for not allowing the parolee to challenge an individual at this time;

5. He is entitled to a fair-minded, impartial parole board;

6. He is entitled to a statement by the parole board members in writing at the conclusion of the hearing, as to the evidence used to reach a decision and the board's reasons for revocation.

The courts are in dispute as to whether the parolee has the right to his own attorney or to a court-appointed attorney at either the preliminary or the parole board hearings.

Probation

Two types of situations may be involved in probation cases. In some instances, the judge actually passes sentence at the time he places the convicted individual on probation. In other cases, however, the judge may merely release the convicted individual into the community, deferring sentence until the defendant completes the prescribed probationary period or again finds himself in trouble with the law. In either type of situation, the person on probation

---

11. According to standards set up by the American Correctional Assn., and according to requirements specified by the courts, per William A. Rutter, *Criminal Procedure*, 5th ed., (Gardena, Cal.: 1973), p. 123.

Also see Morrissey v. Brewer, 408 US 471 (1972), in which the United States Supreme Court stated that "some degree of procedural due process must be afforded in proceedings to revoke probation or parole . . . [but that] these safeguards need not be as extensive as afforded an accused prior to conviction."

must be afforded some type of hearing in which the evidence for and against him can be considered, before probation can be revoked.

If the individual on probation has not been actually sentenced at the time revocation is being considered, he must be allowed to have an attorney during the hearing.[12] Courts differ on the right to an attorney in instances in which sentence was passed at the time the accused was granted probation.

Coordination of Probation and Parole Services

Traditionally, probation has been a function of the state courts, and has usually been handled at the district or county level. Parole, on the other hand, has been a function of the state correctional process. Since probation and parole have much in common, about half of the states have combined probation and parole supervisory services to some degree. In some jurisdictions, supervision of probation and parole have been completely merged. This, of course, is the procedure in the federal court system. In most states this supervisory merger has come under the authority of a state board of probation and parole or adult authority.

MEASURING THE SUCCESS OF CORRECTIONS AND LOOKING AT SOME PROBLEMS

It should be noted that the correctional system is only one of the methods by which we attempt to lower the crime rate. Clearly, crime does not begin in maturity, in the processes of arrest, prosecution, imprisonment, or rehabilitation. Crime begins at the beginning, in the environment in which the youth is reared. A correctional system, after the fact, can never be a substitute for the moral and ethical values heretofore furnished by family and church—values that President Gerald Ford declared "will prevent more crime and corruption than all the policemen and prosecutors . . . can ever deter." As family and social values have broken down, additional strains have been placed on prosecutive and correctional programs. Although the basic causes of crime may be attributable to the moral breakdown of family and community influences, many authorities still feel that much can be accomplished through the correctional processes.

12. Mempha v. Rhay, 389 US 128 (1967).

What Society Demands

If we define rehabilitation as causing the convict to change his way of living by giving him inner moral strength, then we are expecting too much. After a time in confinement some convicts do, of course, become completely changed in character. However, the aims of society will be satisfied if the convict can learn to hold back his criminal tendencies.

Changes in the thinking and attitudes of confirmed criminals are difficult to measure. We simply do not have enough basic information about human motivation and behavior to accurately determine when one individual has been rehabilitated, while another offender has not. To ask more than conformity of the convict is to place almost impossible demands on the correctional processes.

Changes in Society's
Approach to Corrections

For thousands of years, criminal justice systems were based on the idea of retribution, or socialized vengeance. People believed that the criminal had done wrong and should suffer punishment. This was a basic premise of early English law, and some of this thinking was carried over into the justice systems in the American colonies.

The colonial courts believed that punishing the offender would cause this individual to give up all inclinations toward crime. Therefore, the colonial courts placed convicted persons in stocks, tied others to the ducking stool, gave lashes in public, or marked them with a branding iron. Prison sentences usually involved confinement for several years. Of course, there may have been other factors in the society of that time that kept criminal violations at a low figure.

Today, few persons agree with punishment as a correctional method. From the standpoint of practicality, however, it must be admitted that colonial society benefitted from this method, since there were relatively few criminal repeaters.

Colonial correctional philosophies were modified considerably by the influence of the kind-hearted American Quakers, who believed that meditation and moral urging would cause the violator to turn away from evil ways. From about 1830 to 1870, the leading prisons in this country allowed little verbal contact between prisoners, stressing the importance of religious visitors to preach morality and the gospel of reformation to prisoners.

The Quaker influences continued until shortly after the time of the Civil War. During this period, parole systems, as well as the idea of the indeterminate sentence, were introduced. For the first time, the importance of work programs and education was also stressed.

Gradually, the so-called reformation approach to corrections was introduced. This is the prevailing philosophy at the present time. The reformation approach looks on a prisoner as someone with a curable disease. If the causes of the problem are isolated and the prisoner is properly treated, then rehabilitation should follow. Under this idea, improvement should occur, just as a medical patient can usually be expected to respond to hospital care.

In utilizing the reformation approach, classification systems are set up. The prisoner is completely interviewed, and his or her background thoroughly explored. The idea here is that analysis, classification, and basic investigation can determine those causes or factors that led the individual into crime. After isolating the causes, the system furnishes individual therapy, group or individual counseling, and psychiatric techniques to make the prisoner aware of these causes and to help in overcoming these influences.

Widely acclaimed as an enlightened, logical, humane approach, many individuals working in criminology and correctional occupations never paused to consider whether this system would prove successful in the end. What was expected of this approach was a system which could deal with large numbers of people. Criminologists hoped that these individuals would emerge from the other end of the tunnel modified in both their thinking and behavioral patterns.

There is no doubt that many individual criminals have been led away from crime by the reformation approach. From an overall viewpoint, however, this approach has made little headway in solving the basic problems of the criminal repeater. Without dwelling on statistics, it must be pointed out that roughly two-thirds or more of all serious crime in the first five years of the 1970's was committed by criminal repeaters—individuals who were unreformed. This, of course, has serious implications for society as a whole.

Failure of the reformation approach was acknowledged publicly in 1975 by Norman A. Carlson, Director of the Federal Prison System. Other authorities on correctional techniques—officials like William E. Amos, Chairman of the Youth Correction Division of the U.S. Board of Parole, and United States Attorney General William

Saxbe, have stated frankly that correctional officials do not know how to reform prisoners.[13]

The Societal Guilt Idea

With the reformation approach under fire, another school of thought has developed in the United States, advocating a "societal guilt approach" to the corrections problem. Proponents of this idea view all offenders sympathetically, contending that most violators are not responsible for criminal acts, because outside agencies led or forced them irresistibly into criminal pursuits.

As Clarence Kelley, Director of the FBI, has stated, this is an "admirably humanistic perspective," that has "seriously discounted the possibility that criminal offenders are mainly rational—albeit unprincipled—individuals who see crime as an easier means than lawful industry of gaining what they want. It is no doubt true that a significant number of offenders have grown up gravely deprived through a host of social inequities. For each of them, there are thousands of other persons who have suffered the same misfortunes without succumbing to the temptations of crime."[14]

Exactly what is proposed by the theorists of the societal guilt approach is not certain. Proponents of this idea feel that society should be restructured, and that relatively few offenders should be put in jail. How this group intends to curb crime until society is perfected is not clear.

One viewpoint concerning the correctional problem was expressed by Christopher T. Bayley, former Deputy United States Attorney General, founder of the White Collar Crime Clearing House, and Prosecutor for King County, Washington:[15]

13. See William E. Amos, "The Philosophy of Corrections, Revisited," *Federal Probation,* December, 1975, pp. 43–47. Attorney General Saxbe's speech was quoted verbatim in newspapers on April 17, 1975.

In this speech, Attorney General Saxbe pointed out that " . . . we are catching more people than we can digest in our system of justice."

See also the interview with Senator Ted Kennedy of Massachusetts, reported in *Time,* May 31, 1976. This article pointed out that Senator Kennedy had "introduced a crime bill that called for a mandatory two-year sentence without parole for violent crimes, and four years for repeat offenders." Kennedy thinks rehabilitation approaches have failed, and he has taken the blunt position that punishment is society's best deterrent.

14. *Los Angeles Times,* September 1, 1975, p. 15. Also see Gopal C. Pati, "Business and Ex-Offenders: A Case of Holy Alliance," *Security Management,* March, 1975, pp. 22–23.

15. Christopher T. Bayley, "Certainty of Punishment: A Deterrent to Crime," *Security Management,* March, 1976, pp. 36–38. (American Society For Industrial Security.)

There has developed in the past year a national debate that I think is fundamental to the future of our free society . . . 'What do we do with criminal offenders once they are caught, prosecuted, convicted, and they're before us, in our hands, so to speak, for sentencing?' The debate has centered around two very different concepts of what we should do with these people. On the one hand, there are some who feel the purpose of sentencing is to treat or rehabilitate criminal offenders. It is known as the individual treatment model. On the other hand, there is developing a new approach, which is gaining more and more support, and can be labeled the certainty of punishment model.

The treatment model sounds good. It is based on the premise that for any person ready for sentencing, a program for him or her can be devised that will solve the individual problems the person has which led to the commission of the crime. It is further based on the idea that crimes are committed because someone has problems. He had, for example, a broken home or an alcoholic father or is economically deprived or something else exists in his situation which has led to this crime. If this premise is accepted, then it follows that if we as sentensor or society, can only solve that underlying problem, we will prevent commission of another crime. Those who argue this side of things really believe that the best way to prevent recidivism, namely new crimes being committed, is to treat the person for whatever the problem might be.

There are two things wrong with that approach. The first is that it is not just. If we treat people and give criminal sentences based on a person's problems, rather than on what he did and is convicted of having done, we do not have a system of justice. . . . The decision on sentencing is based on who the person is rather than what he did. It may be for the best of reasons. It may be that the treatment model is advocated because it sounds better than punishing. If we can only treat them, it will be more humane, more up to date, more civilized. But it is not a system of justice.

The second thing that's wrong with the treatment model is that it doesn't work. Robert Martinson in New York is the head of the Department of Sociology at the City University of New York. He conducted a study of 250 treatment programs of all kinds throughout the country: those in prison, those in the community, group therapy, individual therapy, psychological counseling, education, work release, and other programs. He

271

began basically disposed toward those various programs. His goal was to ascertain which methods worked in reducing recidivism and which did not. The study was conducted for the state of New York. They were about to put millions of dollars into treatments and wanted to know where those dollars should go.

The state was apparently embarrassed by the conclusion: none of them had any effect on recidivism. In Martinson's words 'with few and isolated exceptions' none of them had any effect on recidivism . . . Martinson's report was suppressed by the state of New York for almost three years. It finally came to light when a court ordered the results produced, . . . So the treatment model, the idea that we can somehow change peoples' lives by putting them into some kind of a program has failed because it doesn't work.

The reason why it fails and the reason why it is so wrong is that it completely destroys the idea that as individuals we are responsible for our actions. To illustrate, imagine a person who has been convicted of a crime being interviewed. . . . He is asked about his family. Did he have a broken home? Was his father an alcoholic? Often the presentence workup report begins to indicate that these are the problems which somehow caused the crime and the solution will be some kind of a treatment program. A serious side effect in asking all those questions is to gradually convince a person that it really wasn't his fault that he committed that burglary or robbery. Because of all those terrible things that happened to him, it was more or less predetermined that he was going to lead a life of crime.

. . . The only person who is going to cause a change is the individual, and he is only going to do it if he makes a fundamental decision to change. . . . the common man has felt all along: if someone commits a crime he should be punished for it . . . you are probably not going to have any results and will instead end up with a system that he can manipulate and one that does not prevent him from committing another crime. The flag under which the new popularly supported reform is flying is called 'certainty of punishment' . . .

. . . If we replace the model with something that clearly signals to those who would commit crimes that if you break the law you will be punished. That certainty would have more effect than anything else on reducing criminal activity.

Some crimes, of course, are committed by irrational, crazy people, but the vast majority of crimes are committed by people

272

who know what they are doing, and they think they can get away with it. These are the people to whom our system must send a signal.

. . . Timing is very important to certainty. A system cannot function in slow motion if it's going to produce an effect of certainty.

A number of authorities have been outspoken in questioning the worth of the entrenched reformation approach to corrections. Professor Gordon Tullock of Virginia Polytechnic Institute stated:

The standard criminologist has been living in a dream world for at least 150 years. They've thought that the cause of crime is not the economic return sought by some people, but an illness or some sort of disease. Eighty percent of the people who seriously think about crime think of punishment as a deterrent—except for the sociologists, and they wrote all the books.[16]

Professor James Q. Wilson of Harvard has pointed out:

For a long time, and to our great disadvantage, we clung to the myth that there was a bureaucratic or governmental alternative to familial and communal virtue, . . . We struggled to maintain the hope that the police and schools could prevent crime and that prisons and treatment programs could rehabilitate criminals.[17]

The *Wall Street Journal,* in an editorial, expressed the opinion of that publication:

But the main reason for the failure to reverse or even slow down the crime rate is the social theories that prevailed in most courtrooms and legislative halls. Those theories stressed trying to understand crime's causes when the key to crime control, as penologists and politicians are slowly coming to understand, lies less in unearthing motivations than in streamlining courts and promptly punishing offenders. Until this bottleneck in the

16. Michael T. Malloy, "Punishment Is a Deterrence to Crime," *National Observer,* June 19, 1976, p. 1.
17. *Time,* April 26, 1976, pp. 82–84.

criminal justice system is broken, no amount of money for police forces is likely to make more than the most marginal difference.[18]

Some Proposals for the Future

What has been happening with regularity is that the police arrest criminals and have them brought into the courts. The courts dribble a few of these into the penal institutions. The prisons then pour them back onto the streets, where they return to a life of crime.

Authorities like Patrick V. Murphy, President of the Police Foundation and former head of the police departments in Syracuse, Detroit, Washington, D.C., and New York City, feel that getting tough and imposing longer sentences is not necessarily the answer. Murphy has asserted that:

> The key to making a system effective is to convince everyone that justice will be consistent. That 1) A man who commits a crime will almost surely be arrested. 2) If arrested, he will get a fair and speedy trial. 3) If convicted, he will be punished for the crime he committed, not for some minor misdeed of little consequence. 4) After paying his debt to society, he will have a good chance to get a decent job.[19]

Attorney General Saxbe and Los Angeles Chief of Police Edward Davis feel that the answer may be to change correctional procedures for certain types of offenders. This should be for a select group that Saxbe labels "violent strangers," the armed robbers, rapists and burglars who account for much of the public's fear of crime. As Saxbe put it:

> What we want to sell to the 50,000 judges in this country is that when this violent stranger comes into court, that they immediately red-flag the handling of that case . . . accelerate their trials, get them off the streets, get them in the penitentiary. . . . This . . . means . . . that the violent strangers be tried for their crimes instead of misdemeanors, be sentenced to prison instead of probation, and serve much more of their sentences before being released.

18. "Cops and Robbers," *Wall Street Journal*, May 17, 1976. Editorial.
19. Patrick V. Murphy, "Our Disgraceful System of Combatting Crime," *Reader's Digest*, February 1974, p. 169.

The logic behind this is that time, not prison, rehabilitates. Some eighty-one percent of rapists, robbers, and burglars are under twenty-five and ninety percent are under thirty, according to Jerry Wilson, the recently retired chief of the Washington, D.C. police, "Criminal activity is a kind of immaturity . . . We are recognizing that we've got to put some people away until they mature."[20]

Persons who are sentenced to prison do not automatically give up all their rights at the time of conviction. However, they do not continue to enjoy all the rights that are available in free society. It is the purpose of prison to hold individuals committed there. Prisons were never designed to serve as country clubs. On the other hand, prison officials have no right whatever to abuse or mistreat inmates.

Courts had long maintained a laissez faire attitude toward prisons because they felt that the administrators of the penal institutions needed considerable leeway to control convict populations. The new civil rights movement of the 1960's, however brought about a change in prison conditions. In general, judges will no longer tolerate conditions that degrade inmates. On the other hand, the courts will not permit an inmate to have privileges that jeopardize security or safety. Disciplinary rules must be utilized in penal institutions, and they will be upheld by the courts if uniformly applied to all inmates, and if they are not cruel or degrading in application.

The Halfway House

The processes through which a convict returns to society are trying, at best. This transition is doubly difficult for the isolated, the friendless, or the individual who may have some emotional problems. For this reentry into society, the convict should not be any farther away from people than is necessary. The halfway house is a base which frequently helps to ease this transition.

In essence, the halfway house is a supervised residence in the community, through which released prisoners make contact with the outside world. Not a new concept, the use of the halfway house is on the increase, according to correctional authorities. It developed in response to the difficulties and failures of convicts groping for help. Often, a community may be openly antagonistic to the opening of a halfway house, fearing that a crime wave will automatically follow the opening of this facility.

20. Michael T. Malloy, "Reform Is a Flop," *National Observer*, January 4, 1975, p. 1.

In the past, halfway houses have been set up by governmental agencies, by private civic and charitable agencies, or as a cooperative effort on the part of both. Community support is frequently necessary to success. The approach taken here is that there will always be a certain number of ex-convicts in the community. If these individuals are given reasonable support, there is an increased chance that they will be able to establish themselves as responsible members of the community. On this basis, the halfway house therefore deserves community support.

In the community type of house, it is usually necessary to establish two boards or councils to operate the project successfully. One body, which is essentially an advisory board, is made up of influential and prominent members of the community. This group helps to obtain a feeling of commitment from the community in general, and to assist in obtaining financial backing.

The second board, sometimes called a board of directors, is engaged in the day-to-day operation of the house. These directors may be called on to devote many hours of work in setting up the operation and in screening applications of soon-to-be-released prisoners who apply for residency.

It is often advisable to use as much correctional help as possible in the halfway house. In addition to a director who lives in the house, it may be helpful to have counselors from employment offices, job training experts, and a medical and psychiatric professional who is willing to devote time to a civic cause.

There are no absolute methods for testing the effectiveness of a halfway house in the rehabilitation of criminals. However, ex-convicts have frequently reported that residence in a halfway house was a determining factor in their turn away from crime.[21]

THE COMMUNITY WORK PROGRAM: ALTERNATIVE TO PRISON

There is much evidence to support the proposition that prisons frequently serve as "graduate schools," where lawbreakers learn to improve their criminal techniques. There is also good reason to feel that young offenders should not be exposed to the influence of hardened convicts. To avoid these problems, correctional authorities have long been interested in workable alternatives to imprisonment.

21. Edwin M. Lemert, *Instead of Court,* (Rockville, Md.: National Institute of Mental Health, Center for Studies of Crime and Delinquency), 1971.

Community work programs are among the alternatives that are available here. Originating in a Wisconsin law of 1913, community work programs allow convicts or jail inmates to leave the institution for work on a regular basis. The inmates in a program of this kind spend all their nonworking time inside the jail or prison where they have been committed.

Patterned after the original Wisconsin statute (the Huber Law), some jurisdictions have passed laws that permit only those convicted of misdemeanors to become involved in a program of this kind. Other states, however, have extended community work programs to include felony offenders. A program of this kind may be based on a cooperative arrangement between the sentencing judge and the local jail or penal institution. Still other jurisdictions do not allow participation unless the sentencing judge and the state parole board agree that the inmate is suitable for this type of program.

In some states, a portion of the sentence must be served before the inmate is eligible for consideration. Under federal law, prisoners are sentenced to the custody of the Attorney General of the United States, who specifies where and how the sentence must be served. Under the Federal Prison Rehabilitation Act of 1965, a federal prisoner may:

> ... (2) work at paid employment or participate in a training program in the community on a voluntary basis while continuing as a prisoner of the institution or facility to which he is committed, ...
>
> The willful failure of a prisoner to remain within the time prescribed to an institution or facility, designated by the Attorney General, shall be deemed an escape from the custody of the Attorney General ...

Not all Inmates Are Suited
for Community Work Programs

Many inmates are simply not good material for community work programs. If there is little likelihood for immediate rehabilitation, the prisoner should not be considered. In addition, it should be pointed out that this type of program is not a substitute for regular probation or parole.

Before an inmate is chosen for a program of this kind, it is important that there be a detailed diagnosis of the offender and his problems. The prisoner should come to realize that changes are necessary in his conduct and in the things that attract his interests.

A job offer for an inmate must be investigated to verify that the offer is legitimate and will fulfill the correctional objectives deemed desirable for that inmate. It is also important for the prisoner to realize that while he is in the community work program he is in technical custody. The prisoner should understand that prosecution will follow automatically if he decides to run away.

Community Work Programs
Cannot Ignore the Community

In spite of the success that has been gained with community work programs in some areas, there are still many individuals who feel that justice can be served only by incarcerating prisoners. In many cases the prisoner has already been a serious problem in his community, and to release this individual could jeopardize the safety of other citizens. In addition, a release should not be made if the prisoner is likely to deprive a regular worker of a job. It should also be pointed out that there is an increased possibility for prison contraband problems if the releasee under a community work program is allowed to live in the regular part of the prison when not at work.

A program of this kind must work out ways for the prisoner to obtain work clothing and transportation to his job. Work tools may also be a problem. The prisoner should be allowed to keep his earnings, minus charges for laundry, clothing, and transportation. In the ideal situation, the job is one that the inmate may want to retain after final release from the institution.

A program of this kind is not without limitations and problems. Work is usually beneficial, but is not the complete answer to rehabilitation. Properly used, however, a community work program may enable a prisoner to feel useful, to regain lost pride, to keep his family off of welfare, and to help him establish roots in the outside world.

Different programs work for different people. Community work programs may provide a workable alternative to imprisonment in selected cases.[22]

COMMUNITY SERVICE ORGANIZATIONS

The purpose of this section is to point out how community service organizations assist the objectives of the criminal justice system. Usu-

---

22. *Community Work—An Alternative to Imprisonment,* (Washington, D.C.: Correctional Research Associates), 1967.

ally this is accomplished by indirect means, by giving aid and support to the potential offender who may be tempted to engage in crime because of economic or social problems.

Development and Purposes of Community Service Organizations

It is frequently asserted in America that "all men are born equal." In one sense this is true, as society seeks to provide like opportunities to all individuals and to hold all races, sexes, and individuals equals in the sight of the law.

As a practical matter, however, there are noticeable differences between individuals. Some parents may simply be unable to provide the economic opportunities that would be advantageous to their children. Also, some individuals are simply not capable of seizing on the chances that may be available, either from a cultural or economic standpoint.

Community service organizations are usually created to extend a helping hand to the less fortunate, or to those who have failed to understand their own individual needs. Any number of community service organizations are sponsored by church groups, lodges, or sincere groups that have local affiliations. The type of aid varies from organization to organization, and from community to community.

The Salvation Army, for example, operates on the premise that need has no season, and that aid to a distressed, desperate individual or family may steer underprivileged individuals away from crime and enable them to get their own feet on the ground. Some community service organizations do not offer money. Instead, they furnish counseling, guidance, and moral encouragement. A teen-age recreation center may channel young people into wholesome sports and recreational and educational interests that will lead away from delinquency and toward useful careers.

The material that follows describes some of these community service groups, their functions, and their problems. There are a number of other organizations throughout the country that help to maintain society on a law-abiding course.

Teen Drug Information Centers

Community-based drug information centers for teen-agers are found in most major cities, and in some other localities where the citizens are socially aware.

One organization of this kind is located in the South Broadway area of Los Angeles. It is youth oriented, and is designed to both assist and inform young people. The staff includes professionals, ex-drug addict counselors, and community leaders who reach out to youth in the streets, jails, schools, and organized gangs. The object is to point out alternatives to crime, drug abuse, violence, and delinquency.

The services offered include recreational activities, detoxification, information and referral, individual and group counseling, and employment and social opportunities. The object is to turn young persons away from a life style that leads to drugs and clashes with the law. This type of community-oriented program teaches the individual to accept personal responsibility. Drug information centers usually have game tables, ping pong, refreshments, printed anti-drug literature, regular dances, game equipment, and a book library.

Suicide Prevention Centers

There are suicide prevention centers in major population areas throughout the United States. The Suicide Prevention Center of Los Angeles, California, was the first professionally organized service agency explicitly focused on self-destructiveness in this country. It maintains a 24-hour crisis telephone answering service to help individuals who are desperate and want to commit suicide.

The telephones at this agency are staffed by volunteer non-professional and professional counselors, carefully selected and trained to respond immediately to the special needs of desperate people, who are inclined toward self-destruction, violence, alcoholism, and drugs. This service is especially helpful to those troubled by isolation and loneliness, and to those without family, friends, or other resources to fall back on.

Free Clinics

Most metropolitan areas have free clinics, offering medical treatment and counseling to those who are unable to pay. Clinics are sometimes operated in conjunction with either private or public hospitals, with the clinic functioning as a separate unit. In some instances, hospitals charge all who are able to pay, utilizing a part of this revenue to handle destitute patients. Doctors and staff members may devote part of their work hours to maintenance of a free clinic.

Police Enforcement Should Be Unvarying, While the Penalty Imposed May Vary Considerably

The blind application of the prescribed penalties of a law, however wisely written, cannot provide justice in all cases. For example, one person may steal because he observes an opportunity to get rich. Another may steal because he needs food for a hungry child, or to buy medicine for his family. However, the law enforcement officer investigating an incident has taken an oath to uphold the law; it is not within his power to excuse a violator. If the prosecutor brings the matter before the courts, it is the job of the judge and/or jury to determine guilt and to take into account the circumstances in setting the penalty. A judge cannot say, "I think this particular law is stupid, therefore I'm not going to convict anyone who violates it."

A law enforcement officer who closes his eyes to a violation is also doing a disservice to the criminal justice system. An account in a Los Angeles newspaper read:

> . . . [officers] allowed at least a dozen sunbathers to go nude at . . . Beach despite a new ordinance that went into effect Friday prohibiting nudity on . . . County beaches. . . . no arrests were made Friday and that the . . . department would again issue warnings to nude sunbathers today . . . He said there is no warning provision in the ordinance . . . Nude sunbathers covered up when the patrols went by, then removed their clothes as soon as the patrol left the area.[23]

Law Enforcement Agencies Must Abide By the Fundamental Liberties

It is apparent that law enforcement agencies must utilize workable rules that guarantee the fundamental liberties set forth in the federal and state constitutions. Criminal investigations must be conducted to conform to court requirements and decisions.

This necessitates constant training and improved competence on the part of police employees. It also benefits the image of the police with the general public. When the man on the street has confidence in the job that the police are doing, it is easier to obtain information in solving crimes and to gain the cooperation of those

23. *Los Angeles Times,* April 17, 1975, p. 10.

who know the whereabouts of wanted criminals. In short, when the police make an extra effort to earn the respect of the public, then their future efforts may be more effective.

Others who figure in the criminal justice system must also do their part. The average citizen must realize that the system functions imperfectly unless it is supported by the individuals it strives to protect. Every person should be willing to testify when needed in court; to report for jury service; and to support the efforts of investigating officers, prosecutors, judges, the courts, and the correctional agencies that make up the whole system. All this should take place while every right is being extended to the accused. Only when this happens does the nation enjoy adequate procedures for the administration of justice.

SUMMARY

The basic purpose of the criminal justice system is to eliminate or reduce crime and delinquency. This may be done by creating a climate favorable to the growth and change of the criminal's personality and attitudes. In the final analysis, no criminal can be changed except from within. If the shock of arrest, trial, and the imminent actuality of punishment is enough to awaken responsibility, then the judge will usually grant probation. If the judge does not feel the convict is a suitable risk for probation, then the convicted person will be sent to a penal institution. Since hardened convicts will influence inexperienced convicts toward a continuing life of crime, it is beneficial to classify all incoming prisoners and confine the young and inexperienced in minimum or medium custody facilities. In any event, the prisoner must be given something to look forward to— vocational training is a must for those who do not have the basic skills to earn a living on the outside. Education inside the institution will also give the convict better job opportunities, broaden horizons, and better enable the convict to adjust to individual circumstances. Parole is a useful tool in allowing prisoners to prove themselves, and to make the adjustments back into the outside world. Experience shows that almost all prisoners need guidance and counseling in making this reentry. Parole, however, represents great potential for harm to the community if violent individuals are released before they have the capacity to get along when faced with the pressures and frustrations of normal living. When the convict has no job and few prospects, the likelihood of a return to crime is considerable.

For, many years, perhaps the majority of officials in the correctional process have favored a reformation approach. This involves thorough, analytical interviews with the prisoner, in which his or her background is recorded and explored. Authorities feel that analysis, classification, and basic investigation can determine those causes or factors that led the individual into crime. After isolating the causes, the system furnishes individual therapy, individual or group counseling, and psychiatric techniques to make the prisoner aware of the causes and to assist in overcoming these influences. This approach looks on a prisoner as someone with a curable disease. If the causes are isolated and treated, then rehabilitation should follow, just as a medical patient should respond to hospital care. There is no doubt that this approach has been successful in many individual cases, but the total adds up to failure. Roughly two-thirds or more of all serious crime in the first five years of the 1970's was committed by criminal repeaters who had been processed through this system, by individuals who were simply unreformed.

Quite frankly, authorities are divided as to the approach to take in reforming criminals. Some authorities feel that "getting tough" and imposing longer sentences is not the answer. These authorities generally feel that the following factors should be included: (1) prompt and certain arrest processes, (2) a fair and speedy trial, (3) punishment for the crime committed, and (4) an opportunity for a decent job when the prisoner's debt to society has been satisfied.

The public should not overlook the fact that the prevention of crime and delinquency should have at least as high a priority as the treatment and correction of those who are already involved. One is dependent on the other, to some extent. Many individuals feel that an authorization for additional funds for law enforcement and correctional agencies should automatically reduce the extent of crime. Money, of course, will often help a great deal. There are limits, however. Much of the damage to the general public is in full swing before the criminal justice system comes into play. The courts, the prosecutors, the correctional agencies, and the police must bear responsibility, but so too must the home and those social institutions that mold responsibility in the young.

QUESTIONS

1. Would you say that a court conviction singles out the defendant as an individual needing special attention to induce that person to live within the law?

2. Should society seek to be vindictive or rehabilitative in sentencing a convict? Why?

3. What are three classes of individuals who may come before a judge for sentencing? Do all necessarily need to be sent to prison?

4. What kind of specific information does the judge need concerning the defendant at the time he passes sentence?

5. What use does the judge make of this specific background information?

6. In general, what class of persons should be granted probation on conviction in a criminal case?

7. List some of the factors that the judge will usually consider in deciding whether to grant probation.

8. What are some of the advantages of using minimum security facilities for some prisoners?

9. On the average, are prison inmates as literate as other persons in the work force? Give the basis for your answer.

10. What direction should educational programs take in the prison environment?

11. Are work programs of value inside a penitentiary? Is it helpful to offer vocational training to inmates?

12. What are the basic differences between probation and parole?

13. Does every prison inmate have the right to be released on parole? Or is release on parole something that must be earned by the individual inmate?

14. Why is it so important that the state adult authority or parole board grant parole only to those who have demonstrated a desire to rehabilitate themselves?

15. Describe the basic functions of the parole officer.

16. What are the dangers in requiring one parole officer to handle an excessive number of parolees?

17. Should definite conditions for behavior be specified by the parole board, or should the parolee look only to his individual parole officer for rules of conduct?

18. Should the parole board or adult authority have any hesitancy in revoking parole when it is clear that the parolee is in violation? Why?

19. Judged from an over-all basis, how effective is the so-called rehabilitation approach in steering convicts away from a continuing life of crime?

20. Describe some other ideas or approaches that may be tried to prevent criminal recidivism.

GLOSSARY

This is a list of the more common legal phrases used in the administration of criminal justice. Some of these phrases are used in legal circles for civil lawsuits, as well as for criminal cases.

The student should make frequent reference to a standard law dictionary, which can be found in the reference section of almost every library.

Accusatory pleading   The indictment, information, or complaint that charges an individual with the commission of a crime.

Accused   The individual against whom criminal charges have been brought; the defendant.

Acquittal   A verdict returned by the jury in favor of the defendant; a finding of not guilty. A directed verdict of acquittal may be ordered by the judge if all the proof offered by the prosecution does not satisfy all the requirements needed to prove guilt.

Admission   A concession or acknowledgement that a certain fact is true. If there is an admission of all the essential facts by a criminal, it is known as a confession. The accused may make an admission of some facts without necessarily being guilty.

Adversary System   The trial system used in courts in the United States to bring out the facts in both criminal and civil cases. The two sides dispute the issues that are in doubt, presenting evidence to support their individual claims. It is partisan advocacy. Questionable facts are contested.

Affidavit   A voluntary, one-party statement, given under oath and reduced to writing. It is made out of court, without notice to the other party in a legal controversy, and the other side has no opportunity to cross-examine the person furnishing the affidavit.

Glossary

Affirmation   Quakers and members of some other religious groups are opposed to taking an oath. When required to testify, they may give an affirmation. This is a solemn, formal declaration that the witness will tell the truth. It is recognized by the courts as an alternate to putting a court witness under oath prior to testifying.

Allegation   The information or material that one side expects to prove in a trial or legal action. The pleadings are made up of specific allegations.

Amicus curiae   This is an old Latin term, meaning "friend of the court." Occasionally, the issues in a particular prosecution may be of interest to a large segment of the general public, and the judge may allow an outside attorney to come into the court and give opinions and legal counsel as amicus curiae, or "friend of the court." Normally, however, only the legal representatives of the defendant and the prosecution are allowed to participate in a criminal trial.

Appeal   In criminal law, a petition carrying a decided case from a lower court to a higher court (appellate court) for reexamination. Similar procedures are used in the civil courts, and most appellate courts handle both kinds of appeals.

Arraignment   The act of bringing someone before the court to answer a criminal charge.

Arrest   To deprive an individual of his liberty by legal authority. Holding or detaining one to answer a legal charge or inquiry.

Attest   To affirm, or legally acknowledge that a matter is true.

Bail   The procedure for allowing the release of a person under arrest, pending trial. The subject is required to remain under the jurisdiction of the court by delivering the subject (accused) into the hands of a surety, who may be required to pledge money or property to guarantee the appearance of the accused at the time of trial. In some cases, the accused may be allowed to remain at liberty on his pledge to the court that he will appear. This is called release on one's own recognizance.

Bailiff   An official of the court or police officer assigned responsibility to maintain peace in the courtroom, as specified by the judge.

Bench   The judge. Sometimes used to mean the judge's desk or podium in the courtroom.

Bench warrant   A writ issued from the bench, by the judge, calling for the immediate arrest of the individual named. This is the type of process that will be issued, for example, in the event an accused jumps bail.

288

Best evidence rule   The requirement that only the best available evidence should be accepted in a trial in a court of law. Thus, a copy of a document is not admissible when the original can be obtained. It must be proved that the copy is the best evidence available, before it will be allowed in court.

Capital offense   A criminal violation which carries the death penalty.

Certiorari   A writ issued to an inferior (lower) court by an appellate court, instructing that a pending case, or the records thereof, be sent to the higher court for examination for error.

Charge to the jury   Written instructions given by the judge to the jury, as to how jury members should be guided in considering the evidence and arriving at a verdict. This is the final part of a criminal trial.

   The purpose of the charge is to enlighten the jury as to the law, and how the jury is required to act in relation to the evidence. A number of charges may be given, all in written form, phrasing the judge's instructions as simply and as concisely as possible. Some of these instructions are standard in form, and may be passed from judge to judge, and from trial to trial. Other instructions may be needed, however, for the specific applications of the law to an individual trial. Defense attorneys carefully review these, often seeking new trials on appeal on the basis that the charge to the jury did not permit the accused to receive a fair trial.

Civil case   A lawsuit or legal action undertaken in the civil courts to obtain money damages for a civil wrong. As an alternative, the plaintiff in a case of this kind may seek a court order directing or restricting a certain action. (This is an injunction.)

Commitment   The court's judgment, whereby the convicted individual is placed in a jail, prison, or other institution.

Commutation   The alteration of a criminal sentence. The change of a punishment from a greater to a lesser sentence. (The change from a lesser to a greater sentence is illegal under the ex post facto provisions of the U.S. Constitution, and state constitutions.)

   A commutation can be granted by the sovereign authority—the governor in a state, or by a board with this specific authority. Under certain statutory authority, a judge or state board may commute a sentence to "time served." This means, in effect, that there is a pardon for the balance of the sentence remaining to be served.

Complaint   A legal pleading used to charge an individual with a criminal offense.

Confession   An admission of guilt or responsibility for a crime.

Conspiracy   A combination of two or more persons, seeking by joint action to accomplish some criminal or unlawful purpose, or to accomplish a legitimate objective by unlawful means. There must be a joint scheme, but action by only one conspirator is sufficient. The conspiracy may constitute both criminal and civil wrongs.

Contempt of court   Any act which will hinder, obstruct, or embarrass a court in its procedures for administering justice, thereby lessening the court's dignity or constituted authority.

Coram nobis   A procedure whereby a party petitions the court that rendered a judgment adverse to that party, to review a mistake of fact that occurred at the trial. The petition filed by the party making the request must show that the true facts were not known to this individual at the time of trial. It is usually an appeal seeking to set aside a guilty verdict on the basis of fraud, duress, or coercion that did not come to light until after the trial was over.

Coroner's jury   A jury functioning under the authority of the coroner or medical examiner to inquire into the cause of an unexplained death.

Corpus delecti   The substance, the essential elements, or the body of a crime. When a criminal offense is dissected or analyzed, the corpus delecti is the whole of the specific elements needed to spell out a criminal offense. This term is frequently misunderstood, in that some persons believe it is a reference to the body of the victim of a crime. It has no reference to a physical body, and a murder conviction may be obtained by proving the individual requirements of the crime, whether or not the victim's body is ever found.

Counsel   An attorney, a lawyer, a legal advocate, or legal advisor. The terms may be used interchangeably in United States courts.

Cross-examination   The questioning of a witness who has already testified for the other side in a criminal trial, civil trial, or legal hearing.

Degree of proof   The quantity or amount of proof required to support a judgment.

Deposition   A question and answer statement about facts known to an individual. Under certain circumstances it may be used in place of testimony in court. It is taken under oath, generally by a court reporter.

Derivative rule   When evidence is excluded from a trial because it was illegally obtained (see "exclusionary rule"), the courts say that the evidence cannot be used at all. In other words, not only is the illegal evidence excluded, but anything derived from that evidence is also kept out of the case. This applies to leads or material indirectly obtained. This is sometimes expressed by the courts as the "fruit of the poisoned tree" doctrine set out by the United States Supreme Court in *Silverthorne Lumber Company* v. *United States,* 251 US 385 (1920) and *Nardone* v. *United States,* 308 US 338 (1939).

Detainer   The placing of a hold on a prisoner, to obtain custody of that individual upon release from a sentence being served or a charge for which this person is being held.

The purpose of the detainer is to get physical custody of the prisoner who is wanted on another charge in another state or jurisdiction. In prison language, a detainer is a "sticker" placed on the file.

By statute in many jurisdictions a convict is not eligible for parole if a detainer is on file. Consequently, prison inmates often seek to have all charges against them disposed of at one time, rather than to have a detainer on file.

Diminished responsibility   A legal doctrine that is now allowed by some courts. Under this doctrine, proof of mental derangement, short of insanity, may be submitted as evidence of a lack of deliberate or premeditated design or intent to commit a crime. The legal effect is that a person with diminished legal capacity may not be held responsible for premeditated murder, but may be convicted of manslaughter, which does not require premeditation.

Direct examination   The first questioning of a witness; examination-in-chief. The presentation of the testimony of the witness on whose behalf this individual was called. This is followed by cross-examination by the attorney for the opposing side.

Discovery   Discovery is a relatively new legal technique in which an attorney is allowed to gain some knowledge of the evidence that will be used by the other side. In most situations, discovery is used by defense attorneys, on the theory that examination of this evidence prior to trial is necessary to a fair trial. This right is usually limited to an examination of statements or confessions given to the government investigators, or to reports on the examination of physical evidence made by expert witnesses.

The prosecution also has the right of discovery of the defendant's evidence but this is seldom of much use to the prosecution from a practical standpoint.

Disqualification   The judge's act in removing himself from the handling of a legal proceeding; stepping down and allowing another judge to preside over a trial in which the first judge may be influenced or prejudiced by prior involvement in the facts. It may be a situation in which the judge has a family or business relationship with any of the parties involved. If the defendant, for example, is represented by the judge's former law partner, then the judge should disqualify himself. This is not to imply that he could not be fair, but that he might be unconsciously influenced. The judge must act to keep the trial system above suspicion.

Double jeopardy   Being twice subjected to the risk of punishment for committing only one crime. In this connection, it should be noted that more than one violation may arise out of a continuing course of action.

En banc   Some of the functions of appellate courts may be handled by a lone judge. The term en banc means a full court, or consideration by all of the judges, together.

Evidence   The kind of proof that will be accepted by a court of law to prove or disprove a matter before the court.

Evidence may take a number of forms—verbal testimony, a physical object used to commit the crime, such as a knife or gun, and physical items from which an inference may be drawn.

Exclusionary rule   The rule of excluding evidence from use in court, if the evidence was obtained by unlawful or illegal means, such as evidence from an illegal search.

Exoneration of bail   Relieving the bail bondsman of liability under the bond.

Ex parte   A legal action undertaken in behalf of, or on the application of, one side only.

Expert Witness   An individual with unusual scientific or technical qualifications, who is used to give an opinion as to the nature or meaning of evidence or conditions that are in issue during a trial.

The technical background necessary to qualify may be acquired by unusual education or unusual experience and training in a specific field. It is up to the trial judge as to whether the witness has the expert qualifications that will satisfy the court.

Ex post facto law   If an act occurred before it was prohibited by statute, then the act is not a crime. A law which attempts to set a punishment for acts in the past is illegal, or ex post facto, under the

United States Constitution. However, under English law, a statute of this kind is allowed.

In addition, a statute is an ex post facto law if it attempts to increase the penalty for an illegal act that occurred prior to the setting of the increased penalty.

Extradition   The legal process involved in removing a wanted individual from a state to which he has fled.

Felony   There are varying definitions as to a felony. We generally think of it as any serious crime. In some jurisdictions it is any crime punishable by more than one year imprisonment. In other jurisdictions it is a crime that can be punished by incarceration in a penitentiary.

Fresh pursuit   The immediate pursuit of a criminal by a peace officer. The pursuit must be continuous. If the pursuit is lost at any time, then the fresh pursuit principle no longer applies. Under this doctrine the peace officer may continue his chase into another state, even though he normally does not have power to arrest beyond the state line. This type of authority is provided by statute in many states, frequently by reciprocal agreement with adjoining states.

Grand jury   The investigative jury that acts for the general public when an indictment should be returned. The word comes from the French invaders of England, and means "large jury" as distinguished from the smaller trial, or petit jury.

Habeas corpus   A legal action that requires an explanation as to whether someone is being held legally. The court orders the individual supposedly holding the prisoner to come into court with that person, for an adjudication as to the legality of continuing to hold that person. It prevents persons from being jailed without good cause.

Hung jury   If a jury cannot agree on a verdict after reasonable consideration, it is called a hung jury and is dismissed by the judge. A mistrial is then declared, and a criminal case may be tried again, with a completely new jury.

Impeachment   The word has two legal meanings. In a court trial, impeachment is the process for showing by other testimony that a witness is unworthy of belief.

293

An impeachment is also a proceeding to legally remove an office holder for wrongdoing in connection with his official duties.

Indeterminate Sentence   A sentence for imprisonment for a maximum period specified by law, subject to earlier termination by an adult authority or parole board at any time after a minimum period set by law has been served. A typical sentence might be five years to life for burglary.

Indictment   The finding by a grand jury that there is reasonable grounds to believe an accused person may be guilty of a crime. An indictment is a prerequisite for a felony prosecution in federal court and in some state jurisdictions.

Information   A type of pleading used by the prosecuting attorney in lieu of an indictment in some jurisdictions, charging an individual with the commission of a crime.

Inquest   An inquiry by the coroner or medical examiner into the cause of any unexplained death, or any sudden death. The purpose is to make certain that if death resulted from a crime, the facts are developed for prosecution.

Jeopardy   The peril in which an accused is put when charged before a court properly organized and competent to try the accused.

Joinder   A joinder is the coupling together of two or more legal defendants in some legal step, such as prosecution, in one proceeding for individual involvement in a single offense.

Jurisdiction   The authority, capacity, power, or right of a court to act in a particular case; the power of the individual who has the right of judging.

Magistrate   An official of a court, or any judge, with power to issue warrants and/or conduct arraignments.

Mandamus   A writ of mandamus is an order of a court to a lower court or governmental agency (police department or prosecutor), to compel some act which is a legal duty.

Mens rea   The specific mental intent to commit an act that is criminal in nature. The guilty state of mind that is a requirement for most true crimes.

Nolle prosequi   Sometimes abbreviated as nolle pros. A binding entry into the court records by the prosecuting attorney that he will not further prosecute a case, or will not further prosecute a specific count or one of multiple defendants.

Nolo contendere   A plea that is allowed in most jurisdictions, but not in all. For purposes of the criminal prosecution, it has the same effect as a plea of guilty.

Nolo contendere means "I will not contest it," in Latin. The difference between this plea and a plea of guilty is that it cannot be used as proof of wrongdoing in a civil lawsuit that is an outgrowth of the same incident that resulted in the criminal prosecution.

Objection   A verbal protest by one of the attorneys during a trial. It is an appeal to the judge, claiming that the material or evidence being offered is not the proper kind to be heard by the jury.

Opening statement   A speech made by one of the attorneys in the opening stages of a trial, outlining the case that will be presented and developed through the presentation of witnesses. It gives a summary of the evidence that can be expected, so that the jury can better understand it as the presentation develops.

Peremptory challenge   A means of striking an individual, or barring that person from jury service, for which no reason need be given.

Plaintiff   The side that initiates action in a court trial. In a criminal case the prosecutor is always the plaintiff.

Polling the jury   When the jury reaches a verdict, the members of the jury are ushered into court. In a criminal case the accused has a right to have the judge or court clerk ask each juror how he or she voted. If a juror states that he voted not guilty, the jury is sent back out by the judge, with instructions to come to an agreement.

Recidivist   A criminal repeater.

Reprieve   A reprieve withholds or stays the execution of a sentence for a time, to give the executive time to study the facts in a particular case, or to enable the convicted individual to obtain some relief or reduction of a sentence.

The power to grant a reprieve is statutory. For example, in California the governor has the power to grant reprieves, pardons, and commutations of sentence, after conviction . . . (Constitution of California, Article VII, Section 1.)

Severance   The granting of separate trials to two or more individuals accused of involvement in the same crime. If the rights of one individual may be jeopardized by a joint trial, then a severance will be granted by the trial judge. The power to grant or refuse a severance lies with the trial judge, but appellate courts may grant a new trial if some of the evidence against one defendant should not have been heard in connection with another defendant.

Special verdict   The verdict of the jury as to facts only.

Stare decisis   The legal principle that a court should follow the opinion of a previously decided case which involved identical circumstances.

Statute of limitations   A period of time set by statute, within which a person may be prosecuted for a crime, or a civil lawsuit filed. If action is not taken within the prescribed time, prosecution can never be undertaken. There is no statute of limitations on some serious crimes, such as murder.

Subpoena   An order from the court, prepared by the court clerk, compelling an individual to testify in court as a witness.

Subpoena duces tecum   A subpoena or writ by which a court directs an individual to produce a specific article of evidence for introduction at the time of trial.

Summons   An order to appear in court that may be used in misdemeanor cases in place of an arrest warrant.

Surety   The individual who places money on deposit with the court clerk, or pledges property for a defendant being released on bail.

Unlawful flight   The Federal Unlawful Flight statute, commonly called UFAP by FBI Agents, is Title 18, United States Code, Section 1073.

This law was written to enable the FBI to file federal criminal charges against individuals wanted for certain serious state crimes (murder, manslaughter, robbery, burglary, arson, rape, kidnapping, and assault), and who have fled the state. FBI agents in the state of flight locate the fugitive, and apprehend. The wanted person is then held on the federal charge until local officials extradite. As a matter of policy, the federal process is almost always then dismissed.

Venue   The location or the place of a criminal trial.

Verdict   The decision of the trial jury as to the guilt or innocence of the accused.

Voir dire   This is the procedure involved in the preliminary questioning of a prospective juror by the judge or one of the attorneys in the preliminary part of a trial. If the questioning shows that the individual is not competent for jury service, has a personal interest in the outcome, or is prejudiced, then he will not be seated as a juror. It is a technical challenge that enables the attorney for one side or the other to eliminate the prospective juror for cause.

INDEX

299